Internet Explorer 4
One Step at a Time

Internet Explorer 4
One Step at a Time

Craig Witherspoon and Barbara Kasser

IDG Books Worldwide, Inc.

An International Data Group Company

FOSTER CITY, CA · CHICAGO, IL · INDIANAPOLIS, IN · SOUTHLAKE, TX

Internet Explorer 4 One Step at a Time

Published by

IDG Books Worldwide, Inc.

An International Data Group Company
919 E. Hillsdale Blvd., Suite 400
Foster City, CA 94404
www.idgbooks.com (IDG Books Worldwide Web site)

Library of Congress Catalog Card No.: 97-076681

ISBN: 0-7645-3104-2

Printed in the United States of America

10 9 8 7 6 5 4 3 2 1

IE/SQ/QS/ZY/FC

Distributed in the United States by IDG Books Worldwide, Inc.

Distributed by Macmillan Canada for Canada; by Transworld Publishers Limited in the United Kingdom; by IDG Norge Books for Norway; by IDG Sweden Books for Sweden; by Woodslane Pty. Ltd. for Australia; by Woodslane Enterprises Ltd. for New Zealand; by Longman Singapore Publishers Ltd. for Singapore, Malaysia, Thailand, and Indonesia; by Simron Pty. Ltd. for South Africa; by Toppan Company Ltd. for Japan; by Distribuidora Cuspide for Argentina; by Livraria Cultura for Brazil; by Ediciencia S.A. for Ecuador; by Addison-Wesley Publishing Company for Korea; by Ediciones ZETA S.C.R. Ltda. for Peru; by WS Computer Publishing Corporation, Inc., for the Philippines; by Unalis Corporation for Taiwan; by Contemporanea de Ediciones for Venezuela; by Computer Book & Magazine Store for Puerto Rico; by Express Computer Distributors for the Caribbean and West Indies. Authorized Sales Agent: Anthony Rudkin Associates for the Middle East and North Africa.

For general information on IDG Books Worldwide's books in the U.S., please call our Consumer Customer Service department at 800-762-2974. For reseller information, including discounts and premium sales, please call our Reseller Customer Service department at 800-434-3422.

For information on where to purchase IDG Books Worldwide's books outside the U.S., please contact our International Sales department at 650-655-3200 or fax 650-655-3295.

For information on foreign language translations, please contact our Foreign & Subsidiary Rights department at 650-655-3021 or fax 650-655-3281.

For sales inquiries and special prices for bulk quantities, please contact our Sales department at 650-655-3200 or write to the address above.

For information on using IDG Books Worldwide's books in the classroom or for ordering examination copies, please contact our Educational Sales department at 800-434-2086 or fax 817-251-8174.

For press review copies, author interviews, or other publicity information, please contact our Public Relations department at 650-655-3000 or fax 650-655-3299.

For authorization to photocopy items for corporate, personal, or educational use, please contact Copyright Clearance Center, 222 Rosewood Drive, Danvers, MA 01923, or fax 978-750-4470.

 is a trademark under exclusive license to IDG Books Worldwide, Inc., from International Data Group, Inc.

ABOUT IDG BOOKS WORLDWIDE

Welcome to the world of IDG Books Worldwide.

IDG Books Worldwide, Inc., is a subsidiary of International Data Group, the world's largest publisher of computer-related information and the leading global provider of information services on information technology. IDG was founded more than 25 years ago and now employs more than 8,500 people worldwide. IDG publishes more than 275 computer publications in over 75 countries (see listing below). More than 60 million people read one or more IDG publications each month.

Launched in 1990, IDG Books Worldwide is today the #1 publisher of best-selling computer books in the United States. We are proud to have received eight awards from the Computer Press Association in recognition of editorial excellence and three from *Computer Currents'* First Annual Readers' Choice Awards. Our best-selling *...For Dummies®* series has more than 30 million copies in print with translations in 30 languages. IDG Books Worldwide, through a joint venture with IDG's Hi-Tech Beijing, became the first U.S. publisher to publish a computer book in the People's Republic of China. In record time, IDG Books Worldwide has become the first choice for millions of readers around the world who want to learn how to better manage their businesses.

Our mission is simple: Every one of our books is designed to bring extra value and skill-building instructions to the reader. Our books are written by experts who understand and care about our readers. The knowledge base of our editorial staff comes from years of experience in publishing, education, and journalism — experience we use to produce books for the '90s. In short, we care about books, so we attract the best people. We devote special attention to details such as audience, interior design, use of icons, and illustrations. And because we use an efficient process of authoring, editing, and desktop publishing our books electronically, we can spend more time ensuring superior content and spend less time on the technicalities of making books.

You can count on our commitment to deliver high-quality books at competitive prices on topics you want to read about. At IDG Books Worldwide, we continue in the IDG tradition of delivering quality for more than 25 years. You'll find no better book on a subject than one from IDG Books Worldwide.

John Kilcullen
CEO
IDG Books Worldwide, Inc.

Steven Berkowitz
President and Publisher
IDG Books Worldwide, Inc.

VIII
WINNER
*Eighth Annual
Computer Press
Awards ≥1992*

IX
WINNER
*Ninth Annual
Computer Press
Awards ≥1993*

X
WINNER
*Tenth Annual
Computer Press
Awards ≥1994*

XI
WINNER
*Eleventh Annual
Computer Press
Awards ≥1995*

IDG Books Worldwide, Inc., is a subsidiary of International Data Group, the world's largest publisher of computer-related information and the leading global provider of information services on information technology. International Data Group publishes over 275 computer publications in over 75 countries. Sixty million people read one or more International Data Group publications each month. International Data Group's publications include: **ARGENTINA:** Buyer's Guide, Computerworld Argentina, PC World Argentina; **AUSTRALIA:** Australian Macworld, Australian PC World, Australian Reseller News, Computerworld, IT Casebook, Network World, Publish, Webmaster; **AUSTRIA:** Computerwelt Osterreich, Networks Austria, PC Tip Austria; **BANGLADESH:** PC World Bangladesh; **BELARUS:** PC World Belarus; **BELGIUM:** Data News; **BRAZIL:** Annuario de Informática, Computerworld, Connections, Macworld, PC Player, PC World, Publish, Reseller News, Supergamepower; **BULGARIA:** Computerworld Bulgaria, Network World Bulgaria, PC & MacWorld Bulgaria; **CANADA:** CIO Canada, Client/Server World, ComputerWorld Canada, InfoWorld Canada, NetworkWorld Canada, WebWorld; **CHILE:** Computerworld Chile, PC World Chile; **COLOMBIA:** Computerworld Colombia, PC World Colombia; **COSTA RICA:** PC World Centro America; **THE CZECH AND SLOVAK REPUBLICS:** Computerworld Czechoslovakia, Macworld Czech Republic, PC World Czechoslovakia; **DENMARK:** Communications World Danmark, Computerworld Danmark, Macworld Danmark, PC World Danmark, Techworld Denmark; **DOMINICAN REPUBLIC:** PC World Republica Dominicana; **ECUADOR:** PC World Ecuador; **EGYPT:** Computerworld Middle East, PC World Middle East; **EL SALVADOR:** PC World Centro America; **FINLAND:** MikroPC, Tietoverkko, Tietoviikko; **FRANCE:** Distributique, Hebdo, Info PC, Le Monde Informatique, Macworld, Reseaux & Telecoms, WebMaster France; **GERMANY:** Computer Partner, Computerwoche, Computerwoche Extra, Computerwoche FOCUS, Global Online, Macwelt, PC Welt; **GREECE:** Amiga Computing, GamePro Greece, Multimedia World; **GUATEMALA:** PC World Centro America; **HONDURAS:** PC World Centro America; **HONG KONG:** Computerworld Hong Kong, PC World Hong Kong, Publish in Asia; **HUNGARY:** ABCD CD-ROM, Computerworld Szamitastechnika, Internetto online Magazine, PC World Hungary, PC-X Magazin Hungary; **ICELAND:** Tolvuheimur PC World Island; **INDIA:** Information Communications World, Information Systems Computerworld, PC World India, Publish in Asia; **INDONESIA:** InfoKomputer PC World, Komputek Computerworld, Publish in Asia; **IRELAND:** ComputerScope, PC Live!; **ISRAEL:** Macworld Israel, People & Computers/Computerworld; **ITALY:** Computerworld Italia, Macworld Italia, Networking Italia, PC World Italia; **JAPAN:** DTP World, Macworld Japan, Nikkei Personal Computing, OS/2 World Japan, SunWorld Japan, Windows NT World, Windows World Japan; **KENYA:** PC World East African; **KOREA:** Hi-Tech Information, Macworld Korea, PC World Korea; **MACEDONIA:** PC World Macedonia; **MALAYSIA:** Computerworld Malaysia, PC World Malaysia, Publish in Asia; **MALTA:** PC World Malta; **MEXICO:** Computerworld Mexico, PC World Mexico; **MYANMAR:** PC World Myanmar; **NETHERLANDS:** Computer! Totaal, LAN Internetworking Magazine, LAN World Buyers Guide, Macworld Netherlands, Net, WebWereld; **NEW ZEALAND:** Absolute Beginners Guide and Plain & Simple Series, Computer Buyer, Computer Industry Directory, Computerworld New Zealand, MTB, Network World, PC World New Zealand; **NICARAGUA:** PC World Centro America; **NORWAY:** Computerworld Norge, CW Rapport, Datamagasinet, Financial Rapport, Kursguide Norge, Macworld Norge, Multimediaworld Norge, PC World Ekspress Norge, PC World Nettverk, PC World Norge, PC World ProduktGuide Norge; **PAKISTAN:** Computerworld Pakistan; **PANAMA:** PC World Panama; **PEOPLE'S REPUBLIC OF CHINA:** China Computer Users, China Computerworld, China InfoWorld, China Telecom World Weekly, Computer & Communication, Electronic Design China, Electronics Today, Electronics Weekly, Game Software, PC World China, Popular Computer Week, Software Weekly, Software World, Telecom World; **PERU:** Computerworld Peru, PC World Profesional Peru, PC World SoHo Peru; **PHILIPPINES:** Click!, Computerworld Philippines, PC World Philippines, Publish in Asia; **POLAND:** Computerworld Poland, Computerworld Special Report Poland, Cyber, Macworld Poland, Networld Poland, PC World Komputer; **PORTUGAL:** Cerebro/PC World, Computerworld/Correio Informático, Dealer World Portugal, Mac*In/PC*In Portugal, Multimedia World; **PUERTO RICO:** PC World Puerto Rico; **ROMANIA:** Computerworld Romania, PC World Romania, Telecom Romania; **RUSSIA:** Computerworld Russia, Mir PK, Publish, Seti; **SINGAPORE:** Computerworld Singapore, PC World Singapore, Publish in Asia; **SLOVENIA:** Monitor; **SOUTH AFRICA:** Computing SA, Network World SA, Software World SA; **SPAIN:** Communicaciones World España, Computerworld España, Dealer World España, Macworld España, PC World España; **SRI LANKA:** Infolink PC World; **SWEDEN:** CAP&Design, Computer Sweden, Corporate Computing Sweden, Internetworld Sweden, it.branschen, Macworld Sweden, MaxiData Sweden, MikroDatorn, Natverk & Kommunikation, PC World Sweden, PCaktiv, Windows World Sweden; **SWITZERLAND:** Computerworld Schweiz, Macworld Schweiz, PCtip; **TAIWAN:** Computerworld Taiwan, Macworld Taiwan, NEW VISION/Publish, PC World Taiwan, Windows World Taiwan; **THAILAND:** Publish in Asia, Thai Computerworld; **TURKEY:** Computerworld Turkiye, Macworld Turkiye, Network World Turkiye, PC World Turkiye; **UKRAINE:** Computerworld Kiev, Multimedia World Ukraine, PC World Ukraine; **UNITED KINGDOM:** Acorn User UK, Amiga Action UK, Amiga Computing UK, Apple Talk UK, Computing, Macworld, Parents and Computers UK, PC Advisor, PC Home, PSX Pro, The WEB; **UNITED STATES:** Cable in the Classroom, CIO Magazine, Computerworld, DOS World, Federal Computer Week, GamePro Magazine, InfoWorld, I-Way, Macworld, Network World, PC Games, PC World, Publish, Video Event, THE WEB Magazine, and WebMaster; online webzines: JavaWorld, NetscapeWorld, and SunWorld Online; **URUGUAY:** InfoWorld Uruguay; **VENEZUELA:** Computerworld Venezuela, PC World Venezuela; and **VIETNAM:** PC World Vietnam.
3/24/97

CREDITS

Acquisitions Editor
John Read

Development/Copy Editor
Kathleen McFadden

Technical Editors
Greg Guntle
Barbara Kasser

Production Coordinator
Ritchie Durdin

Book Designers
Seventeenth Street Studios
Kurt Krames

Graphics and Production Specialists
Linda Marousek
Ed Penslien
Dina F Quan
Trevor Wilson

Quality Control Specialists
Mick Arellano
Mark Shumann

Proofreader
David Wise

Indexer
David Heiret

ABOUT THE AUTHORS

Craig Witherspoon is a freelance writer with more than 25 years of experience in the computer industry. Beginning with RCA in the 1970s, Craig has been involved in the growth of the computer revolution from its roots. He is the author of *Optimizing Client/Server Networks* and the *60 Minute Guide to Netscape Navigator 3*, both from IDG Books Worldwide.

Barbara Kasser considers the Internet her playground. When Barbara's not tooling around the Net, she works as a network administrator for an international corporation. Barbara also teaches and writes training manuals for Computer Coach, a computer training facility in Boca Raton, Florida. Barbara has written several other books, including *Netscape Navigator 4 Browsing and Beyond* from IDG Books Worldwide.

WELCOME TO ONE STEP AT A TIME!

The book you are holding is very special. It's just the tool you need for learning software quickly and easily. More than a book, it offers a *unique learning experience*. Along with our text, the dynamic *One Step at a Time On-Demand* software included on the bonus CD-ROM in this book coaches you through the tutorials at *your own pace*. You'll never feel lost!

See examples of how to accomplish specific tasks. Listen to clear explanations of how to solve your problems.

Use the *One Step at a Time On-Demand* software in three ways:

- **Demo mode** shows you how to perform a task in movie-style fashion—in sound and color! Just sit back and watch the *One Step* software demonstrate the correct sequence of steps on-screen. Seeing is understanding!

- **Teacher mode** simulates the software environment so you can practice completing a task without worrying about making a mistake. The *One Step* software guides you every step of the way. Trying is learning!

- **Concurrent mode** allows you to work in the actual software environment while still getting assistance from the friendly *One Step* helper. Doing is succeeding!

Our goal is for you to learn the features of a software application by guiding you painlessly through valuable and helpful tutorials. Our *One Step at a Time On-Demand* software—combined with the step-by-step tutorials in our One Step at a Time series—will make your learning experience fast-paced and fun.

See it. Try it. Do it.

To Steven C. Scheer, Ph.D.: Here's one more example for your brilliant implied reader/implied writer lecture.

—C.W.

I dedicate this book to my husband and my son. Bill and Richard, without your support I could never start these projects. Without your love and understanding, I could never hope to finish them.

—B.K.

PREFACE

ongratulations! You're using Internet Explorer 4, a great new suite of software from Microsoft that contains everything you need to become an Internet wizard. Internet Explorer has the tools to change the look and feel of your Windows desktop, help you surf the World Wide Web, send and receive e-mail, and read and post messages to newsgroups. Additionally, Internet Explorer includes programs that enable you to communicate across the Internet, both by actual voice communication or in a text-based chat room. Want to create a Web page to announce your presence to the world? With Internet Explorer, you can do that too.

If you think that Internet Explorer sounds mighty complicated, relax. *Internet Explorer 4 One Step at a Time* will get you comfortable with all of Internet Explorer's components in no time. The lessons in this book are designed to teach you what you need to know to make the Internet your playground.

This book is filled with information on how to use Internet Explorer 4 to become an active player on the World Wide Web. And speaking of the Web, remember that it is constantly changing. The Web's ever-evolving nature and fluidity are two characteristics that make it so much fun. But the Web's changeable nature also means that you may come across a Web site mentioned in this book that either looks different, has moved to a different location, or no longer exists.

Who Should Read This Book

Internet Explorer 4 One Step at a Time is for anyone who wants to leap onto the Internet without spending a lot of time learning boring facts and jargon. You should have a basic understanding of Windows 95 and should know how to use your mouse and keyboard. You don't need to have any prior Internet experience. However, if you've used previous versions of Internet Explorer, this book is for you, too. Internet Explorer 4 has a new look and feel and is crammed with new, exciting features.

Since we're real people, just like you, we understand that you don't have lots of free time and want to use this book to become proficient with the Internet Explorer suite of programs as quickly as possible. To make it easy, we've divided the book into lessons that contain the information you need to know.

We don't think that anyone learns how to use Internet Explorer by reading long boring paragraphs, so we've set up exercises for you to work through. With *Internet Explorer 4 One Step at a Time,* you don't learn by memorizing or reading; you learn by doing. Because we respect your time, we show you the shortest and most effective way to accomplish each task. We've provided extra helpers along the way, such as tips, notes, and sidebars, to make the lessons meaningful and fun.

How This Book Is Organized

Internet Explorer 4 One Step at a Time has an easy-to-follow structure. The book is organized into parts and lessons. Each lesson contains a series of easy-to-follow exercises to help you build your skills as you progress through the book.

PART I: STEP UP TO INTERNET EXPLORER 4

Step Up to Internet Explorer 4 is your launch pad to the exciting new features and innovations of Internet Explorer. Lesson 1 introduces all the programs in the suite, shows you how to open the different programs, and teaches you how to switch between them. Lesson 2 introduces the Active Desktop, a new feature of Internet Explorer that adds browser functions to your Windows operating system. Lesson 3 takes you even further into the Active Desktop, showing you how to add active components such as channels to your desktop and have Web information delivered to you automatically.

PART II: UNDERSTANDING BROWSER BASICS

Understanding Browser Basics shows you how to use the new features of the Internet Explorer browser and how to surf the Internet. Lesson 4 teaches you the ins and outs of Web navigation. You find out what all this URL business is about and how to get yourself from place to place and back home again. In Lesson 5, you learn how to harness the search features of the browser and the Internet to find the information you need quickly and easily.

PART III: A STEP BEYOND THE BROWSER

A Step Beyond the Browser shows you how to personalize your Internet Explorer browser and make your Web experience fun and exciting. Lesson 6 covers finding and organizing your favorite sites, subscribing to new sites, and downloading pages for offline viewing. In Lesson 7, you explore the world of multimedia on the Web with Explorer's special add-on features, and get the ins and outs of downloading "try before you buy" software. Lesson 8 shares some tricks on changing the appearance of the Internet Explorer browser. If you're interested in Web security, you want to check out Lesson 9 for tips on keeping your Internet sessions safe and secure.

PART IV: COMMUNICATION TOOLS

Communication Tools introduces you to four other major components of the Internet Explorer suite. In Lessons 10 and 11, you learn about sending and receiving electronic mail and joining Internet newsgroups with Outlook Express. In Lesson 12, you enter the world of Microsoft Chat and share your thoughts with others. Can you imagine sitting at your computer and talking into a microphone to someone across the world? You learn how in Lesson 13, with its step-by-step exercises on Microsoft NetMeeting, a voice and video conferencing tool. When you're ready to announce your presence to the world, Lesson 14 shows you how to create your very own Web page using FrontPage Express.

The Conventions Used in This Book

To make this book both fun and challenging, each lesson is organized to provide useful learning exercises and elements that challenge you to find out about the programs on your own. Each lesson follows a basic structure and includes the following elements:

- **Stopwatch.** Because we live in such a fast-paced world and don't always have enough time for every task, each lesson shows the approximate amount of time required for completion. This scheduling tool helps you determine whether you have enough time to learn a new skill before a business meeting or before taking the kids to school.

- **Goals.** Each lesson begins with a set of goals that identifies the skills and tasks covered in the lesson.

- **Get Ready.** This section identifies the software program in the Internet Explorer suite that you should have loaded on your computer to complete the exercises in the lesson.

- **Visual Bonus.** The Visual Bonus is an illustration or a collection of illustrations with callouts that guides you through the basic elements of each Internet Explorer suite program.

- **Skills Challenge.** At the end of each lesson is an exercise that incorporates all the skills you've learned in the individual exercises. The Skills Challenge does not include step-by-step instructions, but challenges you to remember and apply the tasks you've learned to reinforce your learning and improve your retention.

- **Bonus Questions.** Sprinkled throughout the Skills Challenge section are Bonus Questions. If you want to push yourself a little harder, you can answer these questions and check Appendix C to see if you answered them correctly.

- **Troubleshooting.** The Troubleshooting section contains a list of questions and answers addressing common mistakes or confusing issues that new users of the Internet Explorer suite often encounter.

- **Wrap Up.** This section is an overview of the skills you learned in the lesson.

Each lesson also contains several exercises that teach you how to perform specific tasks. To make the learning process even easier, the exercises contain additional features:

When you see

the text that follows provides some background or detail that is helpful for you to know about the feature being discussed.

When you see

the text that follows offers reassurances or solutions to common problems.

The illustrations in the book appear adjacent to the steps they represent in the text. In addition to text callouts, the illustrations include numbered step callouts. These numbered step callouts correspond to a numbered step in the text and illustrate the actions you take to successfully complete the exercise.

Menu commands that you will perform use the following format: Select File ➢ Open. In this example, Select means to click the menu name, File is the name of the menu, and Open is the name of the command to select from within the menu.

In numbered steps, actual text that you need to type appears in **boldface**.

The Accompanying CD-ROM

The bonus CD-ROM included with this book is loaded with goodies. The full bells-and-whistles version of Microsoft Internet Explorer 4 is included, of course, and it's customized with preset Favorites for many of the best Web sites referenced in this book. You also get the dynamic *One Step at a Time On-Demand* software, an exciting learning tool that coaches you through the lessons at your own pace. And as if that weren't enough, we've also included WinZip and WS_FTP LE, two indispensable utilities for decompressing downloaded files and transferring files over the Internet.

Feedback

Your feedback is valuable to us. If you have any comments about this book or if you have any suggestions for improvement, we want to hear from you. Please register your comments through our IDG Books Worldwide Online Registration form, located at `http:my2cents.idgbooks.com`.

It's Time to Get Started

We know you're excited and can't wait to get busy. It's time to start your Internet journey with Internet Explorer 4. Grab this book and get comfortable at your computer. You're beginning the most exciting journey you'll ever take, as you explore the many facets of the Internet using the tools, features, and enhancements of Internet Explorer 4.

Have a great time. The Internet is quickly changing the way we live and work. We hope that you have as much fun using *Internet Explorer 4 One Step at a Time* as we did writing it!

ACKNOWLEDGMENTS

It takes many people and a lot of effort to create a book. I would like to say thank you to the people at IDG Books Worldwide who made this book possible. To John Read whose support and infinite patience were greatly appreciated. To Susan Pines who kept everyone on track. To Kathleen McFadden for working so diligently to make this book the best it could be. To Barbara Kasser who stepped in at the last minute to help us get this book finished. To Greg Guntle whose technical expertise helped smooth the rough edges. And to everyone else at IDG Books whose indispensable talents and efforts helped put this book in your hands. I would like to offer special thanks to the people at Microsoft for their support and help during the writing of this book. — C.W.

   Putting a book together takes a lot of behind-the-scenes people. A big thank you goes out to all of the people at IDG Books Worldwide who worked to turn my production files and screen prints into the polished, stunning book you're reading now. Special thanks go to Sue Pines and Kathleen McFadden, the best editors in the world. David Fugate of Waterside Productions also deserves a nod for the work he did on my behalf. Steve Lipson of Computer Coach gets a hug for his technical assistance and sense of humor. And, finally, my heartfelt thanks go to my good friend Ken Shenkman, a fellow writer and Internet junkie, who was there when I needed him. — B.K.

   Special thanks to Tom McCaffrey, Marilyn Russell, and everyone at Real Help Communications, Inc. (`http://www.realhelpcom.com`) for creating the several thousand sound files required for the CD-ROMs in this series, under very aggressive deadlines.

CONTENTS AT A GLANCE

CONTENTS

Jump Start

GOALS

In this section, you gain a basic understanding of the following:

- Opening the Internet Explorer browser
- Moving around in the Internet Explorer browser
- Using URLs
- Closing the Internet Explorer browser

20 MINUTES

Get ready

GET READY

You should be seated at your computer, which is powered up and running Windows. You must have Internet Explore installed on your computer (refer to Appendix A for installation instructions). Additionally, you should be dialed in to your Internet service provider.

Since this is just a quick tour, don't worry about remembering all the features you're about to see. Later in the book, you'll learn everything you need to know to use the Internet Explorer browser. The lessons that follow are packed with steps and tips to help you become an expert in no time. When you complete this section, you'll have taken a quick tour of Internet Explorer and visited some Web pages.

TRY OUT THE
INTERACTIVE TUTORIALS
ON YOUR CD!

■ Opening the Internet Explorer browser

You've probably noticed that your Windows desktop looks a little different since you installed Internet Explorer 4. Internet Explorer installs a feature called Active Desktop that changes the way your desktop looks and the way your mouse reacts to some of the icons and shortcuts you've set up. Even though your desktop looks a little different, all of your favorite programs and shortcuts are still available. Internet Explorer isn't just one program. Instead, it provides a suite of programs to help you surf the World Wide Web, send and receive e-mail, and communicate with others through text and real-time conversation. In addition to these programs, Internet Explorer has other features as well. Opening the Internet Explorer browser is easy. When you installed Internet Explorer 4, the installation procedure placed a Quick Launch toolbar on your Windows 95 taskbar.

❶ Look on your Windows taskbar for the Internet Explorer browser shortcut icon. The icon is an *e* with a ring around it.

NOTE

A shortcut is a picture that appears on your Windows desktop that starts programs quickly.

Opening the Internet Explorer browser

2 Place the tip of your mouse pointer on the Internet Explorer browser shortcut icon. The words Launch Internet Explorer Browser pop up above the picture.

3 Click the shortcut icon one time with the left mouse button.

In a few moments, the Microsoft Internet Start page appears on your screen. You're now viewing the Internet through the Internet Explorer browser. You're on the World Wide Web.

TIP

If you're connecting from home, your telephone won't be available for incoming and outgoing calls while you're online with Internet Explorer. If you find that you're missing important calls, you may want to contact your local telephone company and talk about installing a modem–only line.

WHAT IS A BROWSER?

As you work through the lessons in this book, you'll see many references to the term *browser*. If you're wondering exactly what a browser is, you're in good company. Ask ten people and you'll probably get ten answers.

A browser is a program that provides a way to view, read, and even hear all the information on the World Wide Web. Before the Web, the term browser was a general term for programs that let users, mostly students, look at large text files online. When the first Web browser, called Mosaic, appeared, the term was adopted for Web use.

The technical explanation of a Web browser is a client program that uses the Hypertext Transport Protocol, or HTTP, to request pages from Web servers across the Internet on behalf of the user. Simply put, that means that the Internet Explorer browser does all the hard work of going out and fetching the great Web sites that you want to see and displaying them on your computer. All you have to do is point and click!

Moving around in the browser

■ Moving around in the Internet Explorer browser

When you start the Internet Explorer browser, your screen displays the Microsoft Internet Start page. The folks at Microsoft change this page several times a week to show the latest Microsoft information, news, and tips about Internet Explorer, so don't be surprised if the page looks different each time you open the browser. In various lessons throughout this book, you learn about the parts of the Microsoft Internet Start screen. For now, you are going to take a quick tour.

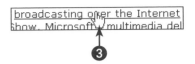

③

1 Place your mouse pointer in the top left corner of the screen and slowly move the pointer around the screen.

As you move the pointer down, you'll notice that as it passes over different areas of the screen, the shape of the pointer changes. The pointer may look like an arrow, a hand, or an I-beam as you move it.

2 Find some underlined text on the page that appears in a different color than the text around it.

Underlined, different-colored text indicates that the text is a *hyperlink*, or a connection to another page or a different section of the same page. When you click a link, you're whisked to the link's location. Whenever your mouse encounters a link on a Web page, the pointer immediately changes to the shape of a hand.

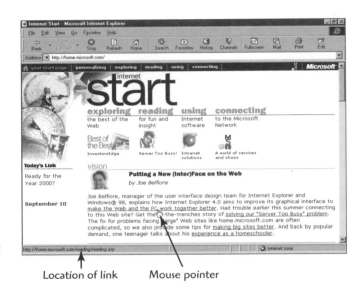

Location of link   Mouse pointer

3 Point the mouse to the underlined text so that the mouse pointer's shape changes to a hand.

In the status bar directly above the Windows taskbar, the word Done is replaced by the location of the link.

4 Click once with the left mouse button to connect to the Web page through the link.

In the top right corner of the screen, the Internet Explorer icon — the blue *e* — becomes animated and changes from an *e* to a globe and then back to an *e* again. In the status bar, various messages flash as the linked page is contacted and then accessed. In a few moments, the new page replaces the one you were viewing previously.

5 Move your mouse over the new page. You'll see that the new page, like the one that was on your screen before, contains links.

As you move the mouse around the new page, make sure that you pass the mouse over some of the pictures. The pictures are called *graphics*. Since pictures, as well as text, can contain links, your mouse assumes the shape of a hand as it passes over some of the graphics.

6 Move your mouse to one of the graphics links on the page.

7 Click once with the left mouse button to move to the link. In a few moments, the linked page appears.

8 Move your mouse pointer to the Back button at the top of the screen. The button has an arrow pointing to the left.

As your mouse arrow rests in the button, the color of the arrow changes from light to dark. The title of the page you visited prior to the current one appears in a balloon.

9 Click the Back button once with the left mouse button. In a few seconds, the previous page appears.

10 Click the Back button again. You're returned to Microsoft Internet Start page, the very first page you visited.

■ Using URLs

Now that you've discovered how to use links to move around, it's time to get a little more ambitious. Besides traveling through the Internet via links, you can specify which page you're going to visit next. The secret of traveling in this way is to know the Uniform Resource Locator (URL), or address, of the page you'd like to visit. You're going to travel to the IDG Books Worldwide site.

1 Move your mouse pointer up to the Internet Explorer icon—the blue *e*—located near the top right corner of the Internet Explorer browser screen.

2 Click one time to load the Microsoft Corporation home page.

Using URLs

③ Move the mouse arrow over the Address bar, the text box located under the Internet Explorer browser toolbar. Notice that the URL for the Microsoft Corporation home page, `http://www.microsoft.com/`, appears in the Address bar. As you move the mouse into the Address bar, the arrow changes to the shape of an I-beam.

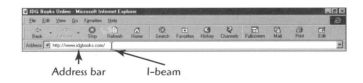

Address bar   I-beam

④ Click one time with the left mouse button. All the text in the box becomes highlighted.

⑤ Type the following text carefully: `www.idgbooks.com/`.

As soon as you start typing, the highlighted text disappears; you don't need to delete it before you type the new text.

⑥ Press Enter on the keyboard. After a few seconds, the home page for IDG Books Worldwide appears.

⑦ Explore the IDG Books Worldwide page. Follow a link to a new location by positioning the mouse pointer on the link and clicking the left mouse button one time.

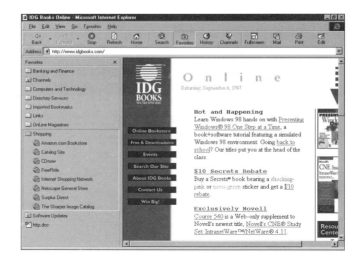

⑧ Click the Back button to return to the IDG Books Worldwide home page.

⑨ Click the Back button again to return to the Microsoft Corporation home page.

⑩ Click the Forward button (the button with the arrow pointing to the right, next to the Back button) to return to the IDG Books Worldwide page.

The Forward button works only if you've just used the Back button, and moves you to the page where you were when you last clicked Back.

⑪ Return to your home base, the Microsoft Internet Start page, by clicking the Home button (the one with the picture of the house) on the toolbar.

■ Closing the Internet Explorer browser

When you're finished using the Internet Explorer browser, you need to close it and break the connection between your modem and your ISP.

1 From within the Internet Explorer browser, select File ➤ Close or click the Close button located at the top right corner of the browser window.

2 Locate the Connected to icon on the Windows taskbar and click it once to display it on your screen.

3 When the Connected to dialog box is visible, click the Disconnect button. In a moment the connection terminates.

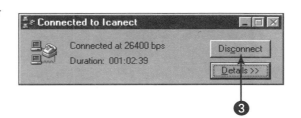

Good work! You're ready to move on to more challenging lessons. In Lesson 1, you learn about the exciting suite of programs included in Internet Explorer 4.

Step Up to Internet Explorer 4

Welcome to the exciting new world of Internet Explorer 4, a complete suite of programs that seamlessly integrates the Web and your desktop. The lessons in this part focus on the basics and introduce you to the individual programs in the suite and the features of the Active Desktop. Lay the groundwork with the following lessons:

- Lesson 1: Meet Internet Explorer 4
- Lesson 2: Welcome to the Active Desktop
- Lesson 3: Integrating the Desktop and the Browser

Meet Internet Explorer 4

25 MINUTES

GOALS

In this lesson, you are introduced to the programs in the Internet Explorer suite. You learn about the following:

- Opening Internet Explorer 4 programs

- Switching between programs

Get ready

GET READY

To complete this lesson, you must install the entire suite of Internet Explorer programs including the Active Desktop (refer to Appendix A for installation instructions). As you work through this lesson, you will be introduced to features of the Internet Explorer suite. When you finish this lesson, you will know how to open the different Internet Explorer suite programs and how to switch between programs.

UPGRADING TO INTERNET EXPLORER 4

Internet Explorer 4 takes a new approach to the task of managing computing resources and offers features and capabilities not found in other browsers or in its predecessors. Internet Explorer 4 is not just a Web browser, but a fully compatible suite of programs that integrates your desktop and the Internet. These new programs and their features reflect some of the best of the rapidly growing technology for smart applications, technology that can help you become more productive by learning your work habits and adapting the program's operation to fit your computing style.

The new integrated tools and capabilities of Internet Explorer 4 are equally applicable to office users, power users, and the casual Web surfer. Everyone benefits from the suite's abilities to display images, provide real-time voice communication and video, and transfer data. The browser's new features can display complex Web content enhanced with interactive components and can provide a secure channel for transferring information and conducting commercial activities across the Internet. The desktop integration brings all of the power of your applications and the resources of the World Wide Web together for you, literally right at your fingertips.

The following list of features highlights how the power of Internet Explorer 4 can not only assist you at work, but also give you some great entertainment options.

■ Offline browsing

Internet Explorer 4 has an enhanced ability to display Web pages stored in the cache, letting you browse sites or newsgroup postings

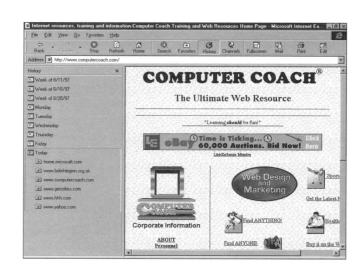

offline. You can set an option to update your Favorites automatically and can then view them offline, perhaps with a laptop computer while you commute or at times when your Internet connection is unavailable. You can also download newsgroup headers, use offline time to select the postings you want to read, and then mark the messages you actually want to see. Internet Explorer downloads the selected messages for offline browsing.

■ IntelliSense features

The smart features in other Microsoft products, like Microsoft Office 97, have been adapted to the Internet Explorer 4 browser. These features include Autoscan and smart toolbars. With Autoscan, the browser automatically completes the URL for a site that you have recently, or regularly, visited when you type in only a few characters. With the smart toolbars feature, the browser displays only the toolbars you need, depending on whether you are viewing a file that is located on your hard drive or the Web.

■ Web page authoring

For everyone who has wanted to create a Web page but didn't have the time or inclination to learn the Hypertext Markup Language (HTML), Internet Explorer 4 includes a What You See Is What You Get (WYSIWYG) HTML editor. The HTML tags are replaced by easy-to-use menus, plenty of options, and simple formatting buttons. This enhancement gives even novices the tools to quickly create outstanding Web pages as shown here.

■ Dynamic HTML

Internet Explorer 4 supports dynamic HTML. More and more Webmasters are developing pages in dynamic HTML because it lets them create a broader spectrum of interactive and multimedia Web pages that respond instantly to mouse movements and keyboard commands. The movement or command does not require a visit back to the server to download the requested information. The information is downloaded when you initially access the Web page, thereby effectively eliminating the refresh rate when you click a

hyperlink or view a Web page element. Screen tips display information about an element when you place the mouse pointer over that element. Hyperlinks and other text elements change style based on mouse or keyboard actions. Information in tables can be sorted, filtered, and viewed using the built-in local database engine. Although all Web pages are written using HTML, not all Web pages contain dynamic HTML features.

■ Security

Internet Explorer 4 offers the broadest support for the Internet security standards available today. Security for transactions and information exchange is an important part of managing the computing environment, and Internet Explorer 4 has developed effective methods for making the network experience secure. The features built into the browser can help keep your documents safe from prying eyes and your transactions safe from tampering or fraud.

LOOKING AT INTERNET EXPLORER 4

So what really is inside Internet Explorer 4? The answer to that question is a whole list of features and functions that this book explores in detail. Here's a preview.

■ Getting online with the Internet Connection Wizard

The Internet Connection Wizard for Internet Explorer simplifies the process of signing up with an Internet service provider (ISP) and connecting to the Internet. In addition to setting up your Internet connection and creating a permanent way to connect to the Internet, the wizard can help you find an ISP.

■ Adding the Active Desktop to your computer

With the introduction of the Active Desktop (shown here), the Windows desktop essentially becomes a customizable Web page. Both the Windows taskbar and the Start menu are now Web savvy, and the desktop supports HTML content. You can drag and drop components

from Web pages directly to the desktop and display live, frequently updated content from a range of channels.

■ Making browsing easier

The new Internet Explorer browser offers a number of innovative features and functions:

- Ability to customize and personalize the browser

- Features that provide access to the widest possible range of Internet content

- Offline browsing to allow for better time management

- Adaptation of the latest Internet security standards and facilities

■ Viewing multimedia with ActiveMovie

ActiveMovie allows you to view multimedia content on the Internet and supports all standard video and audio formats: AVI, QuickTime, MPEG I and II, WAV, AU, and AIFF. ActiveMovie eliminates the need to download helper applications—or plug-ins—to view these types of multimedia elements on Web pages. The audio and video formats played by ActiveMovie require that the entire file download before you can hear the audio or see the movie. Large files can take several minutes to download, so you just have to be patient.

■ Viewing multimedia with NetShow

The NetShow On-Demand Player (shown here), on the other hand, plays streaming audio and video. Streaming technology plays content almost immediately and does not require a full file download before it begins. Web content developers can include larger multimedia files with synchronized productions incorporating audio, graphics, video, URLs, and script commands on their Web sites, and no longer have to consider the long download times that try viewers' patience. On the viewer's end, NetShow works like a cassette or CD player, offering the ability to advance, fast forward, and rewind multimedia files.

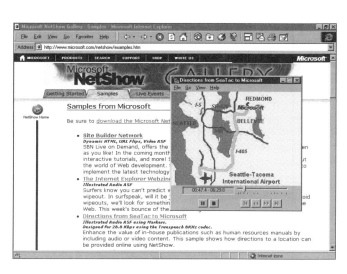

Looking at Internet Explorer 4

■ Going shopping with Microsoft Wallet

Microsoft Wallet is a computerized version of the wallet you carry
around in your back pocket or in your purse. Microsoft Wallet stores
and manages private and confidential information that you need to
conduct business online. It stores digital certificates (ID cards),
personal keys, passwords, credit card numbers, and digital cash. This
information can only be transferred to an online retailer if the user
authorizes the transaction and the transfer of the confidential
information.

■ Corresponding with Outlook Express

Outlook Express (shown at right) is Microsoft's combined e-mail and
newsgroup program. Outlook Express provides all the functionality of
Microsoft Internet Mail and News, along with new features such as the
ability to send and receive HTML messages and to filter incoming mail.

■ Joining real-time discussions with Microsoft Chat

Microsoft Chat is the newly updated version of Comic Chat.
Microsoft Chat has the same fun functionality that Comic Chat offers
with its comic strip interface, but Microsoft Chat has been improved
with the addition of a toolbar, user lists, and additional features.

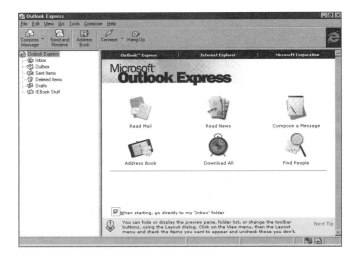

■ Conferencing with Microsoft NetMeeting

Microsoft NetMeeting is an Internet conferencing tool that supports
video and voice conversations. The application enables you to share
software applications and edit files with others in your conference,
participate in chat sessions, and use a common Whiteboard to help
with your meeting. NetMeeting uses industry standards, making it
compatible with other standards-based conferencing software
programs.

■ Creating Web pages with FrontPage Express

FrontPage Express is an easy-to-use Web page editor. FrontPage
Express lacks some of the advanced functionality of many Web page
editors, but is a great tool for novices or for people who want a quick

and easy way to create a Web page. FrontPage Express is fully compatible with Microsoft's FrontPage 97. Files created in FrontPage Express are easily converted to FrontPage 97 format.

INTRODUCING SOFTWARE SUITES

With the introduction of Internet Explorer 4, Microsoft took the concept of program suites and applied it to Internet applications. Like most program suites, you can choose which Internet applications you want to download and install on your computer. For the exercises in this book, however, you should install the full suite. If you want to delete some of the components later, you can.

Opening Internet Explorer 4 programs

With the application loaded on your computer, it's easy to start the Internet Explorer suite programs. Follow these few steps, and you'll be up and running in no time:

1 Select Start ➢ Programs. The program menu displays all of the programs installed on your computer.

2 Select Internet Explorer. Another menu displays that lists the Internet Explorer suite programs installed on your computer.

3 Click the program that you want to start.

4 Click the Close button at the top right corner of the window of the application you just opened.

5 Locate the Quick Launch toolbar. This toolbar is added by default to the Windows taskbar when you install Internet Explorer with the Active Desktop.

6 Click the View Channels button on the Quick Launch toolbar to open the Channel Viewer.

7 Click the Active Channel Guide button on the Channel bar. Internet Explorer opens in full-screen mode, and the preview of the channels appears. These channels are similar to television channels except that they consist of regularly updated Web pages. When you subscribe to a channel, Internet Explorer

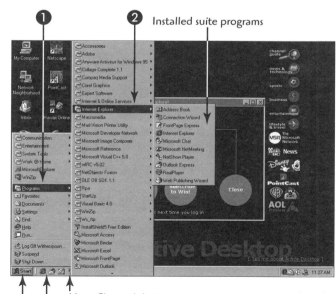

Installed suite programs

View Channels button
Quick Launch toolbar
Windows Start button

Switching between programs

informs you when the content on these Web pages changes. You learn about channels in Lesson 3.

8 Close the Channel Viewer by clicking the Close button at the upper right corner of the Channel Viewer window.

9 Click the Launch Mail button on the Quick Launch toolbar. The Outlook Express mail and news program opens.

10 Close the Outlook Express mail and news program by clicking the Close button at the upper right corner of the Outlook Express window.

NOTE *Your Channel Guide may look slightly different than the one shown in the figure because the appearance of this site changes often.*

Channel bar   Active Channel Guide   Channel Viewer

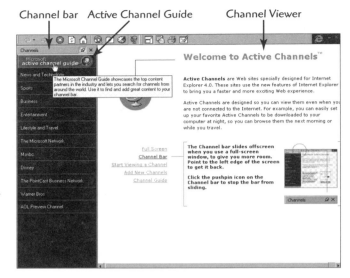

Switching between programs

Because all Internet Explorer suite programs are linked, it's easy to move from program to program. All Internet Explorer suite programs have a Go menu that contains links to all the other programs in the suite. This exercise shows how easy it is to move from one program to the next during a typical online session.

1 Click the Launch Internet Explorer Browser button on the Quick Launch toolbar. The Connection Manager establishes a connection with your ISP, and the default Microsoft Internet Start page displays in the browser window.

2 Click a few hyperlinks and look at the news and features Microsoft includes at this Web site.

3 After you've looked at a few Web pages, it's time to check the mail. Select Go ➢ Mail. Outlook Express opens and displays your Inbox.

4 To switch from Outlook Express to the Internet Explorer browser, select Go ➢ Home Page. The Internet Explorer browser appears with the Microsoft Internet Start Page displayed in the browser window.

Default Start page

Besides the Go menu, some Internet Explorer suite programs even have a toolbar button that opens another program in the suite.

5 Close Internet Explorer by clicking the Close button at the upper right corner of the program window.

6 Close Outlook Express by clicking the Close button at the upper right corner of the program window.

WRAP UP

In this lesson, you learned about the following:

- Upgrading to Internet Explorer 4
- Discovering what's new in version 4
- Opening and switching between programs in the Internet Explorer 4 suite

In the next lesson, you begin to explore the Internet Explorer Active Desktop.

TRY OUT THE
INTERACTIVE TUTORIALS
ON YOUR CD!

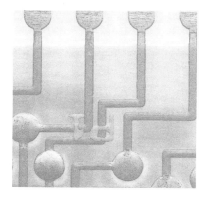

Welcome to the Active Desktop

45 MINUTES

GOALS

In this lesson, you learn about some of the exciting new features of Internet Explorer:

- Installing the Active Desktop
- Working with mouse buttons
- Using the Show Desktop button
- Adding shortcuts to the Quick Launch toolbar
- Adding the Address toolbar
- Adding the Links toolbar
- Adding the Desktop toolbar
- Creating a new toolbar
- Using Find to locate people
- Customizing folders in Windows Explorer
- Automating computer maintenance with Task Scheduler

Get ready

GET READY

To work your way through this lesson, you must install Internet Explorer 4 with the Active Desktop (refer to Appendix A for installation instructions).

When you complete this lesson, you will know how to add toolbars to the Windows taskbar and modify their appearance, use the Internet to search for people, and automate computer maintenance. You will also learn how to select and move files in Windows Explorer using the least number of mouse clicks and how to change the appearance of your folders in Windows Explorer.

MOVING AROUND THE ACTIVE DESKTOP

The Active Desktop is the biggest innovation of the Internet Explorer 4 suite. It adds a new desktop background to the Windows interface that functions like a Web page. One of the advantages of the Active Desktop is its ability to switch from browsing the Internet to browsing the contents of your computer's hard drive to browsing file servers on a computer network.

This book is full of explanations and tips for using the enhancements of the Active Desktop, but the first step is to install it and to look at how it changes the way you move around on the desktop.

Installing the Active Desktop

Before you can complete the exercises in this lesson, you must install the Active Desktop. If you selected the full installation option when you installed Internet Explorer 4, you can skip this exercise. If you didn't install the Active Desktop, you can install it now.

1 Close all open applications before you begin installing the Active Desktop.

2 Select Start ➤ Settings ➤ Control Panel to display the Control Panel window.

③ Double-click the Add/Remove Programs button to display the Add/Remove Programs Properties dialog box.

④ Select the Install/Uninstall tab.

⑤ Select Microsoft Internet Explorer 4.0 from the list of software.

⑥ Click the Add/Remove button to display the Internet Explorer 4.0 Active Setup dialog box.

⑦ Select the option button to Add Windows Desktop Update component from Web site.

⑧ Click the OK button. The Active Setup connects to your ISP and opens the Internet Explorer browser. The Components Download page appears.

⑨ Check the box next to Windows Desktop Update.

⑩ Click the Next button.

⑪ Follow the instructions to download and install the Active Desktop.

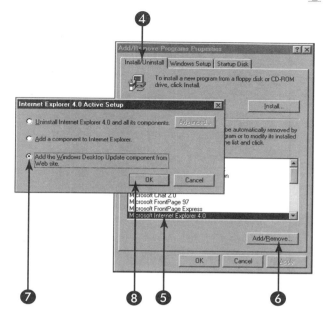

NOTE

To turn off the Active Desktop, right-click an empty area of the desktop and select Properties from the pop-up menu. Click the Web tab, uncheck the box labeled View my Active Desktop as a web page, and click OK.

■ Changing the way you open files

Internet Explorer 4 with the Active Desktop changes the way you open files and programs. Gone are the days of having to double-click the left mouse button. Now you can move around on your computer as easily as you move around on the Internet. Making the switch from a double-click to a single-click takes a little getting used to, but once you become accustomed to it, you will find it an easier way to work.

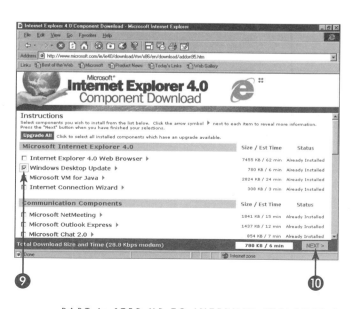

Working with mouse buttons

Working with mouse buttons

This exercise shows you how to set up the Active Desktop's new navigation features and demonstrates how they work with a tour of Windows Explorer.

1. Select Start ➢ Programs ➢ Windows Explorer to open Windows Explorer.

2. Select View ➢ Folder Options. The Folder Options dialog box appears, and the General tab should be displayed. If the General tab is not displayed, click it now.

3. In the Windows Desktop Update section, select the Web style option. This option allows you to browse the contents of your computer in much the same way you browse the Internet. Holding the mouse pointer over a file or folder selects it. Clicking the left mouse button once opens the file or folder.

4. Click OK to apply your changes.

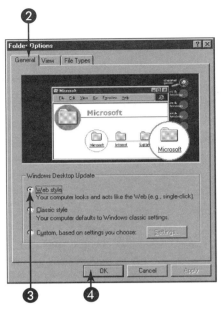

NOTE In Windows Explorer, you will select a folder that contains files you can practice with for this exercise.

5. Click the C: drive, and then select File ➢ New Folder.

6. Type **Exercise** and press Enter.

7. Double-click to select the CD-ROM drive.

8. Double-click to select the Exercise folder.

9. Place the mouse pointer over the file fax.doc but do not click. The file is highlighted.

10. Single-click the file to open it. The file opens in the associated application.

11. Close the file or application.

Working with mouse buttons

⑫ To select a range of files in Windows Explorer, place the mouse pointer over the first file.

⑬ Press and hold the Shift key.

⑭ Place the mouse pointer over the last file. The files are highlighted — without mouse clicks!

⑮ To select random files, place the mouse pointer over the first file. The file is highlighted.

⑯ Press and hold the Ctrl key.

⑰ Place the mouse pointer over each file that you want to select. The files are highlighted — again, without mouse clicks.

⑱ To move the selected files, click and hold the right mouse button on one of the selected files.

⑲ Drag the files to the Exercise folder on the C: drive.

⑳ Release the mouse button. A menu appears giving you a choice of what you want to do with the files.

㉑ Choose the appropriate menu selection. Choose Copy Here.

■ Using the Quick Launch toolbar

The Quick Launch is a toolbar that sits on the Windows taskbar and provides one-click access to your favorite applications. The default buttons are Launch Internet Explorer Browser, Launch Mail, Show Desktop, and View Channels. Microsoft developed this toolbar to provide a convenient way to launch the Internet Explorer suite applications.

Other lessons in this book explain the Internet Explorer browser, Outlook Express, and the Internet Explorer channels in detail, but since this lesson looks at the new navigation methods of the Active Desktop, it is a perfect place for a discussion of the Show Desktop button.

2

Welcome to the Active Desktop

Using the Show Desktop button

Using the Show Desktop button

The Show Desktop button hides open applications and displays the desktop. Although the applications appear to be minimized, they really are not. This feature is useful for multitasking, because you can easily move back and forth between the desktop and your applications. You don't have to minimize an application to open another one from a desktop shortcut.

① If the Quick Launch toolbar does not appear on the Windows taskbar, display the Windows taskbar on your screen and right-click an empty area of the taskbar to display a pop-up menu.

② Select Toolbars ➢ Quick Launch. The Quick Launch toolbar is added to the Windows taskbar.

③ Open an application so it is displayed on the monitor.

④ Click the Show Desktop button on the Quick Launch toolbar. Notice how the application is hidden and the desktop appears.

⑤ Click the Show Desktop button a second time. The application reappears.

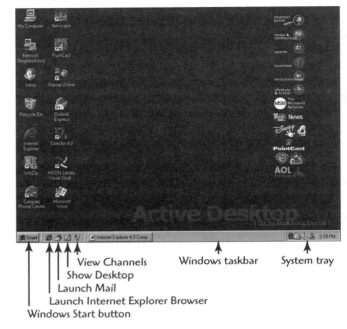

View Channels
Show Desktop
Launch Mail
Launch Internet Explorer Browser
Windows Start button
Windows taskbar
System tray

NOTE

If you have several applications open and maximized, all the applications are minimized when you click the Show Desktop button.

VISUAL BONUS

The Taskbar Loaded with Toolbars

You can customize the Windows taskbar to include toolbars that help you access applications, files, and the Internet faster and easier. You can select from four ready-to-use toolbars or build one of your own.

Web page corresponding to URL typed in Address toolbar

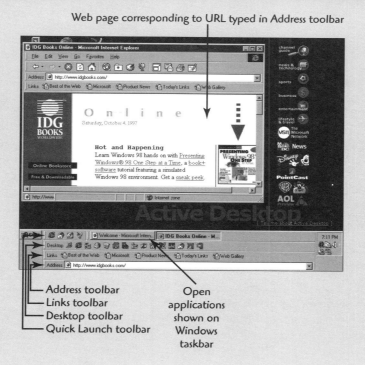

2

Welcome to the Active Desktop

Browser opened after typing a URL into the Address toolbar on the taskbar.

— Address toolbar
— Links toolbar
— Desktop toolbar
— Quick Launch toolbar

Open applications shown on Windows taskbar

MODIFYING THE TASKBAR

One of the new features of Internet Explorer's Active Desktop is the ability to add shortcuts to the Quick Launch toolbar and to add several toolbars to the Windows taskbar.

Adding shortcuts

Adding shortcuts to the Quick Launch toolbar

Although the Quick Launch toolbar comes preconfigured with the Show Desktop button and buttons that launch the browser, mail, and channels, you can add additional shortcuts and customize the toolbar any way you want. This exercise leads you through the steps for adding a shortcut to NetMeeting, a conferencing component of Internet Explorer 4. Refer to Lesson 13 for a detailed look at NetMeeting.

1 Make sure the Quick Launch toolbar is displayed on the Windows taskbar.

2 Select Start ➢ Settings ➢ Taskbar & Start Menu to display the Taskbar Properties dialog box.

3 Click the Start Menu Programs tab.

4 Click the Add button. This action opens the Start Menu Wizard with the Create Shortcut dialog box displayed.

5 Click the Browse button and locate the execution file for NetMeeting. If you followed the default installation for Internet Explorer 4, the path to the NetMeeting execution file is C:\Program Files\NetMeeting\. The execution file is called Conf.exe.

6 Place the mouse pointer over the file to select it.

7 Click Open. The path appears in the command line.

8 Click Next. The Select Program Folder dialog box displays.

9 Select Desktop.

10 Click Next. The Select a Title for the Program dialog box displays with the entry Conf.exe in the text box labeled Select a name for the shortcut.

11 Highlight the entry Conf.exe.

12 Type **NetMeeting** in the field.

13 Click Finish. A shortcut to NetMeeting appears on your desktop, and the Taskbar Properties dialog box appears on the screen.

1

Path to NetMeeting

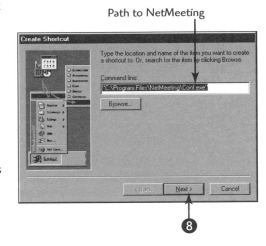

8

⑭ Click OK to close the dialog box.

⑮ Place the mouse pointer over the NetMeeting shortcut on your desktop.

⑯ Click and hold the mouse button while you drag the shortcut onto the Quick Launch toolbar and position it where you want it.

⑰ Release the mouse button to add the new icon to the Quick Launch toolbar.

If you want to remove the icon from your desktop, right-click the icon and select Delete on the pop-up menu. The icon is moved to the Recycle bin.

⑱ To open NetMeeting, click its icon on the Quick Launch toolbar.

You can change the size of the Quick Launch toolbar icons by right-clicking an empty place on the Quick Launch toolbar, selecting View on the pop-up menu, and then choosing Large or Small. You can also display text titles for the icons by right-clicking an empty place on the Quick Launch toolbar and selecting Show Text on the pop-up menu. If you add other toolbars to the Windows taskbar, you can use this method to change the size of the icons located on those toolbars also.

Adding the Address toolbar

The Address toolbar on the Active Desktop works the same way as the Address bar on the Internet Explorer browser, but you don't have to have the browser open to use the Address toolbar. When you type a URL into the Address toolbar and press Enter, the browser opens to display the specified Web page. This feature is useful if you have long Internet sessions but don't use the browser much while you're online.

❶ Right-click an empty area of the Windows taskbar to display the pop-up menu.

Shortcut to NetMeeting

Adding the Links toolbar

2 Select Toolbars ➢ Address. The Address toolbar is added to the Windows taskbar.

TIP *The toolbars discussed in this lesson do not have to be attached to the Windows taskbar. You can move the toolbars to the desktop. Place the mouse pointer over an empty place on the toolbar, click and hold the left mouse button, and drag the toolbar to the desktop. Release the mouse button. You now have a toolbar on the desktop instead of on the Windows taskbar.*

3 Connect to your Internet service provider (ISP).

4 Type the URL for IDG Books in the Address toolbar: `http://www.idgbooks.com`.

5 Press Enter. The Internet Explorer browser opens to the IDG Books Web page.

Browser opens to Web page.

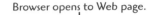
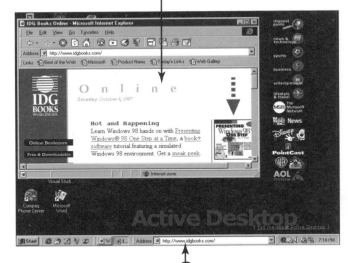

Adding the Links toolbar

If you decide to customize the Links toolbar on the Internet Explorer browser (you learn how in Lesson 8) and use these sites or files often, you may want to put the Links toolbar on your taskbar.

1 Right-click an empty area of the taskbar to display the pop-up menu.

2 Select Toolbars ➢ Links. The Links toolbar is added to the Windows taskbar.

TIP *You can make the Windows taskbar taller by placing the mouse pointer over the top of the taskbar. The pointer turns into a double arrow. Click and hold the left mouse button while you drag the mouse pointer toward the top of your screen. As you move the mouse pointer up, the toolbars stack one on top of another.*

3 Connect to your ISP.

④ Click the Today's Links button. The Microsoft site displays.

Browser opens to Web page.

TIP

To close a toolbar (remove it from the Windows taskbar), right-click the toolbar and select Close from the menu.

Adding the Desktop toolbar

The Desktop toolbar takes all the shortcut icons from your desktop and puts them on the Windows taskbar. Being able to open programs from the Windows taskbar makes it easier to open multiple programs because you don't have to minimize your programs or even click the Show Desktop button to open new applications. Another handy aspect of this feature is that you can hide all the icons on your desktop and make room for the Active Desktop components introduced in Lesson 3.

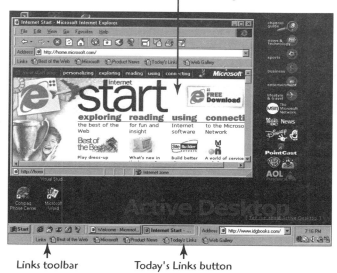

Links toolbar   Today's Links button

① Right-click an empty area of the taskbar to display the pop-up menu.

② Select Toolbars ➤ Desktop. The Desktop toolbar is added to the Windows taskbar.

NOTE

You can use the same method to add shortcut icons to the Desktop toolbar that you used for adding icons to the Quick Launch toolbar.

③ Since all of your Desktop icons are now on the taskbar, you can hide the desktop icons to make more room on your screen. To hide the icons, first open Windows Explorer.

④ Select View ➤ Folder Options. The Folder Options dialog box appears.

⑤ Click the View tab.

⑥ Scroll to the bottom of the list and select the option to Hide icons when desktop is viewed as Web page.

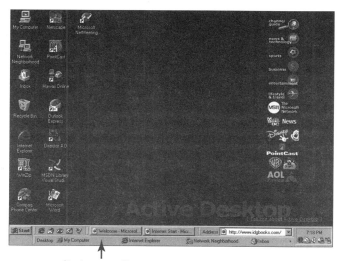

Desktop toolbar

Creating a new toolbar

⑦ Click OK. The icons disappear from the desktop.

⑧ Click the Close button at the top right corner of the Windows Explorer window to close the window.

Creating a new toolbar

In addition to the Quick Launch, Address, Links, and Desktop toolbars you've already learned how to set up, you can build customized toolbars for the Active Desktop. Anything you can put inside a Windows folder can be made into a toolbar. You can put shortcuts to programs into a folder and create a new toolbar from that folder. Or you can put frequently accessed files in a folder and create a toolbar so the files are easy to access at any time.

❶ Right-click an empty area of the taskbar to display the pop-up menu.

❷ Select Toolbars ➤ New Toolbar. The New Toolbar dialog box displays.

❸ Select the Printers folder.

❹ Click OK. You now have a new toolbar that shows icons for each of the printer files and applications in the folder, custom made to fit your computing style.

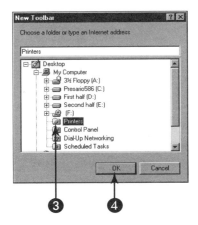

WORKING WITH WINDOWS

The Active Desktop integrates with the Windows 95 operating system and extends the operating system's capabilities. The exercises in this section show you some new Windows tricks: using Start ➤ Find to locate e-mail addresses, customizing folders in Windows Explorer, and automating maintenance tasks.

Using Find to locate people

The Active Desktop Start menu not only includes the same options that are available in Windows 95, but also extends the power of the Find tool beyond the boundaries of the files on your personal

Customized toolbar

Using Find to locate people

computer. Now you can use Find to search for information about people—their e-mail and postal addresses and telephone numbers. This exercise shows you how.

You can use the Find function to locate information such as e-mail addresses, street addresses, and phone numbers—a handy tool for tracking down former friends, past employers, and even lost family members. The Find function gives you access to several directory servers that maintain searchable databases set up in much the same way as the telephone directory. You could use this search tool, for example, to try to find the phone number and address of Cousin Joe to invite him to a family reunion. And although there's no guarantee that you will be able to find information about your cousin, the directories accessible from the Find function are a good place to start looking.

❶ Connect to your ISP.

❷ From the Start Menu, select Find ➤ People. The Find People dialog box displays.

❸ From the Look in drop-down list, select the SwitchBoard directory.

❹ In the Name field, type your name.

❺ Click the Find Now button. The Switchboard directory service searches through its database for the name you typed in the Name field.

❻ A list of possible matches to your search appears in a window on the Find People dialog box.

❼ When you find the person you are looking for, you can add him or her to your Windows Address Book by clicking the Add to Address Book button.

NOTE *To learn more about the Windows Address Book, refer to Lesson 10.*

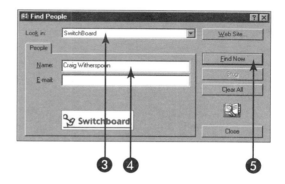

Visit the directory's Web page.

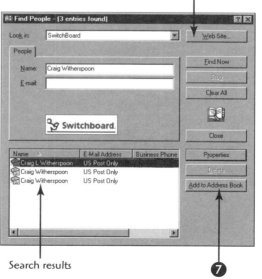

Search results

Customizing folders

8 To search for the same person using another directory service, highlight a different service in the Look in drop-down list and click the Find Now button.

NOTE *To visit the directory service's Web site, select the directory service from the Look in drop-down list and click the Web Site button.*

9 When you are finished looking for people, close the Find People window by clicking the Close button.

Customizing folders in Windows Explorer

The Active Desktop includes an option that allows you to change the appearance of your Windows folders. You can add a colorful background picture and change the color of the text. Folder customization is a just-for-fun feature of the Active Desktop, and the steps in this exercise show you how to take advantage of this personalizing option.

1 Start Windows Explorer.

2 Select the folder you want to customize.

3 Select View ➢ Customize this Folder. This action brings up the Customize this Folder wizard.

4 You are given the choice of creating an HTML document or choosing a background picture. Select Choose a background picture.

5 Click the Next button. The next wizard screen displays a list of available background pictures.

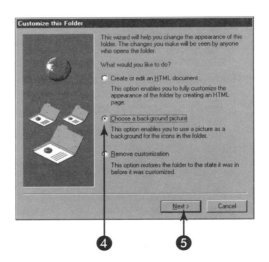

TIP *Refer to Lesson 14 for details on how to create Hypertext Markup Language (HTML) documents in Internet Explorer 4.*

6 Scroll through the picture list and select the background named Clouds.bmp. A preview of the background picture appears in a window on the left side of the wizard screen.

TIP

If you have a picture stored on your computer that you would like to use for the folder's background, click the Browse button and locate the file that contains the picture.

7 With Clouds.bmp highlighted, click the Text button below the picture list.

8 The Color dialog box appears. You use this color palette to choose a color for the folder's text labels. Select a dark blue color.

9 Click OK. The next wizard screen appears.

10 Click the Background checkbox on the wizard screen to enable the Background option. This background is the color that will appear behind your folder's text labels. Use the default color of white.

11 Click the Next button. The final screen of the wizard appears.

12 Click the Finish button. You have set a background picture for the folder, chosen a color for the text that appears in the folder, and selected a color to appear behind the text.

TIP

Remove the background from the folder by starting the Customize this Folder wizard and selecting the option to Remove customization.

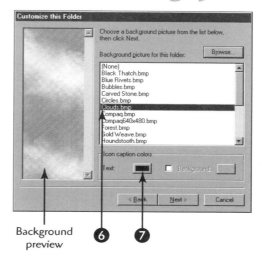

Background preview **6** **7**

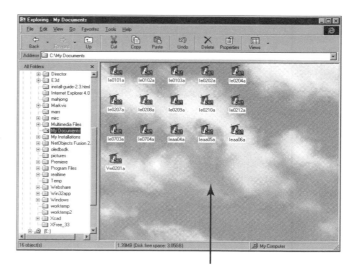

Customized folder

2

Welcome to the Active Desktop

Automating computer maintenance

Automating computer maintenance

The Task Scheduler that comes with Internet Explorer 4 is an improvement over the original Windows 95 version. The scheduler is easy to use and lets you automate the running of scheduled maintenance programs.

1 From Windows Explorer, click the Scheduled Tasks folder in the directory tree. You can find this folder toward the bottom of the list, below the Control Panel and Dial-Up Networking folders.

Clicking the Scheduled Tasks folder adds the Advanced menu item to the Internet Explorer menu bar.

2 Select Advanced > Start Using Task Scheduler. The Task Scheduler icon is added to the Windows taskbar system tray.

3 Click Add Scheduled Task in the right pane of the Windows Explorer window. This action opens the Scheduled Task Wizard.

4 Click Next.

5 Scroll through the list of applications and select ScanDisk.

6 Click Next.

7 The next wizard screen shows ScanDisk in the text box. Select the Weekly option in the Schedule to run section.

8 Click Next.

9 On the next wizard screen, either use the spin controls to set the time for 12:00 p.m. or type the time in the text box.

10 Check the box labeled Friday.

11 Click Next.

12 On the last screen of the wizard, click Finish to add a weekly running of ScanDisk to the list of Scheduled Tasks.

13 You can further automate the ScanDisk task by adding parameters after the file path in the Run field. From the Scheduled Tasks window, right-click ScanDisk.

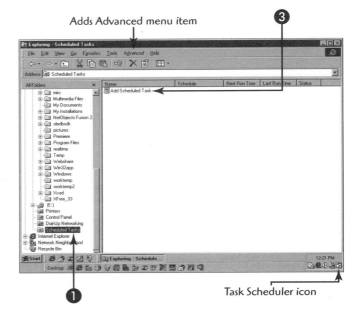

Adds Advanced menu item

Task Scheduler icon

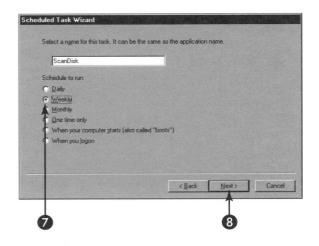

⑭ Choose Properties on the pop-up menu.

⑮ On the ScanDisk dialog box, select the Task tab.

⑯ Add any of the following parameters to the Run command line. Be sure to include a space between the path name and each of the parameters you choose.

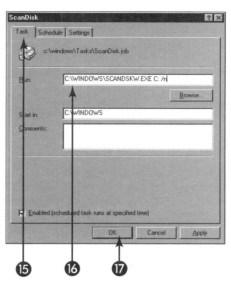

Parameter	Use	Example
drive letter:	To specify the drive(s) you want to check	To check the C: drive for errors, type **C:\WINDOWS\ SCANDSKW.EXE C:**.
/n	To start and close ScanDisk automatically	To open and close ScanDisk without user intervention, type **C:\WINDOWS\ SCANDSKW.EXE /n**.
/p	To prevent ScanDisk from correcting any errors it finds	To set ScanDisk so you can manually correct errors, type **C:\WINDOWS\ SCANDSKW.EXE /p**.

⑰ Click OK to close the dialog box.

SKILLS CHALLENGE: PERFORMING MAINTENANCE AND CREATING TOOLBARS

You have picked up some good skills in this lesson, and now it's time to put them to the test. During the Task Scheduler exercise, you probably thought of some other maintenance tasks you'd like to automate. The customized toolbar exercise probably gave you some good ideas for collecting often-used files and turning them into a handy toolbar. This Skills Challenge lets you put these ideas into practice. You can always refer to the exercises if you need a few tips to help you along.

❶ Open Task Scheduler and start the Scheduled Task Wizard.

❷ Set up the Disk Defragmenter to run on the first day of each month. For a list of parameters that you can use with the Disk

Skills challenge

Defragmenter, look in the Microsoft Knowledge Base (`http://www.microsoft.com/kb`) and search for article number Q155326.

 1 *Where, during the Scheduled Task Wizard process, do you tell the wizard that you want to define additional settings for the scheduled task? What kinds of additional settings are available?*

3 Close Task Scheduler.

4 Open Windows Explorer. Create a new folder and put your most frequently used files in it. For example, if you own a small business, you might put proposal templates, invoices, tracking sheets, and form letters in this folder.

5 Create a new toolbar for this folder.

6 Move the toolbar from the taskbar to the desktop.

 2 *How do you change the size of the icons in a toolbar?*

 3 *How do you hide toolbar titles and the descriptive text for toolbar buttons?*

7 Add, delete, or move your Active Desktop toolbars to fit your personal computing preferences.

TROUBLESHOOTING

Upgrading to a new version of a favorite software program can be a challenge. Here are the answers to a few questions you might have about the Active Desktop.

Problem	Solution
How do I close toolbars that I don't want to view on the Windows taskbar?	Right-click the name of the toolbar (or on an empty area of the toolbar if you have the titles hidden) and choose Close from the menu.
How do I add program icons to the Quick Launch toolbar?	Create a shortcut for the program and place it on the desktop. Drag and drop it onto the toolbar.
I can't get the Disk Defragmenter to start automatically even though I have it set up as a scheduled task in the Task Scheduler. The scheduler opens the Disk Defragmenter, but it just sits there waiting for me to click Start. Is there a command I need to add to the file line?	Use the /NOPROMPT parameter.
How do I remove the Task Scheduler icon from the Windows taskbar system tray?	Double-click the Task Scheduler icon to open Task Scheduler. Select Advanced , Stop Using Task Scheduler.

WRAP UP

In this lesson, you practiced the following skills:

- Familiarizing yourself with the Internet Explorer Active Desktop
- Using the Active Desktop tools on the Internet
- Creating and customizing toolbars to fit your computing needs
- Automating maintenance tasks with the Task Scheduler

In the next lesson, you begin to explore the features and functions of the Internet Explorer browser.

TRY OUT THE

INTERACTIVE TUTORIALS

ON YOUR CD!

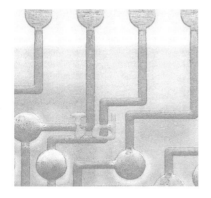

Integrating the Desktop and the Browser

GOALS

60 MINUTES

In this lesson, you master the following skills:

- Subscribing to the Microsoft Network channel
- Subscribing to a new channel
- Viewing updated channel content
- Adding a clock to your desktop
- Adding an active screen saver
- Adding an active Web page to your desktop
- Removing Active Desktop components
- Changing the Active Desktop wallpaper
- Controlling the behavior of your files and folders
- Turning the Active Desktop off and on
- Printing a Web page
- Finding Help

Get ready

GET READY

To complete this lesson, you must have Internet Explorer 4 installed on your computer (refer to Appendix A). Additionally, you must be connected to the Internet before you begin the exercises. When you complete the exercises in this lesson, you'll be able to customize many of Internet Explorer's features. You'll also be able to add active items to your desktop, and know how to access the dialog box for changing the way the items display.

As you work through the exercises in this lesson, you may notice that your computer doesn't look exactly like the screen in an illustration or the title of a button has changed. As more channels are added, Microsoft changes the way they are displayed on the screen.

TRY OUT THE
INTERACTIVE TUTORIALS
ON YOUR CD!

ADDING ITEMS TO THE DESKTOP

One of Internet Explorer's most exciting features is the way it integrates your computer and the Web on your desktop. At any time during the day or night, the Web and its blend of information and fun are available. Click a channel to instantly see fresh information that may have been updated a few minutes ago. Find desktop items at Microsoft's Active Desktop Gallery and place them on your desktop. Your can make your computer an extension of the things you like.

■ Working with channels

Channels allow you to view information that's pushed to your computer. What can you expect to see when you a look at a channel? The best way to describe a channel is as a cross between a Web site and a television program. Although you can preview a channel by clicking its button on the Channel bar, you need to subscribe to take full advantage of the ability to view the new content that's been added to the channel site.

When you subscribe to a channel, you specify how often you want to update the channel and how you'll be notified of the new content. Based on the scheduling options you select, Internet

Adding items to the desktop

Explorer compares the current channel content against the content you viewed last. Internet Explorer copies the new content to the hard drive of your computer when you update your subscriptions. You can update all of your channel subscriptions at one time or select specific ones for update. Once the new channel content has been copied to your computer, you can disconnect from the Internet and view the channel offline.

Start slowly and subscribe to only a few channels instead of to every channel that interests you. Since many files need to be copied to the hard drive of your computer to maintain channel subscriptions, you might find that your computer can't handle several subscriptions—especially if it's an older model or doesn't have a big hard drive. As you subscribe to channels, monitor your system performance carefully. If you notice that your computer seems sluggish or if the display flickers or doesn't look right, unsubscribe from a channel you don't like as much as the others.

CHANNELS — THE LATEST AND GREATEST

In the old days, you got your news from the morning newspaper, the evening television news broadcast, or a weekly magazine that was delivered in the mail. Now, with Internet Explorer, news can come to you as often as you want and you don't need to leave your computer. The technology that enables information to be delivered to your computer at preselected times is called *push*.

Webcasters, also called push applications, deliver the information you select to your computer. By using channels that provide streams of information from Web sources, Webcasting programs send headlines or complete articles directly to your Active Desktop as small desktop items, scrolling tickers, or even screen savers. After you set up your Active Desktop, you can look at the latest stock quotes, football scores, and weather maps on your screen.

Push technology employs some cutting-edge techniques. With Internet Explorer, Microsoft has taken a leap toward making push technology an important way to provide news and other information. In fact, Microsoft is so committed to push that it has developed a standard called Channel Definition Format, or CDF for short, that promises to standardize the way channel content is delivered. Expect to see hundreds, or maybe even thousands, of new push channels in the next few years.

3

Integrating the Desktop and the Browser

Subscribing to the Microsoft Network

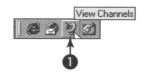

Subscribing to the Microsoft Network channel

When you first install Internet Explorer and the Active Desktop, the Channel bar appears on your desktop. Several preselected channels appear on the bar, including the Microsoft Network. In this exercise, you subscribe to the Microsoft Network.

1 Click the View Channels button on the Quick Launch toolbar, located on the Windows taskbar. If the Quick Launch toolbar isn't visible, position the mouse pointer on a blank space on the Windows taskbar and click the right mouse button one time. Select Toolbars ➤ Quick Launch.

2 The Channel bar appears. To prevent the Channel bar from sliding off the edge of the screen, click the pushpin icon at the top of the Channel bar. The Channel bar remains in place, and the pushpin looks pressed in.

3 Slide the mouse pointer through the channel buttons. Since you haven't set up any channels, only the default channels appear now. As the mouse passes over a channel, the text converts to the channel's icon.

4 Click the channel button for the Microsoft Network. Different graphics about the Microsoft Network appear on the screen.

5 Click the Add Active Channel button when the screen activity stops. The Modify Subscription dialog box appears.

6 On the Modify Subscription dialog box, click the option button next to Yes, but only tell me when updates occur. The dialog box closes, and the Microsoft Network page appears on the right side of the screen.

Whenever an update to the Microsoft Network channel is copied to your computer, a starburst icon, called a *gleam*, appears next to the channel's title on the Channel bar.

7 Close the Channel bar by clicking the pressed-in pushpin. The Channel bar slides off the screen, and the Microsoft Network appears.

Pushpin anchors the Channel bar.

Channels

Microsoft Channel Guide

News and Technology

Sports

Business

Entertainment

Lifestyle and Travel

The Microsoft Network

Msnbc

Disney

The PointCast Business Network

Warner Bros

AOL Preview Channel

Subscribing to the Microsoft Network

TIP

Whenever you want to redisplay the Channel bar, point the mouse at the left edge of the screen. The Channel bar reappears on the screen.

MSN Presents bar   Fullscreen button

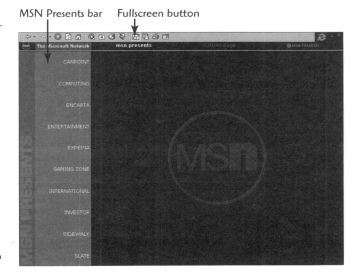

8 Click one of the links on the MSN Presents bar to move to the linked topic.

Hyperlinks can appear as graphic images or as underlined, highlighted text. (You learn all about hyperlinks in Lesson 4). You know you're viewing a hyperlink when the mouse pointer takes the shape of a hand. Other links on a channel page may change color or change shape when the mouse passes over them.

9 Another page of links appears. Click the topic you'd like to see.

10 Look through the channel, clicking any links that interest you to view the linked page.

11 Close the channel by clicking the Close button in the top right corner of the screen.

12 Whenever you want to update only the Microsoft Network channel content, click the Channels button on the Standard Buttons toolbar to open the Channel bar on the left side of the screen.

13 Click the right mouse button on the Microsoft Network icon and choose Update Now from the resulting shortcut menu. Internet Explorer checks the Microsoft Network channel site for new content. If the content has changed since the last time you viewed it, a dialog box that shows files being downloaded to your computer appears briefly.

14 Close the Subscriptions window by clicking the Close button on the Subscription window title bar.

15 A gleam on the left corner of the MSN button on the Channel bar indicates that new information has been added to the channel. Click the MSN button to view the Microsoft Network channel.

Gleam indicates
new content

Subscribing to a new channel

Subscribing to a new channel

In this exercise, you find and subscribe to a sports channel. Subscribing to a channel isn't like signing up for cable TV; there are no fees to pay or long forms to fill out. Best of all, you tell the content provider when and how you want the information displayed.

NOTE *Unless you set up a subscription to dial your ISP and connect to the Internet at a scheduled time, you must issue the command for Internet Explorer to look for updated material.*

1 Click the View Channels button on the Quick Launch toolbar. The Channel bar opens in its own window.

2 The Channel bar initially displays a few featured channels in different categories, including MSNBC News and the Microsoft Network. The bar also contains an Active Channel Guide with more categories of available channels. Click the Microsoft Active Channel Guide on the Channel bar to chose from the available channels.

After a few seconds, the expanded Channel bar slides off the screen. The Active Channel Guide appears in full-screen view with links to channel categories, including Business, Entertainment, Lifestyles, and Sports. Click the Sports link to display the available channels in the Sports category.

3 A list of channel providers appears in the left pane. Position your mouse pointer over the CBS SportsLine channel to display information about that channel's content.

TIP *Your screen may look different than the one shown in the example. Microsoft regularly changes the Active Channel Guide.*

4 If all the channels for a category don't fit on one page, a button to advance to the next screen is included on the page. Click the button to view other channels.

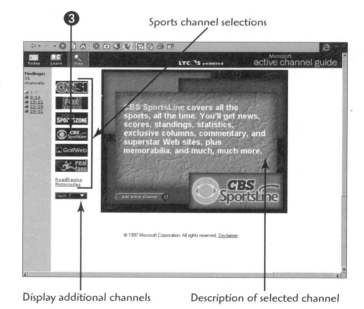

Sports channel selections

Display additional channels

Description of selected channel

Subscribing to a new channel

5 Click the button for the CBS SportsLine channel. A preview of the channel appears in the center of the screen.

6 Click the Add Active Channel button to add a button for the channel to the Channel bar.

7 A dialog box may appear briefly on the screen, indicating that files are being copied to your computer. When the files have been copied, the Modify Channel Usage dialog box appears on the screen. The following options are available:

Option	What It Means
No, just keep it in my Channel Bar	You don't set a subscription, but can click the button to view the channel content when you're connected to the Internet.
Yes, but only tell me when updates occur	When the channel content changes, a gleam appears next to the channel name. You can also request to be notified of content changes by e-mail.
Yes, notify me of updates and download the channel for offline viewing	You receive notification when the channel content changes, and can view the channel when you're not connected to the Internet. If you have a pay-by-the-hour ISP or don't want to tie up your phone line, this option makes good sense.

8 Click the option button next to the third option: Yes, notify me of updates and download the channel for offline viewing.

9 Click Customize. The Subscription Wizard dialog box appears.

10 The Subscription Wizard asks you to choose if you want to download only the channel home page to your computer's hard drive or to download all content specified by the channel.

Click the option to Download only the channel home page.

11 Click Next.

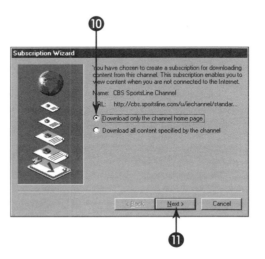

3

Integrating the Desktop and the Browser

Subscribing to a new channel

TIP

Although it's tempting to download all of a channel's content, you need to consider two important points. The first consideration is the size of your computer's hard drive. Channel files are large and take up a significant amount of hard drive space. The second consideration is system resources. Downloading and viewing a channel are memory-intensive operations and may diminish your computer's performance.

12 The next dialog box asks if you'd like to be notified by e-mail when the channel content changes. Click the option button next to No (you learn about e-mail in Lesson 10).

13 Click Next. The next dialog box offers three channel update options:

Option	What It Does
Scheduled	Choose daily, weekly, or monthly updates, or choose the publisher's recommended schedule.
Dial as needed	This option is available only if the Autodial feature of your Dial-Up Networking connection is enabled.
Manually	You decide when to update the subscription and choose Update Subscription from the Favorites menu.

14 Click the option button next to Scheduled and accept the publisher's recommended schedule.

15 Click Finish to end the Subscription Wizard.

16 The Add Active Channel dialog box reappears, confirming the choices you made. Click OK to close the dialog box. The new channel is added to the Channel bar.

17 If the channel you selected has an associated screen saver, the Channel Screen Saver dialog box appears asking if you want to replace your current screen saver with the new one. Click No.

18 The Channel bar slides off the left edge, and the content of the new channel appears on the screen. Explore the new channel, clicking links and hyperlinks to move around.

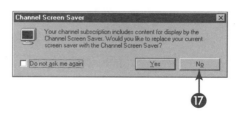

Viewing updated channel content

TIP

The links you encounter while viewing a channel may not appear as hyperlinks. Instead of the mouse pointer taking the shape of a hand when it passes over a link, the screen may change color or a sound might play. If an item on a channel page looks like it may lead somewhere else (like an entry on an index or an arrow, for example), try clicking it with the mouse to see if it's a link.

⑲ Close the Channel by clicking the Close button at the top right corner of the screen.

⑳ The new channel appears on the Channel bar on the Active Desktop.

Viewing updated channel content

Before you can view updated channel content, you need to update your channel subscriptions so that the new information is copied to the hard drive of your computer. In this exercise, you update your channel subscriptions and view the content offline.

When you update your channels, Internet Explorer obtains the new material from the channel content providers for each of your channel subscriptions. The channels are updated based on the schedule you specified when you set up each subscription. Internet Explorer checks the date and time of the last update and the time a new update is scheduled for each of your channel subscriptions and updates only the ones that are due.

❶ If it's not already open, launch the browser by clicking the Launch Internet Explorer Browser button on the Quick Launch toolbar.

❷ Select Favorites ➢ Update All Subscriptions.

❸ The Downloading Subscriptions dialog box appears as files are transferred from the content provider to the hard drive of your computer.

When the updated content has been copied to your computer, the Downloading Subscriptions dialog box closes.

Status bar

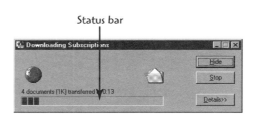

Viewing updated channel content

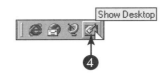

Show Desktop

④ If you want to look at the new content while you're connected to the Internet, click the Show Desktop button on the Quick Launch toolbar.

④

⑤ When the Active Desktop appears, click the button on the Channel bar corresponding to the channel you want to see.

⑥ When the channel opens, look through it, clicking any links that interest you.

⑦ When you're finished, close the channel by clicking the Close button in the top right corner of the screen.

⑧ If you want to look at the new content offline, first disconnect from the Internet as you usually do when you conclude your browsing session.

⑨ When you're no longer connected, select File ➤ Work Offline. A checkmark appears to let you know that you've activated offline mode.

⑩ Follow the instructions in step 5 to look at the content of channels that you've subscribed to.

⑪ When you've finished looking at channels in offline mode, select File ➤ Work Offline to clear the checkmark and deactivate offline mode.

TIP

Always remember to select File ➤ Work Offline to remove the checkmark when you're finished working offline. Otherwise the Internet Explorer browser will start in offline mode the next time you launch it.

⑫ If you want, reconnect to the Internet and continue browsing through Web sites and exploring new channels.

Adding a clock to your desktop

CUSTOMIZING THE ACTIVE DESKTOP

In addition to adding channels to the Active Desktop Channel bar, you can customize the look and feel of your Active Desktop. You can add desktop items like a clock, scrolling stock ticker, or a weather map. You can even add Web content, such as your company's home page, to the desktop. You can use an active item, like a page of stock listings and a scrolling ticker, as a screen saver. Or you can restore the settings that were in use before you installed Internet Explorer's Active Desktop. Your desktop is your own, so why not customize it to reflect your personal preferences?

Adding a clock to your desktop

Viewing real-time information on your desktop is a great way to personalize your computer. Microsoft furnishes several desktop items that offer regularly updated news, weather, and a "cool" clock. In this exercise, you place the clock on your desktop.

NOTE *Avoid the temptation to place too many desktop items on your Active Desktop. These items use valuable system resources and can make your computer seem slow and unresponsive when you work with other programs. Start small, with a simple item like the clock. Make sure you're happy with your computer's performance after you install each item.*

1 Close or minimize all open applications on your computer.

2 Open the browser by clicking the Launch Internet Explorer Browser button on the Quick Launch toolbar.

3 Click inside the Address bar to highlight the existing text.

4 Type `www.microsoft.com/ie/ie40/gallery/`, noticing that as you type, the existing text is replaced by the new text you enter.

5 Press Enter when you've typed the URL. (You learn all about URLs in Lesson 4.)

3

Integrating the Desktop and the Browser

Adding a clock to your desktop

6 When The Microsoft Active Desktop Gallery appears, scroll down the page to the section of Cool Utilities links. Position the mouse pointer on the link to the 3D Java Clock. The pointer takes the shape of a hand, signifying that the text is a hyperlink.

7 Click the hyperlink one time with the left mouse button. The Internet Explorer icon in the top right corner of the browser window becomes animated and several messages flash across the status bar. In a few moments, the download page for the 3D Java Clock appears.

8 Click the Add to Active Desktop button.

9 Click Yes in response in the question, Do you want to add a desktop item to your active desktop? The Add item to Active Desktop dialog box displays.

10 Click OK. The Downloading Subscriptions dialog displays briefly as the components needed to display the clock are downloaded to your computer.

11 Minimize the Internet Explorer browser to view your desktop. The clock is displayed on your desktop in its own window.

12 You can move the clock around the desktop by dragging its title bar. Position the mouse pointer on a blank area on the desktop item's title bar and click and drag the window to another area of the desktop.

13 After you install the clock, open a few of the programs that you normally use. Once you're sure that your computer doesn't seem sluggish or slow, repeat the steps in this exercise to set up additional desktop items.

TIP

You need to be connected to the Internet for the Active Desktop items to display properly. If you don't have a direct connection, your Active Desktop items will appear as gray boxes when you're not logged on.

Adding an active screen saver

Adding an active screen saver

Instead of the average screen savers you're used to, you can use an active item as a screen saver. After your computer is idle for a prespecified time period, the screen saver displays. Move your mouse or touch the keyboard to dismiss the screen saver.

Not all active items are available as screen savers. In this exercise, you subscribe to the StockPoint channel and use the channel's active content as your screen saver.

❶ Close or minimize all open applications on your computer.

❷ Click the View Channels button on the Quick Launch toolbar.

❸ Click the Active Channel Guide button on the Channel bar to display the available channel categories.

❹ Click the Business category to display the available channels that provide active content about business-related topics.

❺ If the StockPoint channel button is visible on the left side of the screen, click it to display the StockPoint channel. If the button isn't visible, type **stockpoint** in the text box.

❻ Click Find. The StockPoint channel appears.

❼ Click the Add Active Channel button.

❽ When the dialog box appears, you should see the third option button selected: Yes, notify me of updates and download the channel for offline viewing. Click OK to continue.

❾ The Active Channel appears, displaying a stock ticker across the top of the screen. Click the Customize button to display a page of custom options you can add. Although many of the customizable options look enticing, for now make sure only the box next to Screen Saver is checked.

❿ Click the Update Channel Settings button.

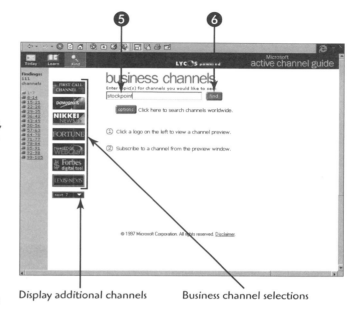

Display additional channels   Business channel selections

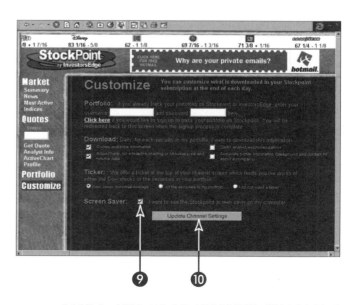

Adding an active screen saver

NOTE *If the Security Alert dialog box appears, click Yes. The Security Alert dialog box appears whenever you exchange information with another computer over the Internet.*

⓫ The Add item to Active Desktop dialog box appears to confirm your subscription to the StockPoint channel. Click OK to close the dialog box. The Downloading Subscriptions dialog box appears as files are copied to your computer.

⓬ Your screen saver is set. To verify the screen saver, click the Start button.

⓭ Select Settings ➢ Active Desktop ➢ Customize my Desktop. The Display Properties dialog box appears.

⓮ Click the Screen Saver tab. The Channel Screen Saver is shown in the Screen Saver box.

⓯ If you want, use the spin controls next to Wait to change the time interval that your computer must be inactive for the screen saver to appear.

⓰ Click the Settings button. The StockPoint screen saver appears in the Channels section of the Screen Saver Properties dialog box.

⓱ Click OK to close the Screen Saver Properties dialog box. You're returned to the Display Properties dialog box.

⓲ Click OK to close the Display Properties dialog box. You're returned to the Active Desktop. The StockPoint Channel appears in the Channel bar on the desktop.

⓳ If you minimized the Internet Explorer browser, click its button on the Windows taskbar to make the Internet Explorer browser the active window. (If you're not sure, point the mouse pointer at each button on the taskbar and read the program name in the resulting screen tip.)

If the browser was not open when you started this exercise, click the Launch Internet Explorer Browser button on the Quick Launch toolbar.

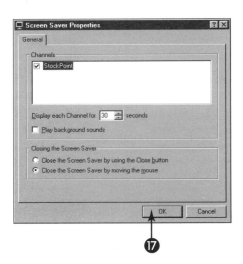

Adding an active Web page

⑳ When the Internet Explorer browser is visible on the screen, click the Home button on the Internet Explorer browser Standard Buttons toolbar to move to or refresh the Microsoft Internet Start page.

Whenever your computer is inactive for the amount of time you specified and you're connected to the Internet, the StockPoint screen saver will display.

Adding an active Web page to your desktop

You can add any Web page to your desktop. You might want to add your company's home page, a page you particularly like, or a page that contains links to other sites.

In this exercise, you add the IDG Books Worldwide page to your desktop.

❶ Close or minimize all open applications on your computer so that your Windows desktop is visible.

❷ Click the right mouse button on an empty area of the desktop. A pop-up shortcut menu appears.

❸ Select Active Desktop ➢ Customize my Desktop. The Display Properties dialog box appears.

❹ Click the Web tab.

❺ When the Web settings appear, click New. The New Active Desktop Item dialog box appears.

❻ Click No in response to the question asking if you'd like to connect to the Active Desktop Gallery.

❼ In the resulting dialog box, type www.idgbooks.com in the Location box.

TIP

Always jot down the URL (Web address) of a page that you want to place on your Active Desktop before you begin the process to add it. That way, you'll be able to complete the steps quickly, instead of fumbling for the Web address.

3

Integrating the Desktop and the Browser

PART I: STEP UP TO INTERNET EXPLORER 4 **55**

Removing Active Desktop components

8 Click OK. The Add item to Active Desktop dialog box appears, advising you that you are subscribing to the IDG site and including it on your desktop.

9 Click OK to confirm that's what you're doing. The Downloading dialog box appears briefly as files are copied to your computer.

When the download is complete, the Display Properties dialog box reappears and the new item is added to the Web tab.

10 Click OK to close the Display Properties dialog box and return to the Active Desktop.

11 The IDG Books site appears in its own window on the desktop. Make the window that contains the IDG page larger by placing the mouse pointer in one of the perimeter borders around the page.

12 When the mouse takes the shape of a double-headed arrow, click and drag the border outward. The window is enlarged.

If you decide to change the way your Active Desktop looks, it's a snap to remove desktop items.

Removing Active Desktop components

After you've loaded up your Active Desktop with gizmos, you might find that you've added too many items or decide that an item isn't as useful as you thought it would be. In this exercise, you remove the IDG Books Worldwide page that you added to your desktop.

1 Close or minimize all open applications on your computer so that your Windows desktop is visible.

2 Right-click an empty area of the desktop to access the pop-up menu.

3 Select Active Desktop ➣ Customize my Desktop. The Display Properties dialog box appears.

4 Click the Web tab to display all of the items you've added to the Active Desktop.

5 Click the IDG Books item so that it appears highlighted.

6 Click Delete.

Web tab

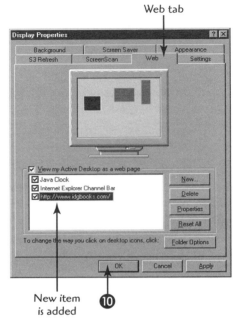

New item is added **10**

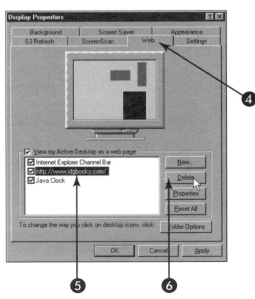

5   **6**

7 The Active Desktop Item dialog box appears, asking if you're sure you want to delete the item. Click Yes.

8 The IDG Books entry is removed from the Display Properties dialog box. Click OK to close the Display Properties dialog box.

9 The Active Desktop appears, with the IDG Books page removed. You can add another page, or even re-add the IDG Books page, any time you want.

Changing the Active Desktop wallpaper

By default, Internet Explorer installs its own wallpaper. It's easy to select a different wallpaper for your desktop background.

1 Close or minimize all open applications on your computer.

2 Right-click an empty area of the desktop to access the pop-up menu.

3 Select Active Desktop ➢ Customize My Desktop. The Display Properties dialog box appears.

4 Click The Background tab.

5 Scroll though the available wallpaper patterns. Click a wallpaper name to see a preview of the wallpaper on the sample monitor.

6 When you find the one you want to use, click Apply. A sample of the wallpaper appears in the Sample box.

7 If the sample screen is acceptable to you, click OK. If you don't like it, choose another wallpaper name from the list.

When you close the dialog box, your desktop reflects your new choice. You can change the wallpaper again, whenever you want.

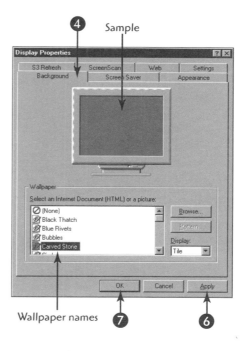

Sample

Wallpaper names

3

Integrating the Desktop and the Browser

Controlling the behavior of your files

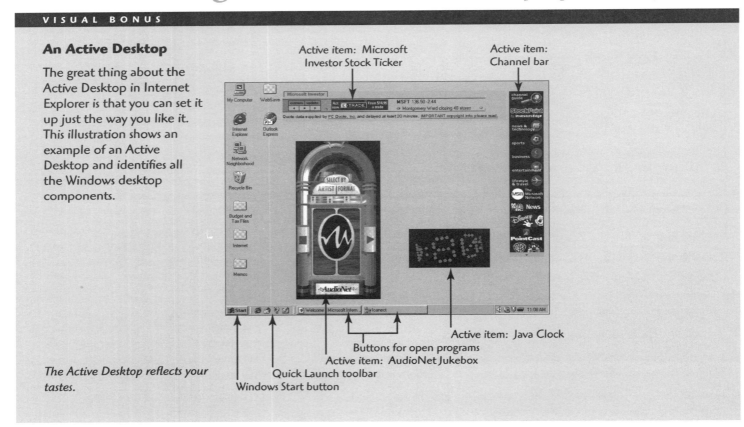

VISUAL BONUS

An Active Desktop

The great thing about the Active Desktop in Internet Explorer is that you can set it up just the way you like it. This illustration shows an example of an Active Desktop and identifies all the Windows desktop components.

Active item: Microsoft Investor Stock Ticker

Active item: Channel bar

Active item: Java Clock

Buttons for open programs

Active item: AudioNet Jukebox

The Active Desktop reflects your tastes.

Quick Launch toolbar

Windows Start button

Controlling the behavior of your files and folders

When you installed the Internet Explorer Active Desktop, the Web default settings were added to your computer. Now your desktop is set so that you point to an item to select it and click it once with the left mouse button to open it. If you're used to double-clicking, you may not want to adopt this new way of dealing with files and folders.

In this exercise, you learn how to change the behavior of your files and folders. You don't need to be connected to the Internet to perform these steps.

Turning the Active Desktop off and on

1. Close or minimize all open applications on your computer so that your Windows desktop is visible.

2. Click the Windows Start button.

3. Select Settings ➤ Folders and Icons. The Folder Options dialog box appears with the General tab displayed.

4. Click the option button next to Custom, based on settings you choose.

5. Click the Settings button to display the Customs Settings dialog box.

6. The box is divided into several sections. In the Click items as follows section, located at the bottom of the box, click the option button next to Double-click to open an item (single-click to select).

7. Click OK to close the Custom Settings box and return to the Folder Options dialog box.

8. Click OK again to close the dialog box and return to the Active Desktop.

Voila! Your folders behave the way they did before you installed the Active Desktop. When you want to open a file or folder on the desktop, in My Computer, or in Windows Explorer, double-clicking does the trick.

Turning the Active Desktop off and on

For the times when you're not connected to the Internet or if you just want to return your desktop to its classic Windows look, you can turn off the Active Desktop interface. To turn it back on, perform the steps in the exercise again.

1. Close or minimize all open applications on your computer so that your Windows desktop is visible.

2. Click the Windows Start button and select Settings ➤ Active Desktop ➤ View as Web Page. The checkmark next to View as Web Page indicates that the feature is enabled.

General tab

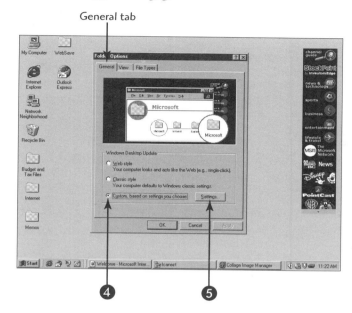

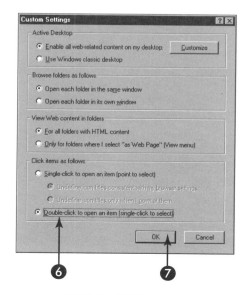

3

Integrating the Desktop and the Browser

Looking at Windows components

③ Click View as Web Page to clear the checkmark and disable the feature.

When the desktop appears, all Active Desktop items are removed.

④ Any time you want to re-activate the Active Desktop, perform steps 1 through 3 in this exercise again.

LOOKING AT INTERNET EXPLORER'S STANDARD WINDOWS COMPONENTS

Even if you've been working with Windows for a while, you may feel a little overwhelmed by such new items as the Active Desktop and channels. Relax! Many of the standard Windows components—like menu bars, dialog boxes, and Help screens—still exist in Internet Explorer. Understanding how these standard Windows components operate makes working with Internet Explorer easier.

■ Working with menus and dialog boxes

The Internet Explorer browser, like most Windows programs, is equipped with a menu bar that holds commands organized by categories, including File, Edit, and Help. To make a selection from the Internet Explorer browser menu, click a menu name in the menu bar to open the list of menu commands. Slide the mouse down the list until the command you want is highlighted, and click the left mouse button. If a menu command has a keyboard shortcut, such as pressing Ctrl+P for printing the current Web page, the keystrokes are shown on the menu. If you change your mind and don't want to select a command from the menu, click outside of the menu to close it.

What happens after you click a menu command depends on the command. Sometimes, clicking the command causes an action, like selecting File ➤ Close. If you click a menu command that's followed by three dots, called an *ellipsis*, a dialog box appears that asks you to select from a list of options or enter additional information. If the menu command is followed by an arrow, clicking the command opens a submenu. Some commands are nested in a few layers of submenus.

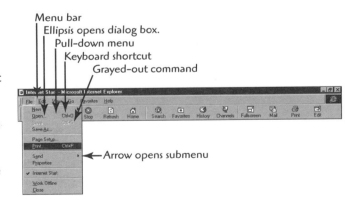

Menu bar
Ellipsis opens dialog box.
Pull-down menu
Keyboard shortcut
Grayed-out command

←Arrow opens submenu

Looking at Windows components

Many times, some of the commands on a menu appear dark while others are dim, or grayed out. A command that's grayed out means the command isn't available at that moment. For example, the Save command may not be available if you're viewing a Web page, but the Save As command, which will prompt you for a name and folder location when you save the page, is available. A grayed-out command doesn't indicate that you've done something wrong; it just means that based on the action you're currently performing, that command can't be used.

Whenever you select a menu command that's followed by an ellipsis (...), Internet Explorer opens a dialog box. Think of a dialog box as a form you need to complete and verify before Internet Explorer can process your request. The Print dialog box and some of its elements are shown in the illustration. The dialog box on your screen may look a little different, depending on the printer you have selected.

Each Internet Explorer dialog box contains one or more of the following elements:

- **Drop-down lists** display only one item and hide the rest. To view all of the items in a list, click the down arrow to the right of the list box.

- **Text boxes** are fill-in-the-blank boxes. Click inside the text box to type an entry. If text already appears inside the box, use the Delete or Backspace keys to delete existing characters before you type or highlight the existing text and type over it.

- **Spin boxes** are text boxes with controls. To change a spin box setting, type the new setting in the text box or click the up and down arrows.

- **Checkboxes** allow you to turn options on or off. Click inside a checkbox to turn an option off if it's on (and vice versa). If checkboxes are grouped together, you can select more than one option.

- **Option buttons** are similar to checkboxes, except that you can select only one option in a group. Clicking one option button de-selects the option that's already selected.

- **Command buttons** appear in every dialog box. The most common commands are OK and Cancel.

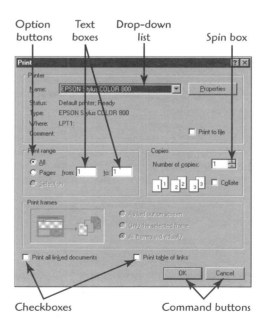

Option buttons   Text boxes   Drop-down list   Spin box

Checkboxes   Command buttons

3

Integrating the Desktop and the Browser

Printing a Web page

Printing a Web page

In this exercise, you print a Web page using the Internet Explorer browser menu. Make sure that the Internet Explorer browser is open and that you are connected to the Internet.

① Click the Home button on the Standard Buttons toolbar to reload the Microsoft Internet Start page.

② Select File. The File menu opens.

③ Slide the mouse down to the Print command and release the mouse button.

④ The Print dialog box appears. Verify that the printer name displayed in the Name box is the same one that's attached to your computer. If not, click the down arrow to open the drop-down list and select the correct printer.

TIP *Always verify that the printer name is correct before you print. If you have another printer or use your computer to send faxes, you might get pages and pages of unrecognizable characters if you select the wrong printer.*

⑤ Web pages, unlike word processing documents, don't have to conform to standard paper sizes. Therefore, one Web page might translate to many printed sheets. Make sure the option button next to All is selected if you want to print the whole page.

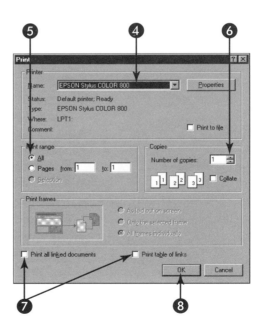

⑥ Set the number of copies you want in the spin box. Use the up or down arrows to increase or decrease the number of copies to print.

⑦ Optionally, if you want to print all the documents linked to the Web page or simply a table of the hyperlinks contained on the page, click the corresponding checkbox at the bottom of the dialog box.

⑧ When you've specified all the options, click OK. In a moment, the Microsoft Internet Start page prints.

■ Using Help

In addition to having this book as a handy reference, you can take advantage of Internet Explorer's online help. You can find information about many topics by using the Help menu's Contents and Index command. You can even perform a keyword search to find a word that's contained within a topic.

If you can't find what you're looking for in the Contents and Index section, you can visit Microsoft Technical Support on the Web. The Web site contains a list of Frequently Asked Questions (FAQs) in addition to links to How-to Wizards and Troubleshooting Guides. You can also click a link to visit the Internet Explorer Support Home Page.

Finding Help

In this exercise, you locate information in Internet Explorer's Contents and Index Help section, and you visit the Microsoft Web site for more assistance. The Internet Explorer browser should be open and on the screen from the previous exercise.

① Select Help ➤ Contents and Index.

② The Internet Explorer Help dialog box appears. Click the Index tab.

③ Type the topic you want to find more information about in the text box. For this exercise, type **Active Desktop**. As you type, the topics list scrolls to entries that match your text.

④ When Active Desktop appears in the list, click it to select it.

⑤ Click Display.

TIP

Help is context sensitive. The topics you find in the Internet Explorer browser Help files are different from the ones available in other Internet Explorer programs such as Outlook Express and NetMeeting.

⑥ A list of the topics that match your text appears. Click the first topic on the list.

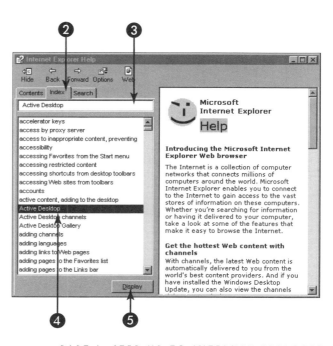

Finding Help

7 Click Display. Information about the topic appears in an information pane on the right.

8 If you can't find the topic in the Index, or want to search with keywords, click the Search tab.

9 Type the words you're looking for in the empty box. Several matching words appear in the second box. The third box contains all of the matching topics.

10 Click a topic that interests you in the third box.

11 Click Display. Information about the topic appears in the information pane.

12 Optionally, narrow your search by clicking one of the matching words, like Print, Printer, Printing. The number of topics in the third box is reduced. Click the topic that you want to see.

13 Click Display. The information about the topic is displayed in the information pane.

14 When you're finished looking through Help, close it by clicking the Close box on the title bar.

15 If you couldn't find what you were looking for, or you want more information, select Help ≻ Online Support.

16 The Microsoft Technical Support page appears. Before you can access the support information, you must register at the site by answering a few questions. You only need to perform this step one time. Click or tab to each text box designated with an asterisk (*) and complete the required information.

17 When you finish, click Next.

18 Click the option button next to Basic, Intermediate, or Advanced Site Options to specify the type of support you want.

19 Click Finish. You may need to use the vertical scroll bar to move to the bottom of the page.

20 The Microsoft Technical Support page appears, with the words Internet Explorer shown in the My question is about box.

21 In the second text box, type **active desktop**.

Select a topic

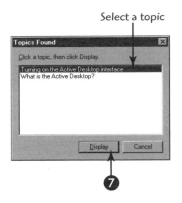

Asterisks denote required information.

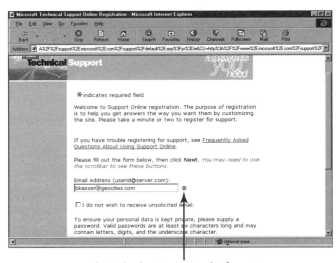

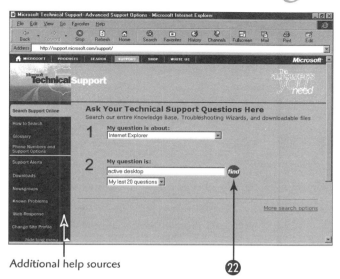

Additional help sources

Skills challenge

22 Click Find.

23 The results appear as a list of hyperlinks. Click a hyperlink to view the associated page.

24 If you want to view another page on the results list, click the Back button and then click the next hyperlink.

25 Return to the Microsoft Technical Support page by clicking the Back button as many times as necessary until the page appears.

26 This time, instead of typing a topic in the text box, click one of the links in the left frame for other sites that offer help.

27 When you're finished, close the Internet Explorer browser by clicking the Close button in the top right corner of the screen.

SKILLS CHALLENGE: TAKING CONTROL OF CHANNELS AND THE ACTIVE DESKTOP

This Skills Challenge provides an excellent opportunity for you to test your understanding of the material covered in this lesson. The steps are deceptively simple; each one may require more than one action or mouse click. If you need help, it's perfectly acceptable to go back and review the exercises you completed in the lesson.

1 Launch the Internet Explorer browser.

2 View the content of a channel on the Channel bar.

3 Open the Active Channel Guide.

4 Find a channel in the Entertainment category and subscribe to it.

 Name the technology that's used to transmit new content to channels.

 Is there a pay-per-view charge to subscribe to a channel?

5 Add the Microsoft Investor Stock Ticker to your desktop.

6 Move The Stock Ticker to a different place on the desktop.

Troubleshooting

7 Optionally, remove the Stock Ticker from the desktop.

8 Turn off the Active Desktop feature.

> **3** *Can you turn off the Active Desktop feature after you've set it up?*

9 Select a new wallpaper pattern.

> **4** *Where can you find help with Internet Explorer questions?*

10 Search the Help Index for information on the Active Desktop.

11 Visit the Microsoft Technical Support page and search for additional information on the Active Desktop.

12 Turn the Active Desktop feature back on.

13 Close the Internet Explorer browser and disconnect from the Internet.

TROUBLESHOOTING

As you view and subscribe to channels and add items to the Active Desktop, you might be puzzled by unexpected questions. The following table shows common problems and offers solutions.

Problem	Solution
I really went overboard and set up too many desktop items. Is there a quick way to restore the Active Desktop to its original look?	Click the Windows Start button and select Settings ➤ Active Desktop ➤ Customize my Desktop. Click the Reset All button to restore the desktop.
Why don't my channels ever get updated? I set up the channel subscriptions properly.	Select Favorites ➤ Update All Subscriptions to download new channel content. To update a specific channel, select Favorites ➤ Manage Subscriptions. On the Manage Subscription window, click the channel you want to update and then click the

Problem	Solution
	Update button on the toolbar. Close the window when you're through.
I've added a lot of items to my Active Desktop, and it seems like my computer isn't working properly anymore. How can I tell if something's wrong?	Active Desktop items can take a big hit on system resources. To check your resources, select Start ➢ Settings ➢ Control Panel. On the Control Panel, click the System icon to view the System Properties dialog box. Click the Performance tab and check the system resources you have available. If the number is low, say below 50 percent, and you don't have many programs open, consider deleting a few desktop items.
Whoa! When I turned on my computer this morning I saw a bunch of gray boxes instead of my Active Desktop items. Where'd they all go?	Active Desktop items only display properly when you're connected to the Internet. If you are connected, open the Internet Explorer browser and click Refresh. The items reappear. If you're not connected to the Internet, connect and they should display properly.
I searched for help on a topic, but even though I found the topic on the list, I didn't see any information about it in the information pane. Why?	You need to click the Display button to change the existing text in the information pane.

Wrap up

WRAP UP

In this lesson, you learned the following Internet Explorer skills:

- Subscribing to and viewing channels
- Changing the Active Desktop
- Working with menus, dialog boxes, and Help

In the next lesson, you learn all about Web addresses and hyperlinks as you gain greater experience with the World Wide Web.

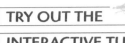

TRY OUT THE
INTERACTIVE TUTORIALS
ON YOUR CD!

Understanding Browser Basics

Learn everything you need to know about surfing and searching from the lessons in this part. Get your bearings with a basic browser introduction and step-by-step search techniques that help you quickly and easily find the information you want. Dive into the Web in the following lessons:

- Lesson 4: Internet Explorer Warm-up Exercises
- Lesson 5: Exploring the Web

Internet Explorer Warm-up Exercises

25 MINUTES

GOALS

The Internet Explorer browser is your escort to Web sites. The exercises in this lesson show you how to use the browser to get around from site to site. You learn the following:

- Moving around with hyperlinks

- Moving backward and forward

- Entering URLs

- Using the History list

- Moving through a framed Web page

Get ready

GET READY

To complete this lesson, you must have Internet Explorer installed on your computer (see Appendix A) and be connected to the Internet.

When you finish this lesson, you'll have learned some important Web techniques, including how to move and navigate to Web pages. You'll also master how to return to pages you've seen before.

TRY OUT THE

INTERACTIVE TUTORIALS

ON YOUR CD!

DISCOVERING THE WORLD WIDE WEB

The World Wide Web is an electronic version of a large, glittering city, filled with shops, cafes, theaters, and libraries that are all interconnected by links. When you use the Internet Explorer browser, you have the opportunity to visit all of the exiting locations in the city, without ever having to leave your computer. Instead of wearing out your shoes and rushing to get from store to store during business hours, you can click hyperlinks in Web pages to tool around the Web any time you'd like. In the course of a few minutes, you can make travel reservations, research a current news story, and find several recipes for amaretto cheesecake.

What are your interests? What would you like to find? You can bet that somewhere on the Web is a document filled with the exact information you want to see. The Internet Explorer browser is your electronic taxi driver and tour guide, whisking you around the Web as you sit back and enjoy the ride!

■ Looking at Web pages

You visit Web sites as you travel through the World Wide Web. Every Web site is made up of one or more documents, called *pages*. A Web page might consist of lines of plain text or it can be an elaborate document filled with different typefaces and colors, graphic images (sometimes animated), and photographs. Some Web pages even contain sound and movies. Most Web pages contain hyperlinks that take you to other, related Web pages. Corporations and large retail organizations, or individuals like you, can create Web pages.

A *home page* is the page at each site that serves as a kind of book cover or index to organize and introduce the other pages and

Moving around with hyperlinks

material at that site. Even if a Web site consists of just one page, you'll hear it referred to as a home page. As you visit sites on the World Wide Web, you'll see many different home pages. In fact, thousands of new home pages appear daily.

■ Working with hyperlinks

Hyperlinks connect Web pages. Most times, hyperlinks appear in Web pages as colored, underlined text or graphics. Hyperlinks are easy to follow; when you click one, the Internet Explorer browser moves you to the linked site. If you want to know where a link will take you, point to the link with your mouse and note the address of the Web site in the status bar at the bottom of the screen. You'll learn more about Web addresses, called URLs, later in this lesson.

Most text hyperlinks are blue before you click them. As soon as you click a link, its color changes to purple, letting you know that you've visited the linked site. When you've looked at hundreds of sites, it's helpful to see an indication of the sites you've already visited. However, Web designers can override this feature and direct that the color of visited hyperlinks does not change from their original color.

Moving around with hyperlinks

In this exercise, you visit some Web sites by clicking links.

❶ Open the Internet Explorer browser by clicking the Launch Internet Explorer Browser icon on the Quick Launch toolbar. If the toolbar isn't visible, display it by clicking the right mouse button on a blank spot on the Windows taskbar and selecting Toolbars ➢ Quick Launch from the pop-up menu.

Alternatively, click the Windows Start button and select Programs ➢ Internet Explorer ➢ Internet Explorer. In a moment, the browser opens and the Microsoft Internet Start page appears as shown in the adjacent figure.

❷ Place your mouse pointer in the top left corner of the screen and slowly move the pointer around the screen. As you move the pointer down, notice that the pointer's shape changes to a hand as it passes over different parts of the screen.

4

Internet Explorer Warm-up Exercises

PART II: UNDERSTANDING BROWSER BASICS   **73**

Moving around with hyperlinks

3 Point the mouse to some underlined, colored text so that the mouse pointer's shape changes to a hand.

Underlined, different-colored text usually indicates that the text is a hyperlink—a connection to another page or to a different section of the same page. When you click a hyperlink, you're whisked to the hyperlink's location.

4 Click the underlined text one time with the left mouse button. In a moment, a new page appears on the screen.

TIP
Hyperlinks connect two locations on the World Wide Web. The portion of the link that causes the mouse arrow to change shape is called an anchor.

5 Place the mouse on some underlined, colored text on the new page. Again, the mouse pointer takes the shape of a hand, indicating that the text is a hyperlink.

6 Click the hyperlink, or *link* for short, one time with the left mouse button. A different site appears on the screen.

7 Graphics, as well as text, can contain links. Move the mouse around on the page. Notice that the mouse pointer assumes the shape of a hand as it passes over graphic links.

8 Position the mouse pointer over a graphic link so that the arrow pointer takes a hand shape.

9 Click one time with the left mouse button. A new page appears on the screen.

Text link

> Online delivery of audio and video -- broadcasting over the Internet -- is coming of age, explains Jim Durkin, manager for NetShow, Microsoft's multimedia delivery product. And there sure is a heck of a lot of content out there to see and hear. Interested in vaudeville? Well, now you can listen to vaudeville music recordings from the early 1900s via the Internet as libraries make their collections available online. Because the store of human knowledge on the Web is vast and growing, a good search tool can be your best online

5

■ Clicking an invalid link

Sooner or later, you're going to click a link that doesn't work. When you click an invalid link, an error message pops up on your screen after the Internet Explorer browser tries to bring up the site. Links don't work for many reasons, and none of them is your fault. As more people publish pages on the Web, failed links are becoming a commonplace experience. When you encounter a failed link, don't worry.

Table 4-1 contains a list of common error messages and what they mean.

TABLE 4-1 ERROR MESSAGES AND THEIR MEANINGS

Message	What It Means
File not found	The page has moved to a new location or has been removed from the Web.
Document contains no data	The address of the link is incomplete. If the address contains a specific file, try entering the URL manually, without the last part. For example, if the URL of the link is something like `http://www.computercoach.com/barbara.html`, enter it as `http://www.computercoach.com` and press Enter. You may be able to connect to the location and then navigate to the specific page.
A connection to the server could not be established	The most common reason for this message is that you were accidentally disconnected from your Internet service provider. Reconnect and try the link again. If you are connected when you receive the message, it generally means that the page the link refers to doesn't exist.
Too many users, try again later Or Connection refused by host	These messages are rare but occur if too many people try to connect to the same page at the same time. Wait a few minutes and try the link again.

Moving backward and forward

Sometimes traveling around the Web can seem like a giant maze. As you click links and move to new and different sites, you leave a lot of interesting sites behind. Don't worry; it's easy to move back and

Moving backward and forward

forward to sites you've visited previously during your current Internet Explorer session.

❶ Click the Back button on the Standard Buttons toolbar. The Back button takes you backward (one page at a time) through the Web pages that you have accessed during your current Internet Explorer session.

❷ Click the Back button again.

❸ Continue clicking the Back button until the button appears dimmed out, indicating that you've moved back though all the sites you have visited.

❹ Click the Forward button on the Standard Buttons toolbar to move forward (one page at a time) through the Web pages that you have accessed during your current Internet Explorer session. You can only use the Forward button if you previously used the Back button.

❺ Click the Forward button again. The browser displays the page you visited after the one currently shown in the browser window.

TIP

To speed things up while you are using the Back and Forward buttons, click the down arrow to the right of these buttons to display a drop-down list. Select a Web page from the list to display that site.

❻ Select Go ➤ Home Page. The page that you see when you first open Internet Explorer appears on the screen.

UNDERSTANDING URLS

So far in this lesson, you've moved to new sites by clicking links. Although jumping from site to site through links is fun, you can lose control of where you're going. Accessing pages with URLs provides a more precise way to travel. What is a URL? Read on.

Every page on the World Wide Web has its own unique address. The address, called a Uniform Resource Locator, is made up of letters, slashes, and periods (usually called *dots*). Although the characters in a URL look like they're randomly placed, each letter and punctuation mark has its own important function.

Typing URLs correctly can sometimes feel like playing with alphabet blocks. If you don't type the name correctly—with every dot, slash, and colon in the right place—the Internet Explorer browser won't be able to find the page you're looking for. Breaking a URL down into distinct parts makes it a little easier to understand. Here's an example of a URL, followed by an explanation of its parts:

```
http://www.computercoach.com/
```

`http://`	Protocol type	Specifies the type of page that's being accessed. The `http://` prefix means that this Web site uses the Hypertext Transfer Protocol, the standard for most Web pages. Some pages you visit may start with other protocols like `ftp://` or `telnet://`.
`www.computercoach.com`	Domain name	Identifies the name of the host computer and its particular Internet address. Every computer that's connected to the Internet has a unique domain name. Customized names, like the ones you see on television and in magazines, are called virtual domain names and must be registered with a special Internet agency.

As you can see, the format of a URL is a complete addressing scheme. As you become aware of URLs, you'll notice that some URLs contain the name of the page after the domain name portion. For example, in the URL `www.computercoach.com/aboutframe.html`, **the page name is** `aboutframe.html`. If the name of the page isn't included in the URL, you'll connect to that site's home page.

Entering URLs

You've probably heard someone give an Internet address that contained the phrase "dot com." Now you know that they're referring to the domain name of the host computer that stores the page. The last portion of the domain name lets you know the primary use of the host computer. For example, in the URL http://www.computercoach.com, the .com means that the host is a commercial enterprise.

Although .com is the most common domain name extension, you'll come across several others.

For example, if a name contains a .edu extension, the host is an educational institution like a university or college. The extension .net stands for an Internet service provider, .gov indicates a government facility, and .int is short for international. Additionally, .org (nonprofit organizations) and .mil (military) are valid domain name extensions. To further identify a domain name, the three-letter extension may be followed by a country code. If there is no country code, the domain is probably in the United States.

Entering URLs

URLs are everywhere. You'll find them displayed on billboards, mentioned on radio and television, and splashed across the newspaper. It's simple to move to a site if you know its URL.

1 Make sure that the Address bar is displayed by selecting View ➤ Toolbars. In the resulting submenu, a check should appear next to Address Bar. If the Address bar menu selection is not checked, click it once to select it so that the Address bar is displayed on the Internet Explorer browser screen.

2 Click the mouse inside the Address bar. The URL of the page that's currently displayed in the browser window appears highlighted.

3 Without deleting the highlighted text, type www.computercoach.com/. The URL that was previously displayed is overwritten by the one you typed.

TIP

When you type a URL, you don't need to enter the http:// portion of the address. The Internet Explorer browser automatically fills in the full URL, searches the Web, and brings up the page you want.

④ Press Enter. The Computer Coach home page appears on the screen. If your computer has a sound card and speakers, you hear music!

⑤ If you're more comfortable using menu commands, you can use an alternate method for accessing Web pages. Select File ➤ Open to bring up the Open dialog box.

⑥ Type the URL of the page you want to view in the box. In this case, type `www.idgbooks.com`.

⑦ Click the OK button. The box closes and in a few moments, the IDG Books page appears.

⑧ To view the URLs of the sites you've typed in the Address bar, click the down arrow next to the Address bar. A drop-down list appears.

⑨ Click the URL of the site you want to revisit. In a moment, the page appears on the screen.

TIP

> *If you find yourself muttering portions of URLs in your sleep, carry a small notebook with you to jot down the URLs you come across during the day. You'll have a list of potentially interesting sites that you can then access*
whenever you have some free time.

RETURNING TO PAGES YOU'VE SEEN BEFORE

So many pages, so little time! You might be thinking that you'll never see all of the pages on the World Wide Web (and you're probably right). But, just as you love to see new and different pages, there are probably a few sites that stay in your mind after you've ended your Internet Explorer session. It's a snap to go back to pages you've already visited.

Address bar

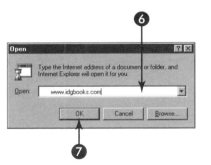

Address of site you're viewing now   Down arrow

Using the History list

Using the History list

In the last exercise, you returned to a site that you'd visited previously by finding its URL in the Address bar. But URLs can begin to look dizzyingly alike after a while. When you just can't remember the URL of that great Web site you visited a few days ago, don't fret. The Internet Explorer browser stores the titles of Web sites you've seen so you can return to them later.

① Click the History button on the Internet Explorer Standard Buttons toolbar. A History bar appears on the left side of the Internet Explorer browser window that displays folders for each of your Internet Explorer sessions. The folders are arranged by weeks and then by days.

② If a folder is closed, click it one time to expand it. For example, if the Today folder appears closed, click it. The folder opens and the titles of all the sites you visited today appear. Conversely, click an expanded folder one time to collapse it.

③ When you find the title of the page you want to access on the History list, click it. The page you requested opens in the browser window on the right side of the screen.

④ When you're finished with the History bar, close it by clicking the Close button on the right side of the bar.

TIP

To hide the History bar fast, click the History button on the Standard Buttons toolbar. The button works like a toggle, so you can display and hide the History list as often as you like.

STEERING THROUGH FRAMES

As you journey around the Web, you'll come across pages that are divided into two or more rectangular windows. Each of the separate windows has the characteristics of an individual Web page. These windows within a page are called *frames*. By using frames, Web page

History bar

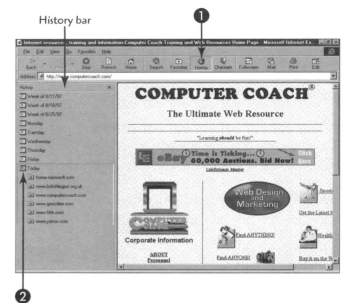

Closed folders   Selected site

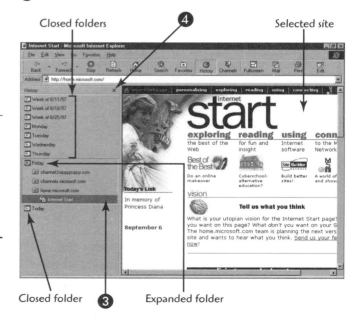

Closed folder   **③**   Expanded folder

Steering through frames

designers can organize information into discrete areas on the page. On a framed page, locating the information you're looking for is easy because you can jump from frame to frame.

Web page designers use frames in different ways. You'll find some Web pages with only two frames, while other pages are divided into several. Many different effects can be achieved with frames. You'll often come across sites that present advertising information or site indexes in a frame.

VISUAL BONUS

Recognizing Frames

The information on this site is organized into two frames for easy navigation.

Frames provide a tool for arranging different types of information on the same page.

Frame 1

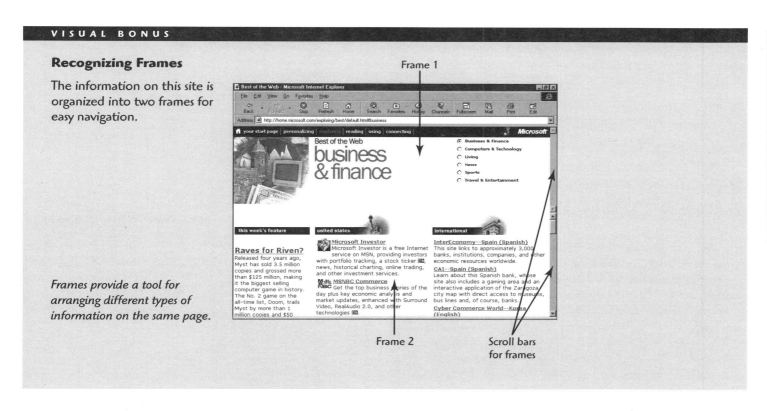

Frame 2

Scroll bars for frames

Moving through a framed Web page

▶ *Moving through a framed Web page*

Moving through a Web page with frames is easy—as long as you know the tricks.

❶ Click the mouse pointer inside the Address bar. The URL in the box appears highlighted.

❷ Type the URL www.florida.com/realestate/.

Remember that it's not necessary to type the http:// portion of the address because Internet Explorer fills it in for you.

❸ Press Enter. The FloridaCom Real Estate Web page appears. Notice that the site has four frames.

❹ Click the New Homes link in the frame on the left. The information appears in the frame on the right.

❺ Use the scroll bars to look at the portion of the page that doesn't fit on the screen.

❻ Click another link to change the view in the frame again.

❼ Click the Back button to return to the frame you viewed previously.

When you're moving through frames, the Back and Forward buttons work in a different way. Instead of moving you back to the *page* you visited last, you return to the *frame* you visited last.

TIP

If you're hung up in a frame and the Back button isn't moving you where you think it should, click the Back button with the right mouse button. Click the page you want to revisit from the resulting pop-up menu.

Advertising frame   Identification frame

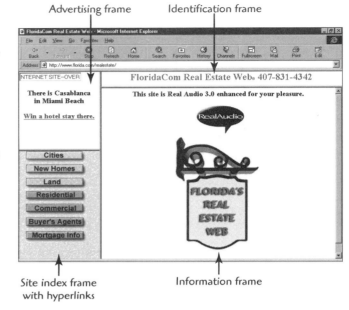

Site index frame   Information frame
with hyperlinks

Vertical scroll bar

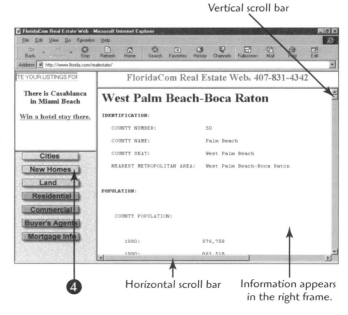

Horizontal scroll bar   Information appears
in the right frame.

SKILLS CHALLENGE: CRUISING AROUND THE WORLD WIDE WEB

You've done a great job with this lesson. Now it's time to test your Web-cruising knowledge. Don't worry if you don't know how to perform one of the steps; you can always refer to the exercises for a little help. As you complete this Skills Challenge, be prepared to pick up a few quick tricks along the way!

1 Make sure that you're connected to the Internet with the Internet Explorer browser open on your screen.

2 Click the Home button on the Internet Explorer Standard Buttons toolbar.

3 Once the page loads, find a text link and click it.

 How do you know when your mouse passes over a hyperlink?

4 When the new page appears, move the mouse over the page, looking for a graphics link.

5 Click the first graphics link you find.

6 Move to a new page on the World Wide Web by typing the following URL in the Address bar: `www.idgbooks.com/`.

 What is a URL?

7 Click the Online Bookstore link.

8 Move down through the page to the Find a Book section. (Hint: You may have to use the vertical scroll bar on the right edge of the page.)

9 Type your favorite author's name (like Kasser or Witherspoon) in the text box and click the Search button.

10 After you've viewed the resulting page, click the Back button.

11 Click the Back button one more time.

Troubleshooting

 3 *What happens when you click the Back button?*

12 Click the down arrow to the right of the Address bar.

13 Click the URL for Computer Coach on the list.

 4 *Why do only some of the URLs of sites you've visited appear on the list when you click the down arrow to the right of the Address bar?*

14 When the Computer Coach home page appears, click the link to Florida Sites.

15 The Florida Sites page contains frames. Navigate through the bottom frame that contains links to many Florida attractions. Notice that the menu bar of links on the left side doesn't move.

 5 *What are frames?*

16 Click any link on the list of Florida attractions.

17 Follow as many links as you like.

18 When you're finished, close the Internet Explorer browser by clicking the Close button to the right of the title bar.

TRY OUT THE
INTERACTIVE TUTORIALS
ON YOUR CD!

TROUBLESHOOTING

Here are some potential problems that you may encounter while you are surfing the Net. The solutions for these problems are easy to implement and can get you back on track quickly.

Problem	Solution
Internet Explorer doesn't keep a History list that goes back far enough to suit my needs. Is there a way to keep addresses in the History list longer?	Select View ➤ Internet Options. Click the General tab. In the History section, increase or decrease the number of days you want to keep pages in History.

Wrap up

Problem	Solution
I tried to access a site, but it took forever to download. What should I do if I find another site like this and don't want to continue downloading the page?	First, click the Stop button on the Internet Explorer Standard Buttons toolbar to stop the transfer of the page. Next, click the Back button to return to the page you were viewing previously.
I clicked the Back and Forward buttons on the toolbar, but I couldn't get to the page I saw yesterday.	You're right; the Back and Forward buttons only work on sites you've been to during the current Internet Explorer session.

WRAP UP

In this lesson, you exercised the following skills:

- Moving to Web sites with hyperlinks
- Understanding and using URLs
- Using the History list
- Moving through a framed Web page

In the next lesson, you begin to use the Internet Explorer browser to search for information and places on the Web.

4

Internet Explorer Warm-up Exercises

Exploring the Web

GOALS

Knowing how to use the Web's search resources efficiently will help you find information quickly. This lesson teaches you techniques for:

50 MINUTES

- Using Internet Explorer's Autoscan
- Searching from the Address bar with Autosearch
- Using the Search button
- Searching from the Microsoft Internet Start page
- Finding a reference on a Web page
- Performing a search using HotBot
- Using HotBot's advanced search techniques
- Finding sites with Yahoo

Get ready

GET READY

To complete this lesson, Internet Explorer must be installed on your computer. (If it's not, refer to Appendix A.) Make sure that you're connected to the Internet before you begin the exercises.

Until now, you've been clicking links and entering URLs to view Web sites. Now it's time to learn how to look for the Web sites you specifically want to see. In this lesson, you learn how to perform an Internet search to find a specific Web page or sites containing information about a particular topic. You also learn how to take advantage of Internet Explorer's special search tools. When you complete this lesson, you'll be able to take control of the Web by setting up search queries and finding matching Web sites.

TRY OUT THE

INTERACTIVE TUTORIALS

ON YOUR CD!

STARTING YOUR SEARCH

Millions and millions of pages reside on the World Wide Web, and new ones appear daily. Finding the Web pages that match what you're looking for can be a frustrating experience. No master directories index every Web site, and even if such directories existed, the rate at which sites appear, move, and disappear would make them impossible to maintain. So what do you do when you want to find a specific Web page or sites about a particular topic?

Indexing tools called *search engines* and *site directories* help you find the pages you want to see. Think of search engines and site directories as personal research assistants, waiting to help you track down information. You tell the indexing tool what you want, and the tool goes out to the Internet to find sites that match your request. When it's finished looking, the indexing tool provides a list of hyperlinks, called *hits*, to matching sites. After you look at the list, you can click the links to move to the matching sites, or you can modify the query and start the searching process again.

Which indexing tool is better? The answer, unfortunately, is another question: What are you looking for? Just as two or three human research assistants might approach the same project a little differently and find different information, each search engine and site directory has its own way of finding the documents you want.

Using Explorer's search features

Therefore, it's always a good idea to use a few different tools to find information on the Web.

Depending on the types of sites you're trying to find, you'll discover that one tool or the other works best. After a little practice with the various tools, you'll be able to find sites covering just about any topic on the Web. Whether you're doing serious research or just poking around for the latest gossip about your favorite movie star or pop singer, search engines and site directories help to make the information on the Web more accessible.

The Web offers two main types of indexing tools:

- **Search engines.** Search engines send electronic spiders, worms, or robots crawling through the Web looking for pages to add to a database. When the spider finds a site that isn't already in the index, it adds a new entry to the database with the page title, URL, and an excerpt of the text. (Different search engines use different sections of the text.) Since it might take a spider years to come across a new site, Webmasters can furnish a search engine with the URLs of their sites and invite the spider to visit.

- **Site directories.** Site directories sort Web sites into categories and sometimes include comments or reviews. Each top-level category is divided into subcategories, which can also have subcategories (similar to the folder structure on a computer). For example, the Government category can be divided into Military, Politics, Law, Taxes, and so on. Site directories are essentially a catalog of sites. Webmasters and sponsors generally register the URLs listed in site directories.

USING INTERNET EXPLORER'S SEARCH FEATURES

Microsoft understands that you want to spend less time searching for Web sites and more time viewing them. Accordingly, Internet Explorer is packed with features to help make the searching process easier. Autoscan and Autosearch both help you with your search. The Explorer bar, another exclusive Internet Explorer feature, makes it easy to jump between the search page and the linked results. The Exploring link on the Microsoft Internet Start page provides multiple search options.

5

Exploring the Web

Using Internet Explorer's Autoscan

Using Internet Explorer's Autoscan

If you've entered an incorrect URL in the Address bar or the URL doesn't work, Autoscan searches for Web addresses that are close to the one you've typed. If you're a bad typist, like I am, Autoscan can save you lots of time and energy! Before you can harness Autoscan's power, you need to set it up.

1 Launch the Internet Explorer browser by clicking the Launch Internet Explorer Browser button on the Quick Launch toolbar.

2 Select View ➤ Internet Options.

3 When the Internet Options dialog box appears, click the Advanced tab.

4 Scroll down the list to the Searching heading. First, select the option to Autoscan common root domains. The domain portion of a URL identifies the type of Web site, like .gov for government. Choosing this option enables Internet Explorer to check through the other domains to find a match, even if you type the wrong domain name, such as .net instead of .com. (For more information on URLs, go back to Lesson 4.)

5 Next, select the option to Always ask. The Internet Explorer browser will ask to perform a search when a Web site cannot be found or the URL is misspelled.

6 Click Apply to apply the changes you made to the current session.

7 Click OK to close the dialog box and return to the Internet Explorer browser screen.

8 Click inside the Address bar to highlight the current URL.

9 Type **idgbooks**.

10 Press Enter. The Internet Explorer icon in the top right corner becomes animated as Internet Explorer tries all possible combinations of Internet protocols (http:// and ftp://, for example) and domain extensions (like .com and .net) until it finds a combination that corresponds to a valid Web

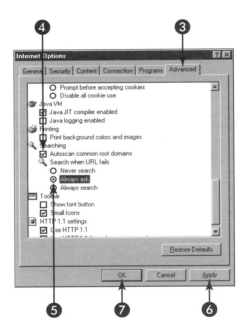

address. In this example, the IDG Books Worldwide Web page displays.

⑪ After you've looked at the IDG site for a few minutes, click the Home button on the Standard Buttons toolbar to return to the Microsoft Internet Start page.

When you complete this first exercise, immediately move to the next exercise.

Searching from the Address bar with Autosearch

Autosearch is another Internet Explorer exclusive feature that lets you perform a search directly from the Address bar. Instead of having to move to the page of a search engine or search service, you type your search criteria directly into the Address bar. Autosearch finds the matching documents and displays the hyperlinks.

Using Autosearch is a quick and easy way to check facts or locate the new URL of a moved site that has a dead page posted at its old address. However, Autosearch only looks through Yahoo, a search service, to find matches, so your search results may be limited.

① The Internet Explorer browser is open and visible on your screen from the preceding exercise. If it's not, launch the Internet Explorer browser now.

② Click inside the Address bar to highlight the current URL.

③ Type **? Santa Claus**.

TIP

*Begin your Autoscan search with a **?** character or the words **go** or **find**. Use any of the three search commands; all three return the same results.*

④ Press Enter. The Internet Explorer icon becomes animated for a moment as Autosearch looks through Yahoo to find Web documents containing the name Santa Claus.

Yahoo returns a page of search results that lists hyperlinks to matching Web sites and brief descriptions of the information

③

Using the Search button

available at the site. The words you typed for the search query are shown in bold text inside the description.

⑤ Click a hyperlink to one of the Santa sites. In a few seconds, the Web page displays in the browser window.

⑥ Click the Home button on the Standard Buttons toolbar twice to return to the Microsoft Internet Start page.

Some search tools refer to Web sites as documents on the results list. Don't get confused; the word document is another way of saying Web site or page.

Using the Search button

The Search button on the Standard Buttons toolbar is another great Internet Explorer innovation. When you click the Search button, an Explorer bar opens on the left side of the browser window. The bar allows you to select a Web search engine or indexing tool, like HotBot or Yahoo, to conduct a search. Once the search is concluded, your results and the Web pages that you accessed from the search results page can be viewed in the same browser window.

Keep in mind that although accessing a search engine from the Explorer bar is convenient, you don't have full use of the custom search features usually provided on each search engine's home page.

① If the browser isn't open and visible on your screen, launch the Internet Explorer browser now.

② Click the Search button on the Standard Buttons toolbar. The Explorer bar opens in its own frame on the left side of the browser window, with the Provider-of-the-day search tool displayed.

③ Type the words **Norwich terrier** in the empty text box on the Explorer bar.

④ Click the button to initiate the search. Although each search engine has a different look, every one contains a text box for

Hyperlink to Santa   Search query in bold text   Search results

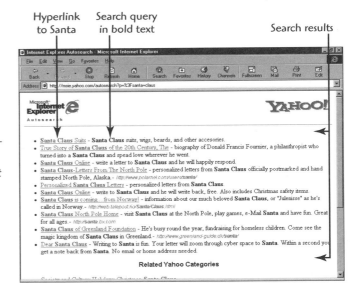

Explorer bar
Provider-of-the-day search engine
Text box for search criteria
Click to begin search.
Click to see a list of other search tools.

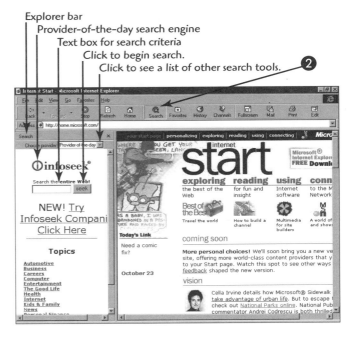

you to type in what you're looking for and a button that you click to begin a search of the Web.

5 The search engine returns a list of pages, called *hits*, that match your search criteria. Read through the list of hits and click the link that most closely matches what you are trying to find. The associated Web page appears in the right side of the browser window.

TIP

To see more of the Web page and less of the Explorer bar, position the mouse pointer on the border between the Explorer bar and the browser window. Hold down the left mouse button and drag the border to the left. Release the mouse button when the window is sized the way you like it.

6 Click the down arrow next to the Select provider field in the Explorer bar and choose another search engine from the list.

7 Again, type **Norwich terrier** in the box and click the appropriate Search button. The hits provided by this search engine are different from the results you got in the previous search.

8 Notice that the Explorer bar only shows hyperlinks in the search results lists. To find out more information about the linked Web site, hold the mouse pointer over the hyperlink until a screen tip appears that shows both the URL and some of the keywords of the linked site. The screen tip may give you a better idea of whether the information on the Web page meets your needs.

9 Close the Explorer bar by clicking the Close button or clicking the Search button on the Standard Buttons toolbar.

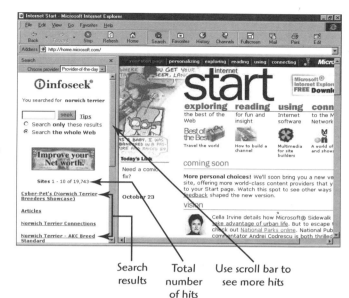

Search results   Total number of hits   Use scroll bar to see more hits

5

Exploring the Web

Searching from the Start page

The better your search query, the better your results will be. (You've heard the saying, "Garbage in, garbage out.") Improve your search results by using the following guidelines:

- **Use phrases.** Using several words instead of just one word when performing a search can help you find Web sites that fit your information needs more precisely. If your search query is just the word *cats*, the resulting hit list will be quite lengthy and may include information on lions and tigers. To narrow the search and restrict the hits to a specific type of cat, for example, you could search for *Siamese cats*.

- **Be specific.** You'll get better results if your search query includes specific words that apply uniquely to the information you are trying to find. If you're looking for information about the Hawaii state flag, for instance, enter all three words in your search. A search for Hawaii flags may return a list of pages that contain references to Hawaii flags but may not contain any information about the state flag.

- **Use all words.** Many search engines give you the option of returning search results that contain all the words you included in your search query or just any of the words. By electing to have the search engine only return a list of Web pages that contain all the words in your query, you will have a shorter list that more closely meets your needs.

- **Don't use articles.** Words like *and* and *the* might limit the search and produce skewed results. Unless you're looking for something specific, like the title *The Old Man and the Sea*, leave articles out of the search query. Apply the same rule to prepositions; leave them out unless you're positive that a preposition or prepositional phrase must be included to obtain the correct results.

- **Type case–sensitive queries.** Internet searches are case sensitive. If you want to find all instances of a word or words, use all lowercase letters. A search for *beach* will turn up different results than a search for *Beach*. If you are searching for a person's name or a city, use the correct capitalization. If you are looking for information on the band Pearl Jam, type Pearl Jam. If you type pearl jam, you may not be satisfied with the results.

Searching from the Microsoft Internet Start page

The Microsoft Internet Start page is another place to begin a search. In addition to links to several search engines, the Search the Web section contains hyperlinks to Web and Chat guides, telephone directories, newsgroups (you learn about newsgroups in Lesson 11), and more. Clicking the Exploring link on the Microsoft Internet Start page takes you to a comprehensive search guide that may be the best search site on the Web.

Searching from the Start page

To complete this and the remaining exercises in this lesson, Internet Explorer needs to be open and on the screen, and you must be connected to the Internet.

1 Click the Home button on the Standard Buttons toolbar to reload the Microsoft Internet Start page.

2 Click the link called Exploring at the top of the page. The Start Exploring page appears. The page contains links to several sites in the Best of the Web section and additional hyperlinks in the Search the Web section.

3 Click the link to Search Engines in the Search the Web section.

4 On the resulting Search the Web page, a list of search engines fills the top frame. The bottom frame contains a variety of search services and guides. Click the option button next to Local City in the Guides section.

5 The top frame changes to a form. In the City field, type **Pittsburgh**.

6 Tab to the State field and type **PA**.

7 Tab to the ZIP field and type **15217**. If you wish, you can substitute another city, state, and zip for the ones shown here.

8 Click Search.

9 The Infospace Ultimate City directory displays a local city guide for the city you typed. Click one of the links on the page to see the weather, area map, restaurant guide, or other types of city information.

10 Click the Back button as many times as necessary until you return to the Search the Web page.

11 Click the option button next to Movies in the Specialty section. A form appears in the top frame.

12 Type **hard days night** in the field in the top frame.

13 Click Search.

Search engines

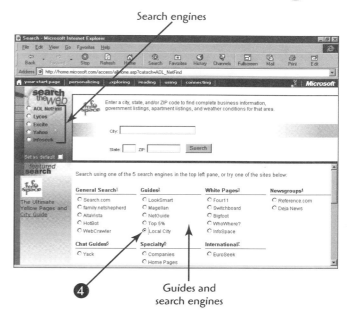

Guides and search engines

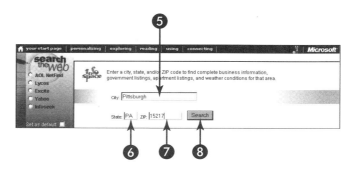

Finding a reference on a Web page

⑭ In a moment, information about the movie *A Hard Day's Night,* starring the Beatles, appears. Explore the page, and if you wish, click any of the hyperlinks to continue exploring.

⑮ When you're finished, click the Back button as many times as necessary to return to the Search the Web page.

⑯ If you wish, click the option button next to another topic and search for more information. Continue searching, clicking the Back button as many times as needed to return to the Search the Web page to start another search.

▶ Finding a reference on a Web page

So far, you've learned how to compile a list of Web pages that may contain the exact information you are looking for. Imagine your dismay if you link to a site and find that it contains page after page of text. Or you open a promising link, but can't find the words you used in the search. The Internet Explorer browser helps take some of the work out of your research project by providing a tool for searching individual pages for keywords.

In this exercise, you search for keywords on a site.

❶ Click inside the Address bar to highlight the URL.

❷ Type `www.geocities.com/~stgregory` in the Address bar.

❸ Press Enter.

❹ When the St. Gregory's Episcopal Church page appears, select Edit ➢ Find (on this page). The Find dialog box displays.

❺ Type **Music Programs** in the Find what field.

❻ Check the Match case checkbox.

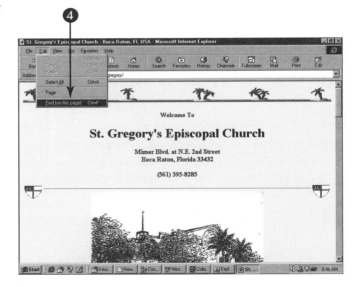

NOTE

Use Match whole word only if you are looking for the exact word and not a word that contains the search term. Use Match case if you want an exact match on uppercase and lowercase letters.

Finding a reference on a Web page

7 In the Direction section, select the Down option.

NOTE *Use the Up option if you want to search from the place where the cursor is located in the document to the beginning of the document. Use the Down option if you want to search from the place where the cursor is located in the document to the end of the document.*

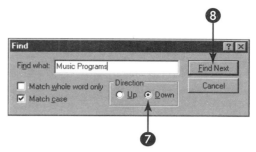

8 Click the Find Next button. Internet Explorer searches the Web page for instances of your keywords. When it finds a match, Internet Explorer highlights the word.

9 To continue searching through the document, go back to the Find dialog box and click the Find Next button. Continue this process until you have found all instances of the word you are searching for.

10 When you are finished looking through the document, click Cancel. The Find dialog box closes, and you are returned to the St. Gregory home page.

11 Click the Home button on the Standard Buttons toolbar to return to the Microsoft Internet Start page.

USING SEARCH ENGINES AND SITE DIRECTORIES

In the early part of this lesson, you learned that search engines and site directories work as your personal research assistants to find the documents you want. Each contains an index of Web pages. When you search for a particular topic, the search engine or site directory looks through its index and assembles the documents that match your criteria.

Since each of the major search engines indexes Web sites differently, you can expect to get different results if you search each service using the same keywords. The differences between the results might vary from a few dissimilar hits to a page of completely different results. Because Yahoo, the major site directory, obtains the pages in its index primarily from registrations by Webmasters and sponsors, its index is compiled in a different way than the search engine indexes.

5

Exploring the Web

Using search engines and directories

The results from a Yahoo search may include sites not found by the search engine spiders.

The following list contrasts the major search engines and Yahoo. Many of the search engines also provide additional services on their pages, like UPS tracking and free e-mail. The list covers only some of the services the search engines and Yahoo offer on their pages.

SEARCH ENGINES AND SITE DIRECTORIES

The following list contrasts the major search engines and Yahoo. Many of the search engines also provide additional services on their pages, like UPS tracking, free e-mail, or a range of other services. The list covers only some of the services the search engines and Yahoo offer on their pages.

- **AltaVista at** `www.altavista.digital.com`. Offers simple and advanced searches and multiple languages. Begun in 1995 and run by Digital Equipment, partnered with Yahoo.

- **AOLNetFind at** `www.aol.com/netfind`. Offers keyword searches, special searches to find people and businesses, newsgroups, AOLNetfind Kids, links to America Online, and Web site reviews. Begun in 1997 and designed by America Online.

- **Excite at** `www.excite.com`. Offers simple and power searches, categories, such as Business, Careers, and Sports, an e-mail lookup feature, maps, and horoscopes. Begun in 1995 and purchased by America Online.

- **HotBot at** `www.hotbot.com`. Offers simple, advanced, and Boolean searches, seven different search classes, links to features, and a comprehensive list of categories. Begun in 1996, powered by Inktomi, and connected with Wired magazine.

- **Infoseek at** `www.infoseek.com`. Offers simple and Boolean logic searches, a broad base of categories and subcategories, and a large assortment of links including UPS tracking, investment tips, news, and reference tools. Begun in 1995 and uses an Ultrasmart/Ultraseek index of Web pages.

- **Lycos at** `www.lycos.com`. Offers keyword, picture, and sound searches, categories including Business, Fashion, and Technology, links to Yellow Pages Online, free software, Companies Online, and classifieds. Begun in 1994 and runs the Top 5% rating service and A2Z directory.

- **Yahoo at** `www.yahoo.com`. Offers keyword searches, a large variety of categories and subcategories, Yahooligans for Kids, Regional Yahoos, What's New, and What's Cool. Begun in 1994 and the oldest Web site directory.

Playing the searching game

Looking at the HotBot Search Page

HotBot, one of the best search engines on the Web, is always a good place to find what you're looking for. You can customize your search and the results list, using HotBot's multiple options and search classes.

Available search sources

Additional services

HotBot lets you search your way.

Access search help

Enter search query

Search for exact phrase or six other combinations

Initiate search

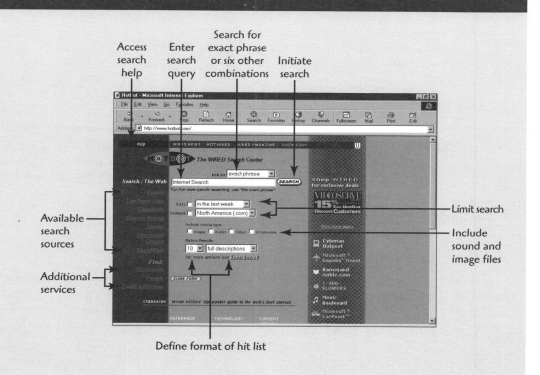

Limit search

Include sound and image files

Define format of hit list

5

Exploring the Web

Approach Internet searching as a game. To play the game, pick a search tool, like HotBot or Yahoo, and then enter a *query* made up of *keywords*. The search tool responds with a *hit list* containing links to Web sites that match your query. You win when you find the sites you're looking for. Here are some other search pointers that will make you a winner every time:

- **Capitalize adjacent names.** Capitalize adjacent names so the search engine treats the words as a single name or title. If you type Honest Abe, your hit list contains Web sites with references to the president. If you type honest abe, your hit list contains sites with the word honest and the name abe, but not necessarily on the same page.

continued

Playing the searching game

- **Keep your query short and to the point.** Search tools cannot effectively process long, rambling queries. Use enough words to fully state your search objective, but keep the query succinct. An example of an effective query is *Internet search technique*. But the query *How can I search the Internet so I get what I want?* isn't going to produce meaningful results.

- **Check for spelling errors.** Typos ruin a great search query. The keywords *Interneet search technique* won't find sites that contain any information whatsoever about the Internet, let alone Internet search technique.

- **Enclose phrases in double quotes.** Some search tools require quotes; some don't. Since you might not be able to remember each time which tools need what, use double quotes consistently to glue phrases together. For example, the query *"Internet search technique"* will find sites that show the exact phrase, rather than every site with the words *Internet* or *search* or *technique*.

- **Use Boolean logic.** Don't panic at the mention of Boolean logic! Here's a quick set of Boolean rules:

  AND. The word AND between keywords limits your search. For example, *Internet AND search AND technique* means that the sites found must contain all of the words. However, it doesn't mean that they need to be together in a phrase or even close together. AND is sometimes represented by an ampersand (&).

  OR. The word OR produces the opposite result of using double quotes around words. In our example, the use of OR means that the search tool will find Web pages that contain the words *Internet* or *search* or *technique*. OR is sometimes represented by the pipe (|) character.

  NOT. Use NOT to exclude a specific word. The query *"search technique" NOT Internet* tells the search tool to dismiss all Web sites that contain references to Internet search technique, but to show you the links to sites that contain references to any other search technique. NOT is often represented by the minus sign (−) character.

- **Start with a broad query and then narrow it.** You don't want to miss anything, do you? Unless you're positive of what you'll find, let the search tool do its job and find as many links as it can. After you've looked at the preliminary results, refine your query and search again.

- **Don't get discouraged.** So many pages are posted to the Web that it may take a few tries before you find what you're looking for. Once you construct an effective query, you'll find what you want.

- **Use site help.** Many search tools contain advanced techniques or helpful hints that explain how to get the most out of each tool.

Performing a search using HotBot

Performing a search using HotBot

Originally an academic experiment, HotBot was developed at the University of California at Berkeley. HotBot is known as one of the fastest search engines and often finds documents that the other search engines miss. HotBot's growing index contains listings for more than 54 million Web documents and more than 4 million Usenet newsgroup articles.

To complete this exercise, the Internet Explorer browser must be open and displayed on your screen. Have a scratch pad and a pencil handy so you can record the number of hits returned for each search.

1 Click inside the Address bar to highlight the existing URL.

2 Type **hotbot**.

3 Press Enter. Autoscan searches the Web and opens the HotBot page.

4 Click inside the Search box.

5 Type **cairn terrier.**

6 Click the HotBot Search button. HotBot searches its index and displays a page of links to Web sites that match the search query. The URL in the Address bar changes to match HotBot's special query language.

7 Scroll through the links shown on the HotBot hit page, which should look similar to the one in the illustration. The links at the top of the results list most closely match the search query.

8 Note the number of hits HotBot found for cairn terrier.

9 The current query is structured to search the Web for all the words. To change the search, click the drop-down arrow next to the phrase all the words.

10 Choose the words in the title option from the drop-down list.

11 Click Search. When the results appear, note the number of matches returned with the revised query. The number of matches is considerably less when you search using the words in the title delimiter.

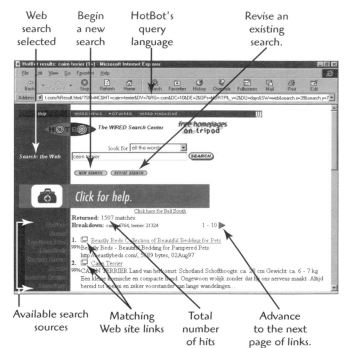

Web search selected · Begin a new search · HotBot's query language · Revise an existing search.

Available search sources · Matching Web site links · Total number of hits · Advance to the next page of links.

all the words
any of the words
the exact phrase
words in the title
the person
links to this URL
the Boolean expression

5

Exploring the Web

⓬ Click Revise Search.

⓭ Click Usenet News from the list of available search sources.

NOTE *Usenet News is an Internet network of newsgroups whose users exchange information, opinions, and news. You learn about newsgroups in Lesson 11.*

⓮ Click the Search button.

⓯ View the new hit list. The list shows links to newsgroup articles instead of to Web pages.

⓰ Note the number of items on the hit list. HotBot found fewer matches looking through the indexed articles on Usenet News than the Web.

⓱ Click Revise Search to return to the original search page displaying your query.

When you finish this exercise, move directly to the next exercise.

Using HotBot's advanced search techniques

In this exercise, you use HotBot's advanced query features to restructure the search you constructed in the preceding exercise. Complete the preceding exercise before you begin this exercise.

❶ Usenet News and words in the title are shown on the HotBot search page from the preceding exercise. Click the Web on the list of available search sources.

❷ Click the down arrow next to words in title and choose all the words.

Your query should now be structured to search the Web for all the words, with **cairn terrier** typed in the search box.

❸ Click the Revise Search button. The original search page appears.

❹ Click the checkbox next to Date.

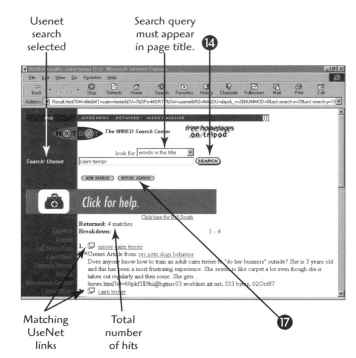

Usenet search selected

Search query must appear in page title. ⓮

Matching UseNet links

Total number of hits

⓱

Finding sites with Yahoo

⑤ Click the down arrow next to in the last week and choose in the last 6 months. Clicking this option narrows the search to Web pages placed on the Web within the last 6 months.

⑥ Click Search. In a few moments, the page appears. Note that fewer matches appear now than when the time frame was unlimited, as when you conducted the search in the last exercise.

⑦ Click the Revise Search button to return to the search page.

⑧ In the Date area, click the down arrow next to in the last 6 months and select in the last 2 weeks from the list.

⑨ Click Search. In a few moments, the results page appears. Mark down the number of matches found, if any.

⑩ Return to the original search page by clicking Revise Search. When the page appears, click the checkbox next to Date to remove the check and extend the date range.

⑪ Click the checkbox next to Continent. Choices include North America and other geographic locations.

⑫ Click the down arrow and choose Southeast Asia from the drop-down list.

⑬ Click Search. When the results list appears, notice how the total number of hits has changed.

By limiting the search query, you limit the total number of hits.

Finding sites with Yahoo

Yahoo, a classic site directory, takes a different approach to finding Web pages than HotBot or other search engines. Yahoo's index of Web sites is arranged by categories. Underneath most categories, you find subcategories.

You can type keywords and let Yahoo look for matches, or you can select a category that interests you from Yahoo's main page. By using Yahoo's hierarchical category structure, you can find Web sites without having to enter any keywords! Of course, to refine your search, you can choose a category and then enter a keyword.

Date checkbox

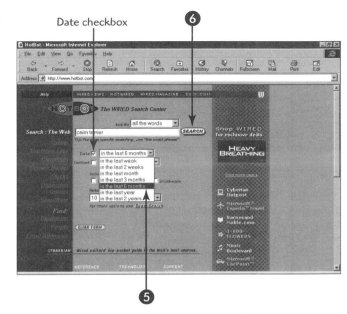

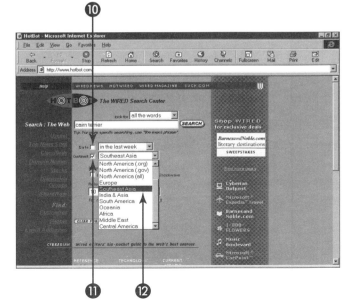

5

Exploring the Web

Finding sites with Yahoo

In this exercise, you find sites that reference old television shows. The first part of this exercise takes you through many of Yahoo's subcategories. The final part of the exercise shows how to jump directly to a specific site.

1 Click inside the Address bar to highlight the existing URL.

2 Type **yahoo**.

3 Press Enter. Autoscan searches the Web and opens the Yahoo page.

4 Click the Entertainment link. An index of entertainment-related categories appears.

5 Scroll down the page and click the Television link. Another index of categories — this time about television — appears. The number of sites grouped under the category appears in parentheses beside the index title.

6 Click the Shows category link.

TIP

As you jump from category to category, you're bound to find a link that doesn't have anything to do with your original search but looks interesting. Feel free to follow another link and see where it takes you. Click the Back button on the Standard Buttons toolbar when you're ready to return to this exercise.

7 Click the Comedies link.

8 Scroll the list of variety shows to find the link to The Dick Van Dyke Show.

9 Click the link.

10 Another page appears, showing links to pages about the show. Click a link to see the page.

11 When you're finished looking, click the Back button.

Yahoo's hierarchical category structure

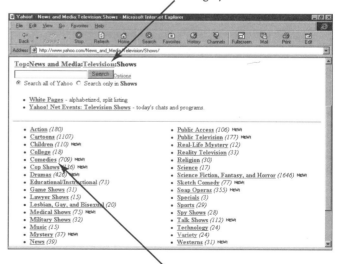

12 If you know what you're looking for, you can search for it directly. Type **"Hawaii Five-O"** in the search box. Make sure you enclose the words in double quotes.

13 For the most comprehensive search, make sure the option button next to Search all of Yahoo is selected.

14 Click Search.

15 Yahoo organizes the links on the search results page into Category and Site Matches. Click any link on the page to visit sites about *Hawaii Five-O*.

Use either of the methods that Yahoo offers to find the pages you're looking for.

SKILLS CHALLENGE: FINDING THE SITES YOU WANT

In this Skills Challenge, you use different search tools to find sites related to William Shakespeare. Now that you've mastered some great search techniques, you can use any search tool. However, if you need help with one of the steps, feel free to look back through the lesson.

1 If it's not already open, launch the Internet Explorer browser.

2 Use the Autoscan feature to open HotBot.

 How does Autoscan work?

3 Type a query in the search box to look for William Shakespeare sites and run the search. Note the total number of documents found.

4 Change the query so that HotBot looks for documents about the person instead of all the words, and run the search again.

Is it necessary to enclose search phrases in double quotes?

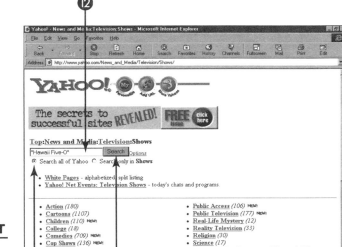

5

Exploring the Web

Skills challenge

5 Click the Search button. When the Explorer bar appears, choose Yahoo from the list of providers. Don't change any of the defaults.

6 Type William Shakespeare in the search box and click Search. Note the total number of documents found.

7 Change the Yahoo search to look for documents about William Shakespeare and literature. Run the search and note the number of hits.

 3 *What's the difference between a search engine and a site directory?*

8 Optionally, to end this Skills Challenge with a bang, you can take a peek at what other people are searching for right now! Type www.go2search.com in the Address bar and press Enter.

9 When the Metacrawler page appears, click the Metaspy link. A list appears showing some of the actual topics that are being searched through Metacrawler, a multithreaded search engine that looks through the indexes of other search engines. The list refreshes (updates) every 15 seconds to show the newest search topics.

10 Close the Internet Explorer browser and disconnect from the Internet.

TROUBLESHOOTING

As you search the Internet, you may find that your search doesn't work or you get some questionable results as you use different search tools. The following table shows how to proceed when you encounter problems.

Problem	Solution
My results list included pages and pages of links. But many of the links don't seem to be working. Why?	Anyone who searches the Internet encounters this frustrating situation. Since Web spiders only go forward finding new pages, pages that have been changed or removed often don't get removed from the index.
I'm doing a research project for school. How do I know for sure that I've found all of the Web pages that match my query?	Unfortunately, you can't be sure. To lower the odds, start searching with a broad query and then make it more specific. Run the same search through a couple of search tools and look at the results closely.
I tried to use Autoscan, but nothing happened after I typed some words in the Address bar.	Two things might have gone wrong. The first one seems obvious, but it happens all the time. Did you remember to press the Enter key after you finished typing? You need to press it to initiate the Autoscan feature. The other thing that might have caused the computer not to move is that you were accidentally disconnected from the Internet. Reset the connection and try again.

WRAP UP

This lesson covered a lot of ground. In this lesson, you learned all about searching as you developed the following skills:

- Using Internet Explorer's exclusive search features

- Learning the difference between search engines and site directories

- Conducting searches with HotBot and Yahoo

In the next lesson, you use the skills you learned in this lesson as you begin to explore how to put together a list of your favorite places in one easy-to-use place.

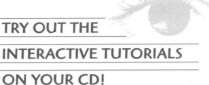

TRY OUT THE

INTERACTIVE TUTORIALS

ON YOUR CD!

PART III

A Step Beyond the Browser

Now it's time to move beyond the basic look and functions of the Internet Explorer browser. The lessons in this part show you how to customize your Start page and the browser toolbars, how to organize and subscribe to your favorite sites, how to use the unique features of Internet Explorer to explore the world of multimedia on the Web, and how to protect your computer with a range of new security features. Extend your skills with the following lessons:

- Lesson 6: Managing Your Web Experience
- Lesson 7: Maximizing Your Web Experience
- Lesson 8: Changing the Look of the Browser
- Lesson 9: Becoming Security Aware

Managing Your Web Experience

35 MINUTES

GOALS

This lesson teaches you how to set some custom options for the Internet Explorer browser. These options make it easier for you to revisit the sites and links you enjoy most. As you work through the exercises, you master the following skills:

- Customizing the Microsoft Internet Start page
- Selecting a different Start page
- Creating a list of Favorites
- Returning to a favorite Web site
- Organizing your Favorites in folders
- Subscribing to Web sites
- Downloading Web pages

Get ready

GET READY

To complete this lesson, you must have Internet Explorer 4 installed on your computer (refer to Appendix A for installation instructions). Additionally, you should be connected to the Internet before you begin the exercises.

When you complete this lesson, you will know how to customize your Microsoft Internet Start page with exciting topics and links that will be available to you each time you open the Internet Explorer browser.

SETTING A START PAGE

By now you've probably noticed that the same page appears each time you open the Internet Explorer browser. For most people, the Microsoft Internet Start page is the first site they see. Or maybe you'd like to see a completely different page—your office's Web site, for example, or a retail mall—each time you begin your Web experience. Either way, the Internet Explorer browser is happy to oblige.

Customizing the Microsoft Internet Start page

Many people like the news and features on the Microsoft Internet Start page, but did you know that Microsoft has provided an array of optional topics that you can add to the page to make your Web experience more personal? You might be interested in current stock prices or want to view the latest sports news. Why not customize your page by adding hyperlinks to the Web sites of recognized and respected content providers such as MSNBC and *Forbes* magazine? Essentially, you can turn your Microsoft Internet Start page into a personal newsstand.

❶ Open the Internet Explorer browser by clicking the Launch Internet Explorer Browser icon on the Quick Launch toolbar. If the toolbar isn't visible, display it by clicking the right mouse button on a blank spot on the Windows taskbar and selecting Toolbars ➢ Quick Launch from the pop-up menu.

Customizing the Start page

2 When the Microsoft Internet Start page appears, click the Personalizing link in the black bar at the top of the browser window to begin customizing your Start page.

3 The start personalizing page appears. The page is divided into three sections labeled step 1, step 2, and step 3. Take a minute to look over the types of additional features you can add to your customized Start page.

4 Under the step 1 heading is a list of available topics—news, technology, money, sports, entertainment, and more. When you click a topic under step 1, the options in step 2 change. For example, select Entertainment and notice how a list of entertainment providers appears in step 2.

5 Check the boxes next to the providers listed in step 2 that you want to add to your Internet Start page. You can check as many boxes as you want.

6 If you want to add additional topics to your Microsoft Internet Start page, click the Next button in step 3 and repeat steps 4 and 5 in this exercise. You may want to add technology providers to your Start page, for example.

7 When you've chosen all the topics you want to include, click the Finish button. The Microsoft Internet Start page reappears on the screen.

8 Scroll down the Microsoft Internet Start page. The topics you selected appear near the bottom the page. In the future, whenever you open the Internet Explorer browser, the topics you chose will appear.

Hyperlinks to the content providers you selected appear as pictures or logos to the left of the topic heading. Underneath the topic heading is a selection of current articles and features.

9 Click a picture or logo on the left side of the Internet Start page to move to the Web site of the provider you chose in step 5 of this exercise.

10 Click the hyperlinked (underlined) portion of an article or feature to move directly to the story.

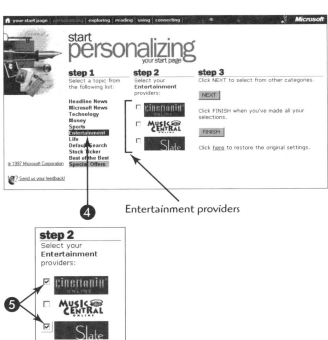

Entertainment providers

Selecting a different Start page

⑪ To return to your Internet Start page from the provider's site, click the Back button or the Home button on the Standard Buttons toolbar.

⑫ To add additional topics to your Start page during the current session or later on, simply repeat steps 2 through 7 of this exercise.

▶ Selecting a different Start page

After you've been on the Web for a while, you may decide that you'd like to start with a page that holds special meaning or interest for you. After some recent abdominal surgery, for example, I changed my Start page to The Adhesions Home Page! Or you might want to open to your company's home page. Internet Explorer allows you to open the browser with any Web page you choose.

❶ If it isn't already open, start the Internet Explorer browser by clicking the Launch Internet Explorer Browser icon on the Quick Launch toolbar.

❷ When the browser loads, move to the page you want to use as your new Start page.

❸ Select View ➤ Internet Options. The Internet Options dialog box appears.

❹ Click the General tab. In the Home page section at the top of the tab is the highlighted address of the Start page currently set as the default.

Address bar

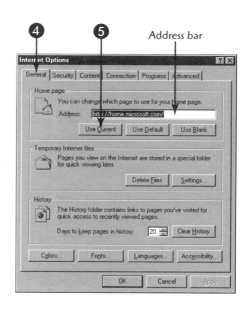

TIP

The Start page is also called the Home page because whenever you click the Home button on the Internet Explorer Standard Buttons toolbar, the browser displays your default Start page.

❺ Click the Use Current button to make the page that's currently displayed on the screen your new Start page. The URL of the page appears in the Address bar.

6 Click OK to close the Internet Options dialog box. The next time you launch the Internet Explorer browser, it opens to the page you selected.

7 Repeat steps 1 through 6 to change the Start page to a new Web site whenever you want.

8 If you decide to change back to the Microsoft Internet Start page, select View ➤ Internet Options.

9 On the General tab screen, click the Use Default button. The original Microsoft Internet Start page is restored and appears the next time you open the browser.

USING FAVORITES

You probably have a lot of favorite places: stores, restaurants, and vacation spots. These favorite places are locations you like to return to again and again. As you browse the Internet, you'll discover some favorite Web places too. The Internet Explorer browser allows you to set up these favorite sites in a special list so you can return to them again and again with just a few mouse clicks.

Creating a list of Favorites

It's a breeze to set up a list of your favorite sites as you cruise around the Web. In this exercise, you set up a few favorite places. Before you begin the exercise, you should be connected to the Internet with the Internet Explorer browser open and displayed on the screen.

1 Type www.switchboard.com/ in the Address bar.

2 Press Enter. The Switchboard Home Page appears.

3 Select Favorites ➤ Add to Favorites. The Add Favorite dialog box appears on the screen.

4 Make sure that the option button next to No, just add the page to my favorites is selected.

5 Click OK to add the Switchboard Home Page to the list of Favorites.

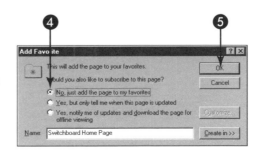

Returning to a favorite Web site

TIP

Another method of adding a Web page to your list of Favorites is to right-click an empty area of the Web page and select Add to Favorites from the pop-up menu that appears.

6 Click the Home button on the Standard Buttons toolbar to return to your Start page.

Returning to a favorite Web site

Using your Favorites list is even easier than creating it!

1 With any Web page displayed in the Internet Explorer browser window, select Favorites on the menu bar. The Favorites menu opens. (I've been using Internet Explorer for a while, so my Favorites may look a bit different from yours.)

2 Slide your mouse down to the entry for the Switchboard Home Page. In a moment, the Switchboard page appears on the screen.

HOW FAVORITES WORK

It almost seems like magic, doesn't it? You click the title of a site on the Favorites list, and you're instantly transported to that Web page. How can the Internet Explorer browser unerringly remember exactly where you want to go?

Actually, it isn't magic that accomplishes the transfer. Instead, like so much of what goes on behind the scenes in Windows and Internet Explorer, *files* are the source of the transaction. Whenever you add a site to the Favorites list,

Windows stores the URL in a file in the C:\Windows\ Favorites folder that's stored on the hard drive of your computer. When you click a site name on the Favorites list, Windows and Internet Explorer open the file, read the code, and move to the corresponding URL of the site.

Now that you know how the whole process works, you can forget about it! Concentrate on setting up and visiting as many Favorites as you want.

Organizing your Favorites in folders ◀

Organizing your Favorites in folders

Before too long, your Favorites list can get mighty long. There's little advantage to using the Favorites feature if you need to scroll through a long list every time you want to return to a favorite site. Fortunately, you can organize these sites in folders, just as you organize the files on your computer.

1 Select Favorites ➤ Organize Favorites. The Organize Favorites dialog box appears.

TIP

> *Don't be alarmed if your list of Favorites looks different than mine. The list is computer-specific. Your computer may contain more or less sites and folders than the example.*

2 Click the Create New Folder button. A closed folder icon appears at the bottom of the list with the words New Folder highlighted in a box.

3 You don't have to delete the words New Folder to assign a name to the folder. So don't press the Delete key, but type **Directory Services** to name the folder. When you begin to create folders on your own, you can call them anything you like.

4 When you've typed the folder name, click outside the folder name box.

5 While holding down the left mouse button, drag the Switchboard Home Page Favorite on top of the Directory Services folder. As you drag, a dim copy of the Switchboard icon appears.

TIP

> *As your Favorites list grows, all of your folders and sites may not fit into one pane of the Organize Favorites dialog box window. Use the scroll bar at the bottom of the window to display the other sites.*

6 Release the left mouse button. The Switchboard Home Page Favorite is now placed in the Directory Services folder. Click the Close button to exit the Organize Favorites dialog box.

7 Whenever you want to return to the Switchboard Home Page, select Favorites ➤ Directory Services ➤ Switchboard Home Page. (To return to another Favorite you've placed in another folder, select Favorites ➤ *Folder Name* ➤ *Title of Favorite*.)

NOTE

To get you started, many of the great Web sites referenced in this book have already been added to the Favorites list in the copy of Internet Explorer on the CD. Look for them in the folder called One Step Collection.

VISUAL BONUS

Working with the Favorites Bar

The Organize Favorites dialog box gives you a limited area in which to work. Instead, click the Favorites button on the Standard Buttons toolbar to open the Favorites bar.

The Favorites bar fills the left side of the Internet Explorer browser screen.

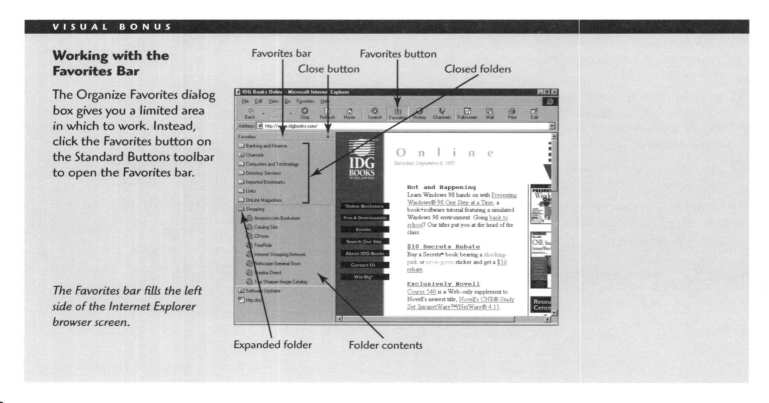

Favorites bar

Close button

Favorites button

Closed folders

Expanded folder

Folder contents

USING SUBSCRIPTIONS

Web pages change all the time. Just like subscribing to a channel, you determine how often you want to update the page and how you'll be notified of the new content. When you subscribe to a site, Internet Explorer compares the current Web page against the way it appeared when you last viewed it. If the site has changed, Internet Explorer copies the new Web page to your computer when you update your subscriptions. You can update all of your subscriptions at once or select specific ones to update. Once the new information has been copied to your computer, you can disconnect from the Internet and view the Web page offline.

Subscribing to Web sites

In this exercise, you set a new Favorites site and then subscribe to it, telling the Internet Explorer browser to track the site and notify you when changes are made. The Internet Explorer browser should be open and on the screen from the last exercise.

❶ Type www.palacebleu.com/ in the Address bar.

❷ Press Enter. In a moment, the Palace Bleu Inn page appears.

❸ Select Favorites ➢ Add to Favorites. The Add Favorite dialog box appears. The following options are available:

Option	What It Means
No, just add the page to my favorites	No subscription, but you'll be able to click the button to view the Web page name at any time when you're connected to the Internet.
Yes, but only tell me when this page is updated	The Web page will appear on the list of Favorites. When the content of the page changes, a gleam will appear next to the Web page name. You can also request to be notified of content changes by e-mail.

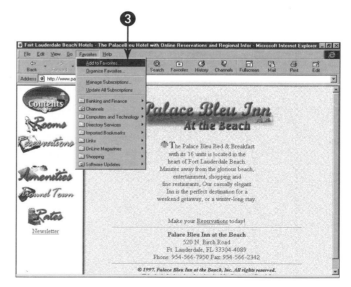

continued

Subscribing to Web sites

Option	What It Means
Yes, notify me of updates and download the page for offline viewing	In addition to receiving notification when the Web page changes, you'll be able to view the page when you're not connected to the Internet.

4 Click the option button next to the third choice, Yes, notify me of updates and download the page for offline viewing.

5 Click Customize. The subscription Wizard dialog box appears.

6 The Subscription Wizard asks you to choose whether you want to download only the Web site to your computer's hard drive, or whether you want to download the Web site and all the pages linked to it.

Click the option next to Download this page.

7 Click Next.

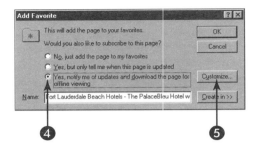

TIP

Unless you're sure how many pages are linked to the Favorite you're subscribing to, don't select the option for downloading the Web site and all pages linked to it. Without meaning to, you could fill your hard drive with unimportant files.

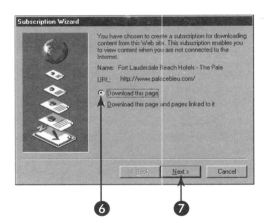

8 The next dialog box asks if you'd like to be notified by e-mail when the Web page changes. (You learn about e-mail in Lesson 10.) Click the option button next to No.

9 Click Next.

10 The next dialog box asks how often you want to update the subscription. You have three options:

Option	What It Does
Scheduled	Choose daily, weekly, monthly, or a custom schedule.
Dial as needed	Select only if your Dial Up Networking connection is set so that the Autodial feature is enabled. If you select this option, the Internet Explorer browser will dial your ISP and download the updated Web page.
Manually	Update the subscription whenever you choose.

Click the option button next to Scheduled.

⑪ Accept the default Daily schedule by clicking Next.

⑫ The next dialog box asks if the site requires a password and provides two text boxes for entering the information. Click No.

⑬ Click Finish to end the Subscription Wizard.

⑭ The Add Favorite dialog box reappears, confirming the choices you made. Click OK to close the dialog box and return to the Palace Bleu Inn page you were viewing previously. The new Favorite is added to the list of Favorites.

⑮ When the Favorite is updated, a starburst icon called a *gleam* appears next to the site name on the Favorites list. Additionally, if you requested e-mail notification, you'll receive an e-mail message telling you that the page has changed.

Downloading Web pages

After you've subscribed to a Web page, you can set Internet Explorer to download the updated Web pages to your computer so you can read them offline. Follow the steps in this exercise to find out how. The Favorites bar that you accessed in the previous exercise should still be open on the screen.

❶ Click the right mouse button on the Palace Bleu Inn entry on the list in the Favorites bar (you'll find it listed as the Fort Lauderdale Beach Hotel). A pop-up menu appears.

❷ Click Update now from the menu. The Downloading Subscriptions dialog box appears as files are transferred from the

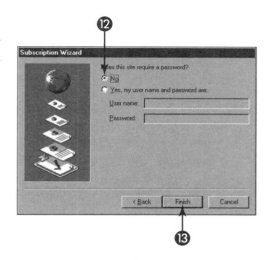

Skills challenge

content provider to the hard drive of your computer. When the updated content has been copied to your computer, the Downloading Subscriptions dialog box closes.

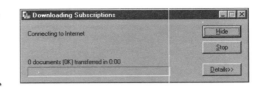

3 When you're returned to the page you were viewing previously, close the Favorites frame by clicking the Favorites button on the Standard Buttons toolbar. The new content of the Web site, if any, appears on the screen.

NOTE

You can update any Favorite to which you've subscribed by opening the Favorites bar, right-clicking the Favorite on the list, and then clicking Update now. If you want to update all your channel and Web site subscriptions at one time, select Favorites ➢ Update All Subscriptions.

4 Even if you're not connected to the Internet, you can view a Web site that has been downloaded to your computer. First open the Internet Explorer browser.

5 Select File ➢ Work Offline.

6 Choose the downloaded site from the Favorites list. Internet Explorer retrieves the page from your History file and displays it in the browser window.

7 When you're finished looking at downloaded sites, be sure and select File ➢ Work Offline again to cancel the offline option.

SKILLS CHALLENGE: PLAYING FAVORITES

This Skills Challenge tests your knowledge of the material covered in this lesson, including changing your Start page, setting and organizing Favorites, and subscribing to Web pages.

These steps don't include all the details for completing the Skills Challenge. However, if you don't remember how to complete a step, look back through the exercises in this lesson for instructions.

1 After you're connected to the Internet and the Internet Explorer browser is open, visit a site you've set up as a Favorite.

2 Move to the following page on the World Wide Web: www.idgbooks.com/.

3 Take the steps necessary to change your opening page to the IDG Books home page. (Once you've opened the Internet Options dialog box and made the necessary changes, click Cancel if you don't want to change the current Start page.)

 Can you change the Web page that the Internet Explorer browser displays when it launches?

4 Add the IDG Books site to the Favorites list.

 Describe two ways to add a site to your Favorites list.

5 Create a new folder on the Favorites list and name it Computer Books.

6 Move the IDG Books Favorite into the new folder.

 What is the advantage of placing Favorites in folders?

7 Subscribe to the IDG Books site so that the icon on the Favorites list changes when the site is updated. Do not sign up for e-mail notification.

8 When you're finished with the challenge, close the browser and terminate your Internet connection.

TROUBLESHOOTING

As you move around the Web, you may encounter an unexpected problem or two. The following table shows some of these common problems and offers simple solutions.

Wrap up

Problem	Solution
I don't want any Web page to load when I open Internet Explorer. How do I do this?	Select View ➤ Internet Options. In the Home page section of the General Tab, click Use Blank.
Now that I've set up all of my Favorites in folders on the Favorites list, I want to reorganize them. Can I do it?	Click the Favorites button to open the Favorites bar. Expand the folders and click and drag a Favorite to its new location.
I went a little crazy with Favorites and set up too many. How do I delete a Favorite after I've set it up?	Open the Favorites bar, click the right mouse button on the Favorite you wish to delete, and choose Delete from the pop-up menu.
Oh no! By accident I deleted some of the Favorites I wanted to keep.	The simplest solution is to return to the sites and set them up again. Find the sites on your History list if you can't remember the URLs.

WRAP UP

In this lesson, you exercised the following skills:

- Setting your Start page
- Creating and organizing a list of Favorites
- Subscribing to Web sites
- Downloading a Web site for offline browsing

TRY OUT THE
INTERACTIVE TUTORIALS
ON YOUR CD!

   In the next lesson, you use Internet Explorer browser add-ons to view multimedia-enhanced and virtual reality Web pages. You also download software from the Internet and install it on your computer.

Maximizing Your Web Experience

85 MINUTES

GOALS

This lesson shows you how to participate in the exciting world of multimedia on the Web by using special add-ons in conjunction with the Internet Explorer browser. You also learn how to download and install software and where to find thousands of free and nominally priced programs on the Internet. In this lesson, you cover the following:

- Viewing NetShow videos
- Determining if the VRML Viewer is installed
- Going virtual with VRML
- Creating a folder for downloads
- Installing WinZip
- Installing WS_FTP LE (Limited Edition)
- Downloading software from the Web
- Installing zipped files
- Downloading software from an FTP site
- Installing self-executing files

125

Get ready

GET READY

Before you begin this lesson, you must install Internet Explorer 4 (refer to Appendix A). You also need to be connected to the Internet and open the Internet Explorer browser.

When you finish this lesson, you will know how to use the Internet Explorer components to view multimedia Web pages and how to find software on the Web that you can download and use.

UNDERSTANDING ADD-ON COMPONENTS

An add-on component is a software program that gives Internet Explorer extra capabilities. Add-on components — you may have heard them called plug-ins or helper applications — can be used to explore virtual worlds and view video. When you did a full installation of Internet Explorer, some add-on components, such as the NetShow On-Demand Player, were included in the installation.

Additional add-on components developed by Microsoft and other software publishers are available for download from the Microsoft Internet Explorer Download site at `www.microsoft.com/ie/ie4/`. Once you install them, these add-on components become a part of the browser and automatically load when you access a file that needs the add-on component in order to display. (Refer to Appendix A for instructions on how to download and install additional components available from Microsoft.)

In addition to these add-on components, the Internet Explorer browser is also equipped with ActiveMovie, an application programming interface. ActiveMovie supports all standard video and audio formats: AVI, QuickTime, MPEG I and II, WAV, AU, and AIFF. ActiveMovie eliminates the need to download several add-ons to view these types of multimedia elements on Web pages. Most of the formats played by ActiveMovie require large file sizes and long download times, but ActiveMovie minimizes the file size and download time without sacrificing quality. One of the major benefits of ActiveMovie is that audio and video files created in the MPEG format play while the file is being downloaded, much like videos created with streaming technology.

TRY OUT THE

INTERACTIVE TUTORIALS

ON YOUR CD!

VISUAL BONUS

Playing with Multimedia

Internet Explorer contains add-on components that allow you to view multimedia such as sound, video, and 3D images. These illustrations show just a sample of the types of multimedia content you can explore with Internet Explorer.

Sit back and watch a broadcast of a performance, a concert, or a classroom lecture with NetShow.

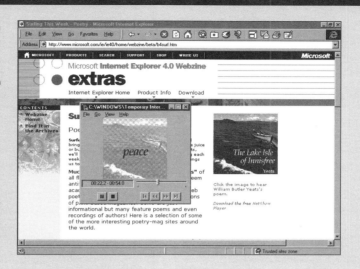

Explore three-dimensional worlds with the Microsoft VRML Viewer.

Viewing NetShow videos

The majority of add-on components for Internet Explorer display the various types of multimedia found on the Web. The exercises in this section show you how to use two popular add-on components: the NetShow On-Demand Player that plays streaming audio and video and the Microsoft VRML 2.0 Viewer, an add-on that lets you view interactive three-dimensional images created with the Virtual Reality Modeling Language.

▶ Viewing NetShow videos

The NetShow On-Demand Player is an ActiveX control that plays interactive Web content such as audio, illustrated audio (images and sound), and video. The NetShow Player uses streaming technology. Video file formats that use streaming technology do not require a full file download before they begin playing; you can see and hear the video as it downloads. Video file formats that do not use streaming technology (such as AVI files) require a full file download before you can initiate play.

This exercise shows you how to operate the NetShow On-Demand Player.

① With the Internet Explorer browser open and displayed on the screen, click inside the Address bar.

② Type www.microsoft.com/netshow/examples.htm.

③ Press Enter. The Microsoft NetShow Gallery Web page appears. This page contains links to several examples compiled by Microsoft to demonstrate how NetShow works.

④ Click the Directions from SeaTac to Microsoft link. The NetShow player opens in a separate window and begins to download the video. The initial download may take a few seconds, but the video begins to play automatically. You do not need to do anything to start the video.

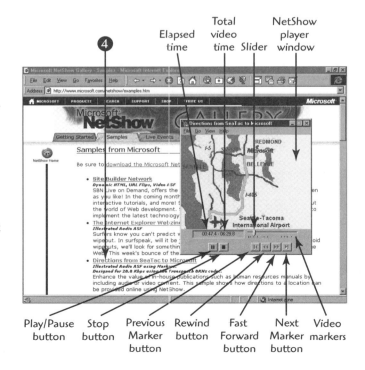

Elapsed time · Total video time · Slider · NetShow player window

Play/Pause button · Stop button · Previous Marker button · Rewind button · Fast Forward button · Next Marker button · Video markers

5 Several buttons along the bottom of the NetShow window control the display of the video. Experiment with these buttons while the video plays. The controls perform the following tasks:

- **Play/Pause button.** Click this toggle switch to pause the video and then to start it again.

- **Stop button.** Use this button to stop the video and rewind it to the beginning.

- **Previous Marker and Next Marker buttons.** Use these buttons to return to a previous marker in the video or to advance to the next marker. Markers work the same as tracks on CDs and are sometimes used by creators of Web videos.

- **Rewind and Fast Forward buttons.** Use these buttons to move backward or forward through a video.

6 The video will play all the way through without any intervention on your part. However, if a video contains markers (you can tell by looking at the slider; the short vertical lines below the slider represent markers), and you want to skip around from marker to marker, you can either click the Next Marker and Previous Marker buttons or use an alternate method.

Right-click the video and select Markers from the pop-up menu. The Microsoft NetShow Player Properties dialog box opens with the Markers tab displayed.

The NetShow Player Properties dialog box displays on top of the player window. To move the dialog box so that you can see the video, click and hold the mouse pointer on the dialog box title bar and drag the dialog box to another part of your screen so that you can see the player window.

7

Maximizing Your Web Experience

Viewing NetShow videos

7 Click Marker 3.

8 Click the Go To Marker button. The video begins to play beginning at marker 3, which in this example shows the instructions for leaving SeaTac Airport.

9 To close the Microsoft NetShow Player Properties dialog box, click Cancel. The dialog box closes.

10 To close the NetShow Player, click the Close button located at the top right corner of the window.

Now you are ready to use NetShow at other Web sites. Remember, anytime you visit a Web page that contains a video constructed in the streaming technology format, the NetShow Player will open automatically and play the video.

ActiveX technology was designed by Microsoft to enable interactive content on the Web. ActiveX can combine multimedia effects, interactive objects, and software applications, regardless of the language in which they were created. This functionality allows you to run applications in Internet Explorer and to run Internet Explorer as a software component in other applications. For example, a Web page might contain access to a product database. When a visitor to the page requests information on a certain product, an ActiveX control accesses the database and displays a multimedia graphic of the product information in Internet Explorer.

Key benefits of ActiveX technology include the following:

- ActiveX controls can be automatically downloaded and set up in the browser with no interaction from the user.

- Authenticode certificates provide protection from potentially damaging code being downloaded to your computer and the unauthorized execution of an applet or script.

- Documents saved in almost any file format can be viewed in the browser.

Sound formats used on the Web

The Internet is filled with audio. You can select from thousands of songs to download, you can tune into talk shows and sporting events, and you can even listen to books online. Depending on the audio file format, you may or may not have to wait for the files to download completely before you can begin listening to the audio files. To really enjoy Web audio, your computer should be at least a 486 66 MHz system equipped with a sound card and speakers and at least a 28.8 bps modem.

Here are brief descriptions of common audio formats:

- **AIFF.** The Audio Interchange File Format is a high-quality audio format. Because of the high quality of the files, AIFF files can take up quite a bit of storage space. A one-minute AIFF file, for example, can take up as much as 10MB of hard drive space. AIFF files can be easily converted to other audio file formats.

- **AU.** The AU format is the most frequently used audio file type on the Internet. This format does not produce a high quality sound (it can be compared to the sound quality of a telephone conversation), but the files are relatively small and almost every computer operating system comes with a player that will play AU files.

- **MIDI.** The Musical Instrument Digital Interface is not actually an audio file format, but a communications protocol that allows the transmission of data between electronic music instruments. Since MIDI contains only instructions for controlling how and when electronic music devices produce sounds, MIDI files are much smaller than most digitized audio file formats.

- **MPEG audio.** The International Standards Organization's Moving Picture Experts Group is responsible for the MPEG format. MPEG was designed for both audio and video file compression. The advantage of using MPEG is its ability to compress large files without sacrificing much quality. Most Web sites that distribute high-quality music use the MPEG format.

- **RealAudio**. RealAudio is a streaming audio format that provides live and on-demand real-time sound.

- **WAV.** Microsoft and IBM are responsible for the Resource Interchange File Format Waveform Audio Format. The WAV file format is used primarily on Windows-based computers and is similar to the AIFF format in that it requires a considerable amount of disk space.

7

Maximizing Your Web Experience

Determining VRML Viewer status

▶ Determining if the VRML Viewer is installed

The Microsoft VRML Viewer integrates with the Internet Explorer browser and allows you to explore three-dimensional virtual worlds. By using the navigation controls in the VRML Viewer, you can move to different areas, look closely at objects, and view the virtual world from different perspectives.

The Microsoft VRML Viewer may or may not have installed when you loaded Internet Explorer 4. This exercise shows you how to determine if the component is installed. If it is not, you must follow the installation instructions in Appendix A before you can go on to the next exercise.

❶ With the Internet Explorer browser open and displayed on the screen, click inside the Address bar.

❷ Type www.microsoft.com/ie/ie40/.

❸ Press Enter. The Microsoft Internet Explorer 4.0 home page appears.

❹ Click the download link. A second window—The Internet Explorer Download Page—opens.

❺ Click the Internet Explorer 4.0 Components link. Another Web page appears that describes the add-on components.

❻ Click the add-on component link that corresponds with your operating system. The Component Download page appears along with a dialog box asking you if it is OK for the Active Setup wizard to determine what components are already installed on your computer.

❼ Click Yes. The Active Setup wizard searches your computer for components that have already been installed and displays the Component Download page after the search. The Status column at the far right of the page shows if a component has been installed or not and may also include information about available upgrades.

   ■ If the VRML component is not installed on your machine, follow the installation instructions in Appendix A before you continue with this lesson.

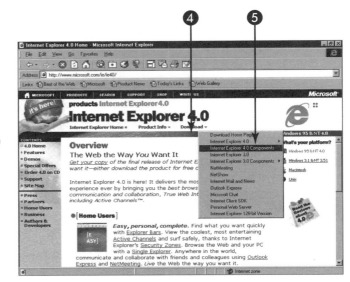

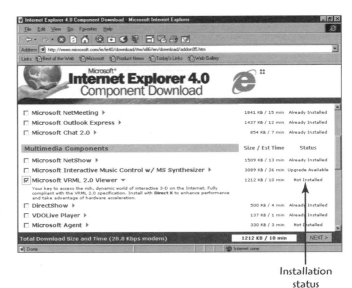

Installation status

- If the VRML component is already installed on your machine, move along to the next exercise.

Going virtual with VRML

Now that you have the VRML Viewer installed, it's time to experience 3D Web effects and learn how to navigate in this brave new world. It takes some practice to become proficient at finding your way around a virtual world, but this exercise helps you get started.

1 With the Internet Explorer browser open and displayed on the screen, click inside the Address bar.

2 Type www.epa.gov/nerlcwww/3dgrafic.wrl.

3 Press Enter. The EPA Microbiology virtual world appears in the browser window. The VRML Viewer controls appear along the left and bottom sides of the browser window.

4 Use the controls that appear along the left side of the browser window to move around in the virtual world. Click the Walk button.

5 Position the mouse pointer just below the E in EPA.

6 Click and hold the mouse button while you move the mouse pointer toward the top of the screen. The image in the browser window appears to be moving closer to you.

7 When the E fills the browser window, release the mouse button.

8 Click the Pan button.

9 Position the mouse pointer in the middle of the browser window.

10 Click and hold the mouse button while you move the mouse pointer toward the right side of the browser window. The rest of the abbreviation fills the browser window.

11 When you see all the letters of the abbreviation (EPA), release the mouse button.

12 Click the Goto button.

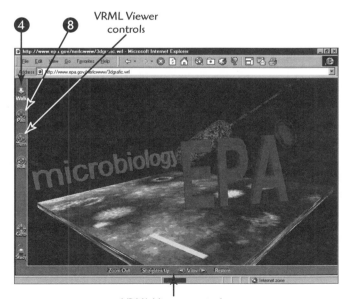

VRML Viewer controls

VRML Viewer controls

Going virtual with VRML

13 Click the green spot with the red outline. The object moves closer to you so that you can view it better.

14 Use the controls that appear along the bottom of the browser window to reorient yourself if you get lost in a virtual world. Click the Restore button. The virtual world returns to its original position.

15 If the world seems to be passing by too quickly as you move the mouse, you can change the speed. Right-click the virtual world.

16 Select Speed from the pop-up menu. A second menu appears.

17 Click Slow. The virtual world moves more slowly and gives you more time to examine it.

18 When you are finished exploring, close the Internet Explorer browser by clicking the close button on the top right corner.

19 Close your Internet connection.

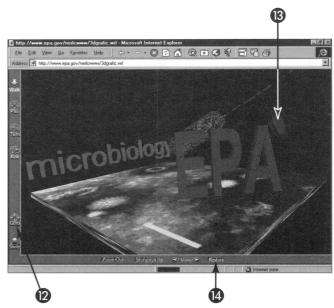

NOTE
To learn more about navigating a virtual world, right-click the virtual world and select Help➤Tour Guide from the pop-up menu.

PREPARING TO DOWNLOAD

Thousands of software programs are available on the Web, ranging from educational games for the kids, to utilities that can keep your computer in good working order, to programs for managing a small business.

But hold on! Before you rush off to explore software download sites and pick a few dozen programs to install, you have to get ready. The exercises in this section show you how to prepare your computer for downloads and how to use two handy programs included on the CD-ROM at the back of this book.

Creating a folder for downloads

Internet Explorer is designed to be compatible with the Java programming language and runs Java programs automatically. Java is an object-oriented programming language that is used to create applets (small applications) and applications that run over the Internet or another type of network.

A Java applet can be included in an HTML page in much the same way as an image or sound file. When you view a page that contains a Java applet, the applet's code is transferred to your system and executed by the browser.

JavaScript is a compact, object-based scripting language for developing Internet applications. JavaScript programs contained in a Web page can recognize and respond to user actions such as mouse clicks, form input, and page navigation.

Creating a folder for downloads

Before you start downloading software, you need to create a folder to store the files that you will be downloading and installing.

1 Open Windows Explorer by selecting Start ➢ Programs ➢ Windows Explorer.

2 Click the C: drive icon in the left pane of Windows Explorer. The list of folders contained on the C: drive appears in the right pane.

3 Right-click the right pane.

4 Select New ➢ Folder from the pop-up menu.

5 A new folder appears in the right pane. The name of the folder—New Folder—is highlighted.

6 Rename the folder by typing **download**.

7 Press Enter. You have created a new folder where you can store files that you download from the Internet.

Leave Windows Explorer open for the next exercise.

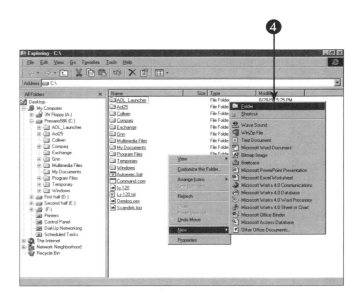

7

Maximizing Your Web Experience

Installing WinZip

▶ Installing WinZip

Most of the files you download from the Internet are compressed. Compressing files makes them smaller so that they transmit over the Internet faster. Before you can work with a compressed file, though, you must decompress it. WinZip is a file decompression and compression program.

In this exercise, you install WinZip from the CD-ROM included at the back of this book. You use WinZip later in this lesson to decompress a file that you download from the Web so you can install the software program on your computer. The copy of WinZip included with this book is a shareware program. You can evaluate WinZip free for 21 days. After that period, if you want to continue using WinZip, you must pay a registration fee of $29.

Before you install a software program, close any programs you may have open on your computer.

1 Insert the CD-ROM from the back of this book in your computer's CD-ROM drive.

2 Windows Explorer should still be open from the last exercise. Locate the file winzip95.exe in the Winzip folder on the CD-ROM.

3 Right-click and hold the file while you drag the mouse pointer to the download folder that you created in a previous exercise.

4 When the download folder is highlighted, release the mouse button.

5 Select Copy Here from the menu. The file is copied to the folder.

6 Open the download folder.

7 Click the winzip95.exe file. The WinZip Setup dialog box appears.

8. Click Setup. Another dialog box appears. The WinZip setup needs to create a directory to install the program. The default directory is C:\Program Files\WinZip.

9. Accept the default installation directory by clicking OK. The files are installed on your computer, and the WinZip Setup Wizard begins.

10. Click the Next button. The License Agreement and Warranty Disclaimer dialog box appears.

11. Click Yes to accept the agreement and to continue with the setup process.

12. Click the option button labeled Start with the WinZip Wizard. Choosing this option causes WinZip to start in wizard mode. Using the wizard is easier for new users.

13. Click Next.

14. On the next screen, click the Quick Search option button. The WinZip installation process searches your computer to find folders where you store zipped files.

15. Click Next. WinZip adds folders to your Favorite Folders List. The Favorite Folders List lists all of your zipped files in date order so that you can find them easily.

16. Click Next.

17. The setup is now complete. Click Close. WinZip is installed on your computer.

18. The WinZip program window appears that shows the program, the help files, and the readme file contained in the WinZip program menu. Click the Close button for this window.

You use WinZip to decompress a downloaded file later in this lesson.

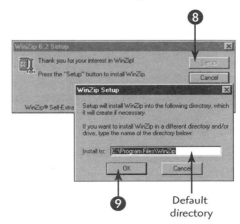

Default directory

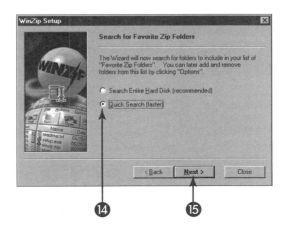

NOTE

To learn more about using WinZip, take one of the WinZip tutorials. To find the tutorials, select Start ➤ Programs ➤ WinZip ➤ Online Manual. The WinZip Help Topics dialog box appears. Double-click Quick

Maximizing Your Web Experience

Installing WS_FTP LE

Start and Tutorials to see the list of available tutorials. Two good ones are the Brief Tutorial and the Step By Step Instructions. For even more information, visit the WinZip Web site at `www.winzip.com/winzip.htm`.

Installing WS_FTP LE (Limited Edition)

Along with Web pages that offer software downloads via the browser, the Internet also has a number of File Transfer Protocol (FTP) sites that are loaded with downloadable programs. The FTP method of transferring files is usually quicker than using a browser to download files.

WS_FTP LE is a Windows-based application for transferring files between two computers over a network, such as the Internet. WS_FTP LE allows you to connect to another computer, browse the other computer's directory structure, and transfer files between both computers. WS_FTP LE is a freeware program and is included on the CD-ROM in the back of this book. The program is freely available to noncommercial home users, school students and faculty, and government employees.

If you removed the CD-ROM after the last exercise, reinsert it before beginning this exercise.

1 Windows Explorer should still be open from the last exercise. Locate the file ws_ftple.exe in the Wsftp folder on the CD-ROM.

2 Right-click and hold the file while you drag the mouse pointer to the download folder that you created in a previous exercise.

3 When the download folder is highlighted, release the mouse button.

4 Select Copy Here from the menu. The file is copied to the folder.

5 From the download folder, click the ws_ftple.exe file. The WinZip Self-Extractor dialog box appears asking if you want to install WS_FTP LE.

6 Click OK.

Installing WS_FTP LE

7 The next dialog box that appears suggests a directory that the setup program can use to unzip the WS_FTP LE files and run the installation files. Click Unzip.

8 A dialog box appears telling you that 18 files were unzipped. Click OK to start the WS_FTP Limited Edition Install Wizard.

9 Click the Continue button. The WS_FTP LE End User License Agreement appears.

10 Read the license agreement and click the Accept button. The Locate Directory Dialog box appears.

11 Accept the suggested directory to install the WS_FTP LE program by clicking the OK button. Another Locate Directory dialog box appears.

12 This dialog box asks for a directory where downloaded files can be stored. Highlight the suggested directory path in the text box.

13 Type **C:\download** so that the files you download from FTP sites will be stored in the download folder you created in a previous exercise.

14 Click the OK button. The FTP Installation dialog box appears.

15 Click OK to accept the recommended version to install. The program begins to install, and the Input dialog box appears.

16 Type your e-mail address in the text box.

17 Click OK. The Program Manager Group dialog box appears.

18 Click OK to accept the recommended program group. The Congratulations dialog box appears.

19 Click OK. WS_FTP LE is now installed on your computer.

20 Close the WS_FTP LE program group window by clicking the Close button at the top right corner of the window.

21 Close Windows Explorer by clicking the Close button at the top right corner of the window.

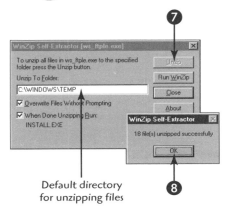

Default directory for unzipping files

Maximizing Your Web Experience

Installing WS_FTP LE

NOTE
For more information about WS_FTP LE, visit the Web site at www.ipswitch.com.

You have the opportunity to use the WS_FTP LE program to download software later in this lesson.

FINDING "TRY BEFORE YOU BUY" SOFTWARE

If you've never explored software download sites on the Internet, you're in for a real treat! Imagine being in a gigantic software store with applications for just about every purpose you can name—from fun time-wasters to serious business applications. Imagine that this software store lets you take whatever programs you want—there's no limit—home for a free trial. The only condition is that at the end of the trial period, if you want to continue using the application, you have to pay a nominal registration fee. What could be easier or more convenient? Well, the Internet is easier and more convenient. Instead of driving to the gigantic software store, you can find it right on your computer.

TYPES OF SOFTWARE AVAILABLE ON THE INTERNET

Three types of software are available for download: shareware, freeware, and commercial software demos.

Think of shareware as evaluation software that you can freely download and try. Use it, evaluate it, and decide if you like it. After a specified time period, generally about a month, you are expected to pay a fee and register the program if you plan to continue using it. When you pay the registration fee, you receive added benefits that are not included with the evaluation copy. You are eligible for technical support and sometimes receive additional program components that the software publisher did not make available in the evaluation copy.

Freeware is software that is free for noncommercial entities such as home, school, and government users. The software publisher does not collect registration fees and generally does not provide technical support or help files.

Commercial software demos are limited versions of a commercial program. Software publishers make these programs available to give potential buyers the opportunity to work with the program. If you decide you like the demo, you can purchase the full version. Commercial programs are generally more expensive than shareware programs.

Downloading software from the Web

The exercises in this section walk you through the steps of obtaining and installing software that you can try before you buy.

Downloading software from the Web

Now that you have your tools ready, it's time to download some software. In this exercise, you find a software program on a Web site and download it. You can apply these steps to different Web sites and different types of programs.

1 Log on to the Internet and open the Internet Explorer browser.

2 Click inside the Address bar.

3 Type www.idgbooks.com.

4 Press Enter. The IDG Books Online Web page appears.

5 Along the left side of the page is a list of links to pages on the IDG site. Click the Free & Downloadable link. The IDG Books Free & Downloadable Web page appears. IDG makes freeware and shareware available to the public on this Web site.

6 Click the Windows Software link to see a list of available Windows-compatible freeware and shareware titles.

7 In this exercise, you download an electronic diary program called OMNIDay. Click the OMNIDay 3.0 link located at the bottom of the first row of titles. A page appears that describes the OMNIDay program and contains a link to download the program.

8 Toward the bottom of the page is a link to download omni.zip. Click the link. The File Download dialog box appears.

9 Make sure the Save this file to disk option is selected.

10 Click OK. The Save As dialog box appears.

11 Select your download folder from the Save in drop-down list.

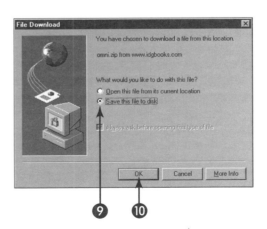

Installing zipped files

⑫ Click Save. The File Download dialog box appears and shows the status of the download. The download may take a while, so feel free to grab a bite to eat or a cup of coffee.

⑬ When the download is complete, a dialog box appears telling you that the file has finished downloading to your computer. Click OK. The program file is now saved in the download folder.

⑭ Close Internet Explorer by clicking the Close button.

⑮ Close your Internet connection.

In the next exercise, you unzip and install the OMNIDay electronic diary.

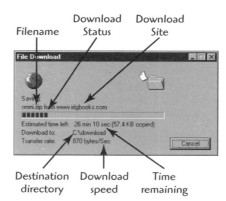

Filename   Download Status   Download Site

Destination directory   Download speed   Time remaining

Installing zipped files

The file you downloaded from the IDG Books Web site has the extension .zip, indicating that it is a compressed file. Before you can run the installation, you must first decompress (or unzip) the file and then locate the setup file for the program. In this exercise, you unzip and install the OMNIDay electronic diary program.

You use the WinZip utility located on the CD-ROM at the back of this book to unzip the OMNIDay files. If you have not already installed WinZip, perform the steps in the installation exercise before proceeding with this exercise.

❶ Open Windows Explorer.

❷ Open the download folder you created in a previous exercise.

❸ Click omni.zip. WinZip opens.

❹ Click I Agree to accept the license agreement and to start the WinZip Wizard.

❺ Click Next to view instructions on how WinZip will unzip the files and start the setup process for the OMNIDay program.

❻ Click Next. WinZip unzips the omni.zip file to a temporary folder created by WinZip. WinZip is ready to start the setup process.

Installing zipped files

NOTE

When the setup process is complete, WinZip deletes the unzipped files and the temporary folder it created for the setup process.

7 Click Install Now. WordPad opens with instructions for upgrading from an earlier OMNIDay version. If this is the first time you have installed OMNIDay, close WordPad by clicking the Close button.

8 The OMNIDay Setup dialog box suggests a directory for installing the program. Click OK to accept the default directory. The setup process begins.

9 When the program has finished installing, a dialog box appears asking if you would like OMNIDay added to your Start Programs menu. Click Yes.

10 Another dialog box appears informing you that the installation is complete. Click OK. The Unicorn Software Applications program group window appears and displays the OMNIDay program and help files.

11 Open the program by double-clicking the OMNIDay icon.

12 When you open OMNIDay for the first time, the program guides you through a series of steps to set up the program. These steps ask you to enter your name, color choices for the OMNIDay program window, a password to protect your journal entries from prying eyes, and the location for saving your journal files. Enter the information as you are prompted.

13 When you finish entering the information for the program setup, a blank page appears with the current date. Use this page to record your diary entries for the day.

14 Once you've finished exploring the program, close OMNIDay by clicking the Close button.

15 Close WinZip by clicking the Close button on the WinZip Wizard.

16 Close Windows Explorer by clicking the Close button.

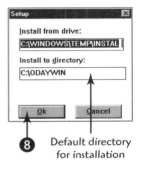

Default directory for installation

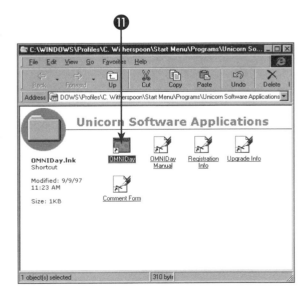

Maximizing Your Web Experience **7**

Downloading software via FTP

NOTE The next time you want to open OMNIDay, start the program by selecting Start ➤ Programs ➤ Unicorn Software Applications ➤ OMNIDay.

Downloading software from an FTP site

Since FTP downloads are generally faster than downloading through the browser, you can save a little time by using the techniques in this exercise to directly access an FTP site and grab programs with the handy FTP utility included on the CD-ROM at the back of this book. Even though Internet Explorer has built-in FTP capabilities, you may find it more convenient to use an FTP program such as WS_FTP LE to search FTP sites and download files. If you have not already installed WS_FTP LE, perform the steps in the installation exercise before proceeding with this exercise.

This exercise shows you how to use WS_FTP LE to download a file from Microsoft's FTP site.

1 Log on to the Internet.

2 Open WS_FTP by selecting Start ➤ Programs ➤ WS_ftp ➤ WS_FTP95 LE. The program opens with the Session Properties dialog box displayed.

3 WS_FTP contains a list of FTP sites and their associated FTP addresses from which you can choose. Select Microsoft from the Profile Name drop-down list.

4 Click OK. WS_FTP connects to the Microsoft FTP site.

TIP The main directory of an FTP site usually contains an index or readme file. This file contains a list of all the directories at the FTP site and a description of the types of files that can be found within those directories. To view this file, double-click it to save it to your computer and then open it in your favorite word processing program.

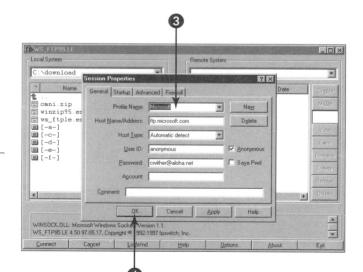

Downloading software via FTP

Several Web sites offer thousands of shareware and freeware programs. Here are a few great places to look:

- DOWNLOAD.COM at www.download.com
- SHAREWARE.COM at www.shareware.com

- Tucows at www.tucows.com
- Jumbo! at www.jumbo.com/
- Happy Puppy at www.happypuppy.com/

7

Maximizing Your Web Experience

5 The left pane shows the directory you specified during installation as the directory where downloaded files are to be saved. The right pane shows the directories available at the Microsoft FTP site. Double-click the deskapps folder. The list of files and folders contained in the deskapps folder appears.

6 Navigate to the games folder, then to the public folder, and finally to the Puzzle folder by double-clicking each of these folders. The files contained in the deskapps\games\public\Puzzle folder appear in the right pane.

7 Double-click MSpuzzle.exe. The Transfer Status dialog box appears showing the status of the file as it downloads to the download folder.

8 When the file has finished downloading, the dialog box disappears. The MSpuzzle.exe file appears in the left pane of the WS_FTP window. Close WS_FTP by clicking the Exit button.

9 Close your Internet connection.

In the next exercise, you install the MSpuzzle file.

Destination directory

Directories available at Microsoft FTP site

5

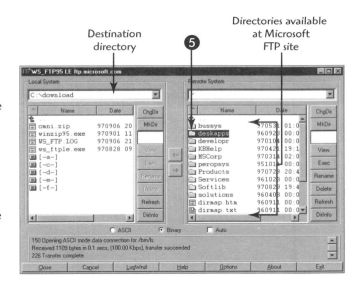

Installing self-executing files

▶ Installing self-executing files

In the previous exercise, you downloaded an execution file (MSpuzzle.exe). Execution files contain all of the setup and installation files needed to install a software program on your computer. Execution files also automate the setup process and do not need to be unzipped before you can begin installing the program. During the setup process, a series of screens asks for information that the program needs to install correctly. In this exercise, you install the Microsoft puzzle program.

NOTE

Web sites and FTP sites can contain either execution files (those with an .exe extension) or zipped files (those with a .zip extension). You will know how these files will install by looking at the file extension.

1 Before you begin this exercise, close all open programs on your computer.

2 Open Windows Explorer.

3 Click the download folder you created in a previous exercise. The folder opens, and the files contained in it appear in the right pane of the Windows Explorer window.

4 Click the MSpuzzle.exe file. The Microsoft Entertainment Pack Puzzle Collection installation screen appears.

5 Click Install. The End User License Agreement appears. Read the license agreement and click Accept. A dialog box appears suggesting a directory path for installing the Puzzle Collection.

6 Accept the default installation directory by clicking OK.

7 When the installation process is finished, a confirmation dialog box appears. This dialog box also includes instructions for accessing the games. Once you've read the instructions, click OK. You are now ready to play with the puzzles.

8 To open a puzzle, select Start ➤ Programs ➤ Microsoft Games ➤ Puzzle Collection Trial. The list of available puzzles appears.

⑨ This puzzle collection contains three puzzles. Select Spring Weekend. The opening window for the program appears.

⑩ Select Game ➢ New. A dialog box appears that gives you simple directions for how to play the puzzle.

⑪ Click OK. You are now ready to see how many moves you need to make the playing area on the left look like the model on the right.

⑫ When you are finished playing, click the Close button at the top right corner of the window.

⑬ Close Windows Explorer.

NOTE

Once you've solved these puzzles, you can uninstall them by selecting Start ➢ Programs ➢ Microsoft Games ➢ Puzzle Collection Trial ➢ Uninstall Puzzle Collection Trial.

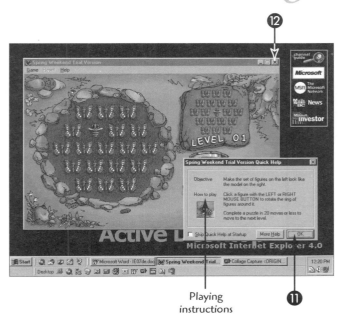

Playing instructions

SKILLS CHALLENGE: FINDING SOFTWARE ON YOUR OWN

The exercises in this lesson showed you how to download software programs from specific Internet sites. In this Skills Challenge, you explore on your own and find a software program that interests you.

❶ Open Internet Explorer and access one of the shareware sites listed in the Where to Find Shareware on the Web sidebar.

❷ Most of these shareware sites have a search box on their main page. Type a search term that describes the type of software you are looking for and submit your request. For example, if you are looking for a software program to help you keep track of your checkbook, try search terms such as personal finance, bookkeeping, or checkbook.

❸ After you find a suitable program, download and install it.

Skills challenge

 1 *Which type of file (execution or zipped) requires the use of an additional application in order to run the program setup procedure?*

4 Open WS_FTP LE and choose one of the FTP sites from the Profile Name drop-down list. The SunSite UNC FTP site contains a number of multimedia files, while the Games site contains, as you might guess, plenty of games.

5 Navigate the FTP site and download a file or two that interests you.

6 Install the programs you downloaded from the FTP site.

 2 *Where can you find information about the files located at an FTP site?*

7 Access the Microsoft Internet Explorer Add-on Component Download Web page and download a multimedia component add-on that you have not already installed.

8 Go to the Microsoft VRML Web page (`www.microsoft.com/vrml/offworld`) and practice your skill at navigating a virtual world.

 3 *How do you know if an add-on component is installed in Internet Explorer?*

9 When you've finished, close the Internet Explorer browser and disconnect from the Internet.

Wrap up

TROUBLESHOOTING

The following table answers a few questions you may have as you continue to work with the skills you learned in this lesson.

Problem	Solution
I would like to explore FTP sites to find software. Where can I find a list of FTP sites?	The largest index of FTP sites is the Monster FTP List at `hoohoo.ncsa.uiuc.edu/ftp-interface.html`. If you have problems accessing the site, try `legolas.mdh.se/~dat94jrh/ftp-lista/`, which is a mirror site.
I downloaded a bunch of programs from the Internet and installed them, but I'm running out of space on my computer. How can I reclaim some space?	Delete the execution and zipped files that you downloaded. Unless you think you will need to reinstall the program later, these files just take up space.
I've been using WinZip with the Wizard interface. How do I switch to the classic interface?	Open WinZip by selecting Start ➢ WinZip. On the first Wizard screen, click the WinZip Classic button located at the lower left corner of the screen.

TRY OUT THE
INTERACTIVE TUTORIALS
ON YOUR CD!

WRAP UP

This lesson included step-by-step instructions for these skills:

- Using multimedia components with Internet Explorer
- Downloading software programs from Web sites and FTP sites
- Using WinZip and WS_FTP LE
- Installing software programs downloaded from the Internet

    In the next lesson, you learn how to customize the Internet Explorer browser to your specifications.

Changing the Look of the Browser

25 MINUTES

GOALS

With the Internet Explorer browser, you can make your own choices for many page display options. This lesson teaches you techniques for:

- Changing the font size for an online session
- Changing the default font style and size
- Displaying pages faster
- Controlling toolbar display and position
- Changing the Links toolbar

Get ready

GET READY

To complete this lesson, you must have Internet Explorer installed on your computer (see Appendix A), have the Internet Explorer browser open, and be connected to the Internet.

When you finish this lesson, you will know how to change the way fonts appear in the Internet Explorer browser and a technique for downloading Web pages faster. You will also know how to customize and move Internet Explorer toolbars.

TRY OUT THE

INTERACTIVE TUTORIALS

ON YOUR CD!

CUSTOMIZING WEB PAGE DISPLAY

Internet Explorer gives you two options for customizing the way Web pages look on the screen. You can change the font style and the font size, and you can choose to manually download individual multimedia elements.

VISUAL BONUS

Same Web Page with Different Viewing Options

Because everyone has personal preferences for how Web pages should display and how quickly they should download, the Internet Explorer browser includes several options for changing the way Web pages look on the screen.

The IDG Books home page displayed using the default Internet Explorer settings

Customizing Web pages

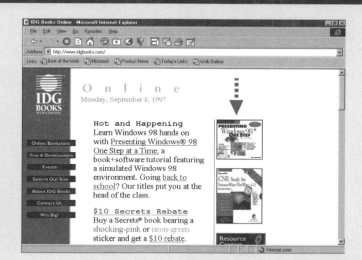

The IDG Books home page displayed using the largest font size available in Internet Explorer

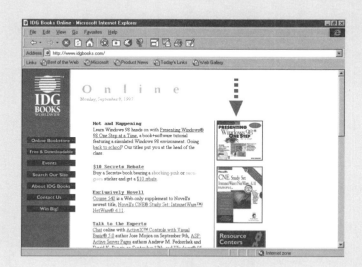

The IDG Books home page displayed using the smallest font size available in Internet Explorer

Customizing Web pages

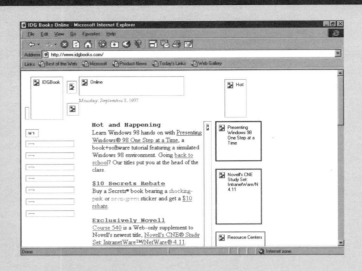

The IDG Books home page displayed without the graphics to reduce download time

The IDG Books home page displayed with a different font style

Changing the font size for an online session

The Internet Explorer browser includes an option for changing the size of the text displayed on Web pages. If you're the type of person who wants to pack maximum content onto every screen, you're a candidate for the smaller font sizes. If you're the type of person who doesn't mind using the scroll bar more frequently as long as the words are large enough to read without your glasses, you're a candidate for the larger font sizes. Of course, plenty of people will be perfectly satisfied with the default that falls right in the middle. It's your choice.

NOTE *This method of changing the font size only affects your current Internet session. The browser reverts to the default font setting when you close it. Refer to the next exercise for instructions on changing the default.*

Here are the steps for changing the size of the font displayed on a Web page:

① Type `www.idgbooks.com/` in the Address bar.

② Press Enter. In a moment, the IDG Books home page appears.

③ Display the list of available font sizes using one of the methods provided by the Internet Explorer browser.

TIP *The term* font size *refers to the height of the letters.*

④ Select View ➤ Fonts to display a menu that lists the available font sizes.

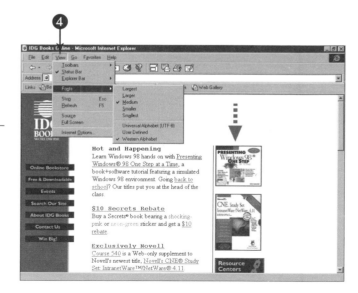

Changing the font size

5 Alternatively, click the Fonts button on the Standard Buttons toolbar to display a drop-down list showing the available font sizes. If you do not see the Fonts button on the Standard Buttons toolbar, select View ➤ Internet Options and click the Advanced tab. Scroll to the bottom of the dialog box, check the Show font button option, and click OK. If the Fonts button does not display on the Standard Buttons toolbar, click the Refresh button.

NOTE *Some Web page designers set the font size for their Web pages. In these instances, the font size set by the designer overrides any browser changes you specify.*

6 The Internet Explorer browser includes five font size choices. Medium is the default, but the other choices include Larger and Largest and Smaller and Smallest. As the font size increases, the amount of text displayed on the screen decreases. Conversely, as the font size decreases, the amount of text displayed on the screen increases.

Select Smallest. Notice how the appearance of the Web page changes.

NOTE *The bottom three entries on the font size menu are MIME-type character sets. MIME stands for Multipurpose Internet Mail Extensions and is a common format used by Internet mail programs to encode messages. The default Western Alphabet set works for most situations.*

7 Select View ➤ Fonts ➤ Largest. Alternatively, click the Font button on the toolbar and select Largest. Notice how the appearance of the Web page changes.

8 Experiment with the remaining two font sizes and choose the one you prefer.

Refresh button

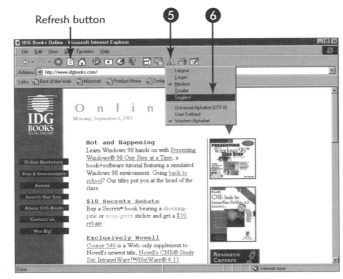

▶ Changing the default font style and size

You may get tired of looking at text displayed in Times New Roman and decide that you want Web pages to display in a font style that doesn't remind you so much of a newspaper. Or maybe you're just burned out on having to switch to a larger or smaller font size every time you start Internet Explorer. You have the option of changing to a different font style and size permanently—or at least until you decide to change the settings again. To change the default font style and size, follow these steps:

1 Select View ➤ Internet Options. The Internet Options dialog box with six tabs appears.

2 Click the General tab.

3 Click the Fonts button at the bottom right of the dialog box to display the Fonts dialog box.

This dialog box gives you the opportunity to change several font settings. The two that you are most likely to change are the Proportional font and Font size options.

NOTE *Proportional fonts use varying widths for each letter of the alphabet, compared to fixed-width fonts that use the same width for each letter. In a proportional font, the letter **w** takes up more space on a line than the letter **l**. Because proportional fonts are easier to read, they are used more often than fixed-width fonts in printed and electronic documents. The list of fonts in the Fonts dialog box is based on the fonts installed on your computer.*

8

Changing the Look of the Browser

Displaying pages faster

④ Use the Proportional font drop-down menu to select a different font style. If you are ready for a switch from Times New Roman, try Garamond to give the text a bold, yet classy, look that's also easy to read.

⑤ Use the Font size drop-down menu to select a different font size. If you want to see as much of a Web page as possible on your screen, choose Smallest. If you want the text to be easier to read, choose Larger or Largest. If you like the display just the way it is, choose Medium.

⑥ If you want to see Web pages with these settings every time you open the Internet Explorer browser, click the Set as Default button.

⑦ Click OK to apply the settings.

⑧ Click OK to exit the Internet Options dialog box.

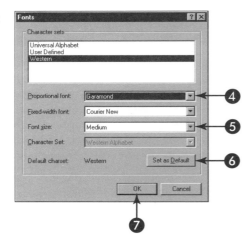

Displaying pages faster

Graphics and multimedia elements are great additions to a Web site, but they can take forever to download. Sometimes when you're in a hurry and need to find information on the Web quickly, you just don't want to wait for the pictures.

You can change the Internet Explorer browser settings so that only text is displayed when you visit a Web site. Access is almost instantaneous when you view pages with text only. Or maybe you want to see some images, but don't have time to enjoy *all* the creative elements that designers put in their Web pages. You can pick and choose which media elements you want to display.

Follow these steps to reduce the amount of time it takes to access Web sites:

① Select View ➢ Internet Options to display the Internet Options dialog box.

② Click the Advanced tab.

③ The tab's Multimedia section gives you the choice to display pictures and to play animations, sounds, and videos. Clear the boxes labeled Show pictures and Play videos.

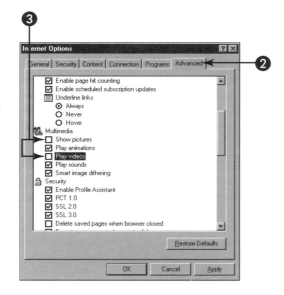

Controlling toolbar display

Icons replace graphics.

The last selection in the Multimedia section, Smart image dithering, is computer-speak for smoothing out the edges and blending the colors of an image to provide a more high-resolution picture.

④ Click OK to apply your changes and close the dialog box.

⑤ The IDG Books home page is displayed with icons in place of the elements that you disabled.

⑥ To display a disabled graphic or video, right-click the icon and select Show Picture from the pop-up menu.

⑦ To restore the display settings, repeat steps 1 through 4 and check the Show pictures and Play videos boxes.

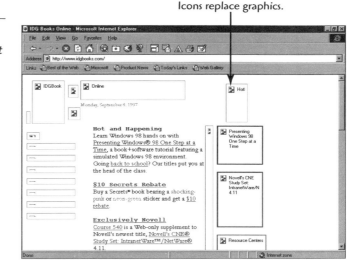

CUSTOMIZING TOOLBARS

You can change the way the Internet Explorer browser toolbars look and operate. You can hide toolbars to increase the available viewing space, stack them one on top of the other, or put them on the same line. You can add hyperlinks to the Links toolbar that give you one-click access to Web sites you visit frequently.

The screen images throughout this book show several different toolbar arrangements. Take some time to experiment with the toolbars until you find a combination that works best for you.

Controlling toolbar display and position

The Internet Explorer browser has three default toolbars: the Standard Buttons toolbar, the Address bar, and the Links toolbar. The browser gives you options for controlling which toolbars display on your screen and where they appear. You can choose whether or not you want text labels on the Standard Buttons toolbar and can even make the icons smaller.

Controlling toolbar display

The Internet Explorer Toolbar

You can create more viewing area for Web pages by changing the toolbars. The first figure shows the default look. The second figure shows a customized version of the toolbars with a different arrangement: the Links toolbar hidden, smaller icons, and no text labels.

Internet Explorer browser default toolbar arrangement

Internet Explorer browser customized toolbar arrangement

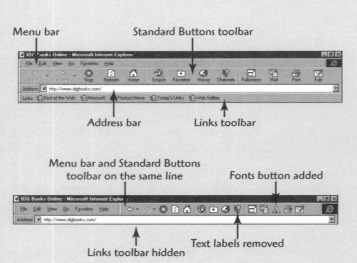

Menu bar   Standard Buttons toolbar

Address bar   Links toolbar

Menu bar and Standard Buttons toolbar on the same line   Fonts button added

Links toolbar hidden   Text labels removed

While most people like having these toolbars handy, sometimes you may want to increase the browser's viewing area by hiding toolbars to display more of a Web page. Maybe you prefer using the Internet Explorer menu bar instead of the Standard Buttons toolbar and want to clear the toolbar from the screen. Or Internet Explorer may have a toolbar that you don't use and don't want to display.

This exercise shows you how to arrange the toolbars to your specifications.

❶ Make sure that the Standard Buttons toolbar, Address bar, and Links toolbar appear at the top of the Internet Explorer browser. If they do not, select View ➤ Toolbars. A second menu appears that lists the available toolbars. A check next to a toolbar means that the toolbar is displayed.

② To move the Standard Buttons toolbar, place the mouse pointer over the vertical line at the left end of the toolbar. The mouse pointer changes to a horizontal double-pointed arrow.

③ Click and hold the mouse button while you drag the mouse pointer upward and to the right of the Help menu item.

④ Release the mouse button. The Standard Buttons toolbar moves to its new position.

If you have the text labels for the buttons turned off (refer to step 12 in this exercise), you should be able to see all of the toolbar buttons on the same line with the menu bar. If you have text labels turned on, some of the buttons will be hidden behind the rotating Explorer logo. A right-pointing arrow lets you know that buttons are hidden. Click the right-pointing arrow to display the hidden buttons.

⑤ To move the Address bar or Links toolbar up or down, place the mouse pointer over the vertical bar on the left side of the toolbar. The pointer turns into a horizontal double-pointed arrow.

⑥ Click and hold the left mouse button and drag the toolbar.

⑦ Another method of moving the toolbars up and down is to place the mouse pointer underneath the bottom toolbar until it changes to a vertical double-pointed arrow. Click and hold the left mouse button.

⑧ Drag the toolbars. As you drag the mouse toward the top of the browser window, the toolbar on the bottom moves to the right of the toolbar above it.

⑨ If two toolbars are on the same line, you can increase the size of one and decrease the size of the other by moving the toolbar on the right horizontally. To move the Address bar or Links toolbar horizontally, first place the mouse pointer over the vertical bar on the left side of the toolbar.

⑩ Click and hold the left mouse button.

⑪ Drag the toolbar on the right to the left or right.

⑪

⑫ Text labels below the buttons on the Standard Buttons toolbar describe the command the button performs. Turning them off saves space. To hide the text labels on the Standard Buttons toolbar, right-click an empty area of the toolbar to display a pop-up menu.

⑬ Locate the Text Labels command on the menu. This command controls the display and acts as a toggle. A check next to the command indicates that text labels are turned on; selecting it turns off the text label display.

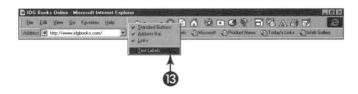

⑬

NOTE

Many of the illustrations of Internet Explorer screens throughout this book show text labels off. If you decide to turn off text labels, you can still find out what a button does by holding the mouse pointer over the button to display the tool tip.

⑭ If you want to save space without giving up the convenience of the toolbar, you can reduce the size of the Standard Buttons toolbar icons. To display smaller icons, select View ➣ Internet Options to open the Internet Options dialog box.

⑮ Click the Advanced tab and scroll to the bottom of the list until you locate the Toolbar options.

⑯ Check the box for Small Icons and click OK.

⑰ To show or hide an individual toolbar, right-click an empty area on any of the toolbars to display the pop-up menu.

⑱ Select the toolbar that you want to hide or make reappear. These menu options act as toggles. A check next to a menu selection means that a toolbar is currently displayed.

⑱

► *Changing the Links toolbar*

The Internet Explorer browser includes five default hyperlinks on the Links toolbar, and each one takes you to a different page of the Microsoft Web site. The toolbar gives you one-click access to special sites selected to keep you up to date on the latest Microsoft news and to introduce you to interesting Web sites. But like just about every other feature of the Internet Explorer browser, the Links toolbar can be customized. You can add or delete links.

But what kind of links? Your list of Favorites is a great place to catalog sites, but you may visit certain Web pages almost every time you connect to the Internet. You can reduce the number of mouse clicks it takes to open these sites by adding them to the Links toolbar. You can add links from a URL displayed in the Address bar, from a hyperlink on a Web page, or from a site in your Favorites list. This exercise guides you through all three options.

1 Make sure that the IDG Books home page is displayed on your screen. If it isn't, type www.idgbooks.com in the Address bar and press Enter.

2 To add a link to the Links toolbar from the Address bar, first place the mouse pointer over the icon to the left of the URL in the Address bar. The mouse pointer changes to a hand.

3 Click and hold the left mouse button and drag the mouse pointer to the Links toolbar.

4 As you move the mouse pointer across the toolbar, a vertical bar appears between the links. Position the vertical bar in the place where you want the link to the IDG Books Web site to appear.

5 Release the mouse button to add the link.

6 To add a link to the Links toolbar from a hyperlink on a Web page, place the mouse pointer over the Win Big! hyperlink on the left side of the IDG Books home page. The mouse pointer turns into a hand.

7 Click and hold the left mouse button and drag the mouse pointer to the desired position on the Links toolbar.

8

Changing the Look of the Browser

Skills challenge

⑧ Release the mouse button to add the link.

⑨ To add a link to the Links toolbar from a site in the Favorites list, select Favorites ➢ Microsoft Software and Service. The menu of favorite sites cataloged in this default folder appears.

⑩ Place the mouse pointer over the site named Microsoft Product Support Services. The Favorite is highlighted.

⑪ Click and hold the left mouse button and drag the mouse pointer to the desired position on the Links toolbar.

⑫ Release the mouse button to add the link.

⑬ To delete a link from the Links toolbar, right-click the link. A pop-up menu appears.

⑭ Select Delete from the pop-up menu.

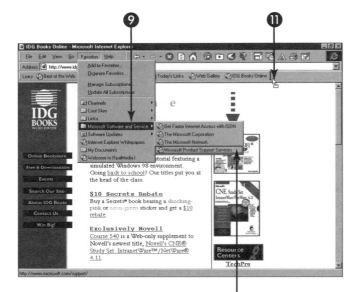

SKILLS CHALLENGE: CUSTOMIZING THE INTERNET EXPLORER BROWSER

This exercise gives you the chance to practice many of the skills you've learned in this lesson for customizing the Internet Explorer browser.

❶ Open the Internet Explorer browser and log on to the Internet.

❷ Change the proportional font to Arial.

❸ Change the font size to large.

 How many font size choices do you have in Internet Explorer?

❹ Make these your default font settings.

❺ Access the SHAREWARE.COM Web site located at www.shareware.com. Add this Web site to the Links toolbar.

 How many different ways can you add a link to the Links toolbar?

6 Move the Links toolbar so that it is located to the right of the Address bar.

7 Restore your preferred font settings and toolbar arrangement.

TROUBLESHOOTING

The following table lists possible problems that you might encounter while customizing the Internet Explorer browser and some suggestions for handling them.

Problem	Solution
When I click a link, my computer makes a sound. Then when the browser finds the link, my computer makes another sound. How do I turn off these sounds?	Internet Explorer 4 adds two sound events to your system, Start Navigation and Complete Navigation. To turn off these sounds, go to Control Panel and click Sounds. Scroll through the Events list until you find Windows Explorer. Highlight Start Navigation. In the Sound Name drop-down list, select None. Do the same for Complete Navigation.
I have added too many buttons to my Links toolbar. How can I remove some of them?	Right-click the link you want to remove and select Delete from the pop-up menu.
My Standard Buttons toolbar takes up too much space. How can I make it smaller?	First turn off the text labels by right-clicking the toolbar and deselecting Text Labels. To make the icons themselves smaller, select View ➤ Internet Options and click the Advanced tab. Scroll down the list to the Toolbar section (it's near the bottom) and check the option for small icons.

Wrap up

WRAP UP

In this lesson, you exercised several skills:

- Changing the font size and style on Web pages
- Turning off the automatic display of multimedia elements
- Specifying different Web pages for the Links toolbar
- Controlling toolbars to provide more viewing space in the browser window

In the next lesson, you begin to explore the security features of the Internet Explorer browser.

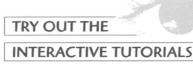

TRY OUT THE

INTERACTIVE TUTORIALS

ON YOUR CD!

Becoming Security Aware

40 MINUTES

GOALS

In a multinetworked environment like the Internet where the possibility of damaging virus code or prying eyes exists, security awareness is a necessary part of participating. To ensure the safety of your equipment, the privacy of your communications, and your ability to control the level of content displayed on your computer, you need to take advantage of Internet Explorer's excellent security features. In this lesson, you learn the following skills:

- Setting Content Advisor ratings
- Setting a custom safety level
- Obtaining a personal certificate
- Using Web site certificates
- Setting up the Profile Assistant
- Setting up Microsoft Wallet

Get ready

GET READY

Before you begin this lesson, you need to have Internet Explorer installed on your computer (see Appendix A), be connected to the Internet, and have the Internet Explorer browser open. When you finish this lesson, you will know how to use the Content Advisor to block access to rated Web sites and how to obtain a personal certificate. You will also learn how the Profile Assistant and Microsoft Wallet make information transfers and shopping on the Internet easier.

TRY OUT THE

INTERACTIVE TUTORIALS

ON YOUR CD!

UNDERSTANDING INTERNET SECURITY ISSUES

The issue of Internet security goes beyond keeping your credit card information confidential, although secure purchasing ability is a big-ticket consideration for Internet shoppers and the retailers who want to sell to them. Similarly, businesses that use the Internet to transact business and transfer data must ensure that the data transfers are confidential.

For parents and schools, though, a major security concern is the prevalence of Web sites that are inappropriate for children and how to prevent them from accessing disturbing, violent, or overtly sexual content. The security focus is similar in the workplace, where employers want to ensure that their employees are only accessing Web sites necessary for their jobs. On the other hand, a primary security issue for heavy Internet users is keeping their computers free of viruses. All of these security concerns are different, but the Internet Explorer browser is equipped with features that address each one.

■ Restricting access to the Internet

As you explore the Internet, you may come across material that you feel is inappropriate for you, your children, or your employees. The Internet Explorer Content Advisor feature gives you some ability to block access to sites on the Internet. The Content Advisor can block sites that are rated by the Recreational Software Advisory Council on the Internet (RSACi) rating service.

Setting Content Advisor ratings

The RSACi is an independent, nonprofit organization that provides information to consumers regarding the levels of violence, vulgar or hate-motivated language, nudity, and sex on Web sites and in computer games. The RSACi uses a five-level rating system that ranges from 0 (allows no objectionable content in a particular category) to 4 (allows explicit display of the content in a particular category).

The RSACi is a supporting member of PICS (Platform for Internet Content Selection) based at MIT. RSACi is working to incorporate their rating system in the standard PICS protocol to be included in browsers all over the world. The RSACi is dedicated to providing a method for parents, teachers, and employers to control Internet content without having to resort to government intervention. The RSACi goal is to achieve self-regulation of Internet site content, while safeguarding the right to free speech.

The RSACi presently rates tens of thousands of Web sites, and new sites are continuously added. For more details, you can visit the RSACi home page at www.rsac.org/.

Setting Content Advisor ratings

Once you activate the Content Advisor and set the rating levels, only the rated sites that meet or exceed the level you set are displayed by the Internet Explorer browser. Access to the Content Advisor is controlled by a password. Anyone who knows the password can change or disable the settings. To ensure that sites remain blocked, keep the password secure.

Open the browser and follow these steps for setting the rating level:

❶ Select View ➣ Internet Options to display the Internet Options dialog box.

❷ Click the Content tab.

❸ Click the Enable button. The Create Supervisor Password dialog box displays.

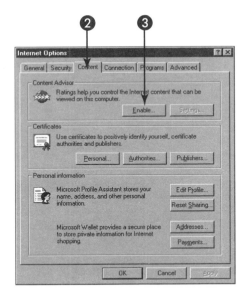

9

Becoming Security Aware

Setting Content Advisor ratings

④ Enter a password in the Password and Confirm password text boxes.

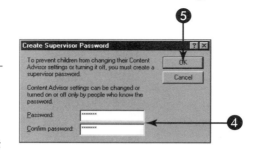

TIP

Select a password that will actually secure the machine by choosing a word or alphanumeric string that would be hard for someone who knows you to figure out. Don't use your pet bird's name as your password. The safest password contains at least eight characters with at least one character being a number (for example, jest4you). You should write down your supervisor password and keep it in a secure place, because you will need it any time you want to change the Content Advisor settings.

⑤ Click OK to enable your Supervisor password and close the dialog box.

⑥ On the Internet Options dialog box, click Settings. The Supervisor Password Required dialog box appears.

⑦ Type your Supervisor password.

⑧ Click OK. The Content Advisor dialog box appears.

⑨ In the Category section of the Content Advisor dialog box, select Language. A slider bar appears in the Rating section.

⑩ Set the level of slang or profanity you want to permit by adjusting the Rating slider.

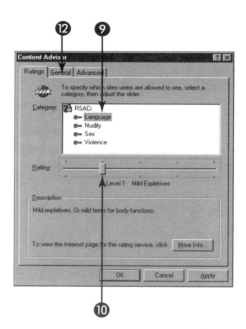

NOTE

A rating level of 0 (the slider bar is at the far left end of the slider) means that the Internet Explorer browser will only display G-rated content. A rating level of 4 (the slider bar is at the far right end of the slider) is equivalent to full Internet access with no blocking.

⑪ Repeat the process explained in steps 9 and 10 for each of the other categories in the window: Nudity, Sex, and Violence.

⑫ Click the General tab.

⑬ If you only want to permit access to rated Web pages, uncheck the box labeled Users can see sites that have no rating.

⑭ If you want to retain password–protected full Internet access, check the next box labeled Supervisor can type a password to allow users to view restricted content.

⑮ Click OK to enable the Content Advisor rating levels and redisplay the Internet Options dialog box.

⑯ Click OK to close the dialog box and return to the Web page.

NOTE
If you want to change the Content Advisor rating levels, select View ➤ Internet Options ➤ Content. Click the Settings button. If you want to turn off the Content Advisor, click the Disable button.

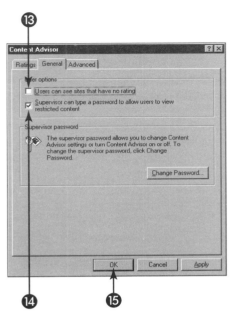

■ Restricting the Internet's access to you

It may seem obvious why you would want to limit access to certain Web sites. But you also want to limit the content downloaded to your computer because of viruses. Although some viruses are merely annoying, others can cause considerable damage and delete important files from your computer.

Another possible problem with downloading content is that software can contain bugs. Bugs are errors in software code that cause the program to work incorrectly and possibly interfere with other software you have installed on your computer. Before you download anything from the Internet, do a little research and only download content from Web sites that can offer assurance that the software available at the site is safe.

NOTE
The security settings used by Internet Explorer do not check for viruses and bugs. You should use a virus detection program such as Norton Anti–Virus or McAfee Virus Scan regularly. Before you download any software from the Internet, always read the readme and release notes files that accompany the software.

9

Becoming Security Aware

Setting a custom safety level

▶ Setting a custom safety level

You can categorize Web sites based on how confident you are that content from these sites won't damage your computer. You can set up a list of trusted sites—sites on your company's Intranet are a good safety bet—and download content without the browser querying you first. You can also set up a list of restricted sites. Whenever you access a Web site with content that causes problems, add the site to the restricted list. Once a site is added, the Internet Explorer browser ensures that you don't accidentally download content from that site, and it maintains the restriction even if you forget past problems.

Microsoft's security zones enable you to divide the Web into special zones with different levels of security. For example, you may be totally confident about the sites on your company's Intranet and have no qualms about downloading content from those sites. You can assign those sites to the trusted zone. Such a confidence level obviously wouldn't extend to the entire Web, so you can assign other Web sites to the untrusted zone. When you attempt to download content from a site in the untrusted zone, the Internet Explorer browser queries and waits for a response before proceeding.

The Internet Explorer browser makes it easy to categorize Web sites. In this exercise, you learn how to assign a Web site to a security zone, set security levels, and control Internet cookie downloads.

① With the Internet Explorer browser open, select View ➤ Internet Options to display the Internet Options dialog box.

② Click the Security tab.

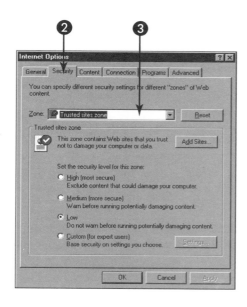

NOTE
The Security tab allows you to change the settings for the different security zones. If you select a security zone from the pull-down menu, the settings change to reflect a default level of security for each zone. In most cases, these default settings provide adequate prompts.

③ Choose Trusted sites zone from the Zone drop-down list.

④ Click the Add Sites button to display the Trusted sites zone dialog box.

⑤ Type http://www.microsoft.com in the text box labeled Add this Web site to the zone.

NOTE *You must type the entire URL for the Web site. The Internet Explorer browser cannot add the site to the list if the protocol designation (such as* http:// *or* ftp://*) is missing.*

⑥ Click the Add button to add the Web site to the list of trusted Web sites. The next time you visit this site with Internet Explorer, the status bar identifies the site as being assigned to the trusted sites zone.

⑦ Click OK to return to the Internet Options dialog box.

⑧ Once you've set the zone, then you set the security level. You can always accept the default. In most cases, a security level of Low is adequate for Trusted sites. But you may want to change the settings for the Trusted sites zone. To change the setting, click the Custom (for expert users) option button.

⑨ Click the Settings button to display the Security Settings dialog box. For each type of download, you have three choices for setting how the Internet Explorer browser should respond to an attempted download:

- The Enable option allows the Internet Explorer browser to download and run content without any interaction from you.

- The Prompt option causes the browser to ask before content is downloaded so you can decide if you want to proceed.

- The Disable option prevents any content from being downloaded to your machine and does not require any interaction on your part.

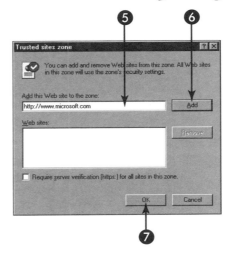

URL added to Trusted sites zone

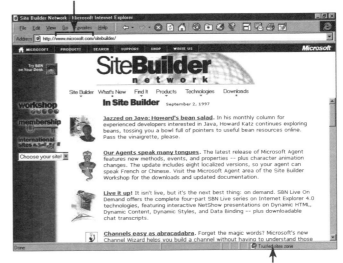

Security zone

9

Becoming Security Aware

Setting a custom safety level

⑩ To change the settings for downloading desktop components to your computer, first scroll down the list until you find Installation of desktop items.

⑪ Select the Prompt option. By selecting the option to have Internet Explorer 4 prompt you before downloading any desktop components, you have the opportunity to decide which components you want.

⑫ Click OK to return to the Internet Options dialog box.

⑬ You can also set the options for accepting Internet cookies. Click the Advanced tab on the Internet Options dialog box.

⑭ Scroll down the list to the Security heading.

⑮ Find the entry for Cookies and select the option to Prompt before accepting cookies.

⑯ Click OK to close the Internet Options dialog box. All your new security settings are applied.

USING CERTIFICATES

Digital certificates are one of the most effective ways of ensuring privacy for your Internet communications. Two types of certificates are used on the Internet: personal certificates and Web site certificates. Personal certificates usually contain your name, e-mail address, and any other information that a Web site needs to verify who you are and ensure that you have permission to access the site. Web site certificates let you know that you are visiting a site that is secure for your communications and transactions. In other words, the certificates assure you that Sears is really Sears, that the content available for download has been tested for viruses and software bugs, and that the information you upload (like your credit card number) will be free from prying eyes.

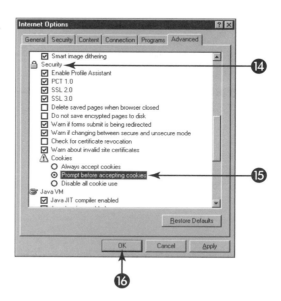

Obtaining a personal certificate

Internet cookies are small files that a Web site automatically downloads to your computer to perform tasks. Two common cookie tasks are to maintain personal information that you supply via registration forms and to keep track of your activities while you are visiting the site. Some shopping sites, for example, maintain a list of your purchases and make the list available to you the next time you visit the site.

A cookie is generally active only as long as you are at the site that set it, but some cookies continue to track your activities even after you've left the site. Many Internet sites use cookies, and if you set the recommended prompt option, you can expect to read many cookie alerts. However, the option to refuse cookies doesn't mean that you can't take advantage of them. If you refuse to allow a cookie to be set, the cookie still functions, but it is only temporarily downloaded to your computer and not saved to disk.

Obtaining a personal certificate

Think of a personal certificate as a digital identification card. You use it to establish your identity like you use a driver's license, passport, or birth certificate. You need a personal certificate to shop online with certain retailers. Your personal certificate assures the retailer of your identity and minimizes the risk of someone else using your name. When you use a personal certificate along with encryption methods, you can be sure that the information you transmit over the Internet will stay private and confidential during the transmission.

The company that issues personal certificates charges a fee for this service, but you can try the digital ID for a free six-month trial period. Having a personal certificate is a convenience because it allows you to access certain sites that require verifiable ID without having to type your user-specific information each time you visit. Personal certificates are downloaded to your computer after you obtain them, and then the Internet Explorer browser supplies your certificate information to sites that request it. You only need one personal certificate for identification, but you may have more than one on a single computer if more than one person uses the machine. With personal certificates, you don't have to take your driver's license out of your wallet any more. Internet Explorer can do that for you.

9

Becoming Security Aware

Obtaining a personal certificate

To perform the steps in this exercise, the Internet Explorer browser must be open and displayed on the screen and Outlook Express (or another e-mail program) must be configured and functioning (refer to Lesson 10 for instructions on configuring Outlook Express).

1 Click inside the Address bar.

2 Type www.microsoft.com/security/.

3 Press Enter. The Microsoft Security Advisor home page displays.

4 Select the hyperlink to download the free VeriSign Digital ID. This link takes you to the VeriSign Web site.

NOTE *VeriSign is a subsidiary of RSA Data Security, Inc. and an independent issuing authority for digital certificates and public and private PGP (pretty good privacy) encryption keys.*

5 Click the Class 1 Digital ID icon to access the enrollment form. You must complete the information on this form to obtain a personal certificate.

6 In step 1 on the Web page, type your name and e-mail address.

7 Choose the options to include your e-mail address in your ID and a challenge phrase.

8 Read the information on the page to help you decide whether or not to provide the information requested by the One Step Registration method.

One Step Registration allows you to add personal information to your digital ID that can be used when you access a subscription-based Web site. For example, if you subscribe to a Web-based information service, such as an online newspaper or magazine, you must type your username and password to enter the site. By adding this information to your digital ID, you no longer need to type the information. It is passed to the site electronically via your digital ID. The directions on the VeriSign Web page provide additional details.

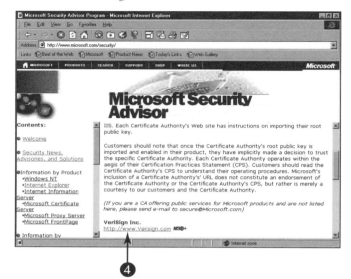

Obtaining a personal certificate

NOTE

A challenge phrase is a method used by VeriSign to identify you when you request information about your certificate. The challenge phrase is used in much the same way that a bank uses your mother's maiden name to verify your identity. Use the same caution when you decide on a challenge phrase as you did when you selected the supervisor password for the Content Advisor. Keep it unique and not too personal.

9 In step 2 on the Web page, select the trial digital ID.

The trial digital ID is dated and is good for six months. When the ID expires, it indicates to requesting sites that it has expired. If you think that you will regularly use a digital ID, add the VeriSign site to your Favorites list so you can return later and obtain the full-featured version when the trial period is over.

10 Because you are only signing up for a trial digital ID, you can skip step 3 on the Web page. Scroll to the bottom of the page and read the Subscriber Agreement in step 4.

11 Click the Accept button. A Security Warning dialog box displays.

12 The Security Warning dialog box alerts you that the VeriSign server is attempting to install an ActiveX control (a portable linked and embedded object code that downloads to your computer and causes it to perform certain tasks). Click the Yes button to install the control. If you do not install the ActiveX control, you cannot obtain the ID.

13 On the next Web page that appears, click the Submit button to start the Credentials Enrollment Wizard. You use this wizard to install your private key on your computer.

14 Complete your selection of a provider by clicking Internet Explorer.

15 Click Next.

16 Type a name for your public key.

Obtaining a personal certificate

Public and private encryption keys provide a method for secure identification of sender and recipient and a method for encrypting messages.

The public key is disseminated publicly so that anyone wanting to encrypt a message to the holder of the private key can have easy access to an encryption method. The message encrypted by the public key can only be decrypted with the private key.

Conversely, the person with the private key who wants to send an encrypted message can use the private key. The recipient can decrypt the message with the public key. This method only ensures that the message was not tampered with between the time it left the sender's computer and the time it arrived at the recipient's computer. To ensure that the encrypted message is only delivered to the intended recipient, it must also be encrypted using the recipient's public key.

The keys themselves are complex algorithms that are installed on your computer to encrypt and decrypt messages automatically. The private key is installed on your computer during the issuing process, and the public one is made available for public download from the VeriSign Web site.

⓱ Click Finish. The VeriSign Enrollment Complete Web page appears in the browser window with the message that you have successfully enrolled and it is time to download your private key.

⓲ Check your e-mail account. You can't proceed until you receive an e-mail message from VeriSign.

NOTE *If you don't receive an e-mail notification right away, click the hyperlink on the Enrollment Complete page. You may be taken to a Services Status page informing you that the enrollment system is not available. If that's the case, you may have to wait a while before your confirmation letter arrives via e-mail.*

⓳ When you receive the e-mail notification from VeriSign, go to the link specified in the letter.

⓴ Type the personal identification number (PIN) shown in the e-mail message in the text box at the bottom of the page.

Using Web site certificates

21 Click the Submit button. Your digital ID is generated. Wait until the process is complete.

22 Click the Install button to download the digital ID to your computer. Once the download is complete, you receive a message that your digital ID was successfully registered.

23 Click OK.

24 To verify that your digital ID is installed and ready to use, select View ➤ Internet Options to display the Internet Options dialog box.

25 Select the Content tab.

26 Click the Personal button. The Client Authentication dialog box appears with the digital ID listed in the Identification list.

27 To view the properties of the digital ID, select it and click View Certificate.

28 The next time you visit a site that requires a certificate, Internet Explorer displays a dialog box asking if you want to send your digital ID to the site requesting it. If you choose to send your digital ID, select it from the list and click OK.

Using Web site certificates

A Web site certificate is a method for offering some security to users who download software from the Internet. Web certificates are issued by the same issuing authorities as personal certificates, but no free trial period is available. Valid certificates take some of the guesswork out of whether or not you should trust downloaded software. At least you can be sure that the download site is maintained by the creator or authorized distributor of the software.

1 With the Internet Explorer browser open, click inside the Address bar.

2 Type www.microsoft.com/vrml/offworld.

9

Becoming Security Aware

22

Using Web site certificates

3 At the VRML (Virtual Reality Modeling Language) page, click the Download link.

4 Read the download instructions on the page that appears. At the bottom of the page is a link labeled Download Microsoft VRML 2.0 Viewer.

5 Click the link. The File Download dialog box appears.

6 Select the Run this program from its current location option button.

7 Click OK.

The file begins downloading to your computer and a Security Warning dialog box appears. This security warning lets you know whether or not the software has a valid certificate (or if it is expired), which certificate authority issued the certificate, and whether the publisher of the software believes the software to be safe.

8 To read more, click the More Info button. A dialog box appears that provides additional details about the certification.

9 Click the Close button at the upper right corner of the dialog box. The Security Warning dialog box reappears.

10 Click the hyperlink for the software publisher—in this case, Microsoft Corporation—in the Security Warning dialog box. The Certificate Properties dialog box appears.

The Certificate Properties dialog box and the information you can access by clicking the Fine Print button provide even more details than you may want to know about the certificate: whether the certificate is valid, whom it belongs to, which certificate authority issued it, and other details about its validity.

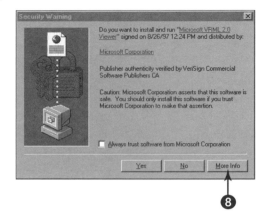

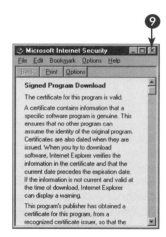

⑪ When you have finished looking at the certificate properties, click the OK button. The dialog box closes and you are returned to the Security Warning dialog box.

⑫ If you wanted to proceed with the software download, you would click the Yes button to accept the certificate. For this exercise, however, click No.

CONDUCTING BUSINESS ONLINE

Microsoft Profile Assistant and Microsoft Wallet are two new technologies in Internet Explorer that simplify information exchange and online shopping. The Profile Assistant stores your personal information and manages the transfer of the information to Web sites that request it. For example, if you need to enter a username and password to access a site, the Profile Assistant can enter the information for you. Microsoft Wallet makes online shopping easier by storing your personal and credit card information and makes the transaction more secure by encrypting the information when it is transmitted over the Internet to a vendor.

Setting up the Profile Assistant

The Profile Assistant helps you manage the transfer of personal information requested by various Web sites. The Profile Assistant notifies you when a site requests data such as your name or e-mail address and lets you decide whether or not to disclose the information.

Before you can take advantage of the convenience of the Profile Assistant, you must first configure the application. You create a profile by entering your personal information. To complete this exercise, the Internet Explorer browser must be open and displayed on the screen.

❶ Select View ➢ Internet Options to display the Internet Options dialog box.

❷ Select the Content tab.

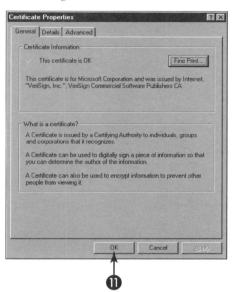

Setting up Microsoft Wallet

3 Click the Edit Profile button. A Properties dialog box appears. The Properties dialog box is an entry form for your Windows Address Book.

4 The Properties dialog box contains six tabs. Make sure the Personal tab is displayed.

5 Notice that your name is already entered in the name fields. If you want to change the way your name appears, click inside the Display text box and type your changes.

6 Click inside the text box labeled Add new and type your e-mail address.

7 Click the Add button.

8 Click the Home tab. Type your address, phone number(s), and Web page address (if you have one) in the appropriate fields.

9 When you finish, click OK. The Profile Assistant is now ready for use.

10 When you access a Web site that uses the Profile Assistant technologies, the program notifies you that the Web site wants to collect information, tells how the information will be used, and provides a list of information requested.

11 From the list of requested information, you can select the data that you want to transmit over the Internet and submit to the Web site.

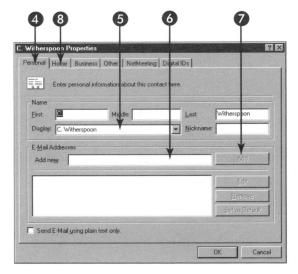

Setting up Microsoft Wallet

Microsoft Wallet provides a convenient and secure way to store and access your payment and address information to make online shopping easier and more enjoyable. Microsoft Wallet consists of the Address and Payment Selectors. The Address Selector provides for the entry, storage, and use of addresses that can be used for shipping and billing purposes. The Payment Selector provides for the entry, safe storage, and use of different payment methods for paying for online purchases.

Setting up Microsoft Wallet

Before you can use Microsoft Wallet, you must set it up. The Internet Explorer browser should be open on your screen from the last exercise.

1 The first step in the setup is to add entries to the Address Selector. Select View > Internet Options to display the Internet Options dialog box.

2 Click the Content tab.

3 Click the Addresses button to display the Address Options dialog box.

4 Click the Add button to display the Add a New Address dialog box.

5 Use this dialog box to record your name, address, and telephone number.

6 When you finish entering the information, click OK. Your new entry is listed in the Address Options dialog box.

7 If you want the items you purchase shipped to an address that is different than the one you entered in step 5, click the Add button again. The Add a New Address dialog box appears.

8 Use this dialog box to record the name, address, and telephone number of the person who should receive the items. You can use this dialog box to add your shipping address, for example, if it is different from your billing address. You can also use this dialog box to enter the names and addresses of gift recipients.

9 When you finish entering the information, click OK. Your new entry is listed in the Address Options dialog box.

10 Repeat steps 7 and 8 to add as many addresses as you want to the Address Selector.

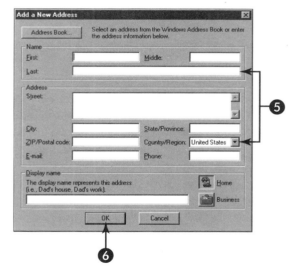

If you go online shopping to purchase a birthday present for a friend and want the present delivered to the friend's address, the shipping information must be available in the Address Selector.

9

Becoming Security Aware

Setting up Microsoft Wallet

⑪ When you have made all your entries to the Address Selector, click the Close button in the Address Options dialog box. The Internet Options dialog box displaying the Content tab appears.

⑫ The next step is to set up the payment options in the Payment Selector. Click the Payments button. The Installing Payment Extensions dialog box appears.

⑬ Click the Install button to continue.

⑭ When the installation is complete, the Payment Options dialog box appears. Click the Add button. A drop-down list with the different types of credit cards supported by Microsoft Wallet appears.

⑮ Select the type of credit card that you want to use for your online purchases. The Add a New Credit Card wizard starts.

⑯ Follow the instructions in the wizard to enter your credit card information, select an address where your bills should be sent, and set a password so that only you can access your credit card information.

⑰ When you come to the last screen in the wizard, click the Finish button. Your credit card is now safely stored in Microsoft Wallet, and you are returned to the Payment Options dialog box.

You can add additional cards to the Payment Selector by clicking the Add button on the Payment Options dialog box, selecting the type of credit card, and completing the necessary information.

⑱ When you are finished entering credit card information, click the Close button. The Internet Options dialog box appears.

⑲ Click the OK button to close the dialog box. You are now ready to begin that shopping spree.

When you access a retail Web site that uses Microsoft Wallet technology, you are prompted for billing, shipping, and payment information while you shop. You can highlight the information in Microsoft Wallet that you want to send to the requesting site. The Wallet provides a safe storage place for your sensitive financial information.

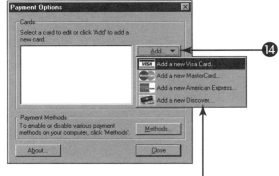

Cards supported by Microsoft Wallet

SKILLS CHALLENGE: DESIGNING A SECURITY PLAN

Now that you've been introduced to all the security options available in the Internet Explorer browser, it's time to design your own security plan. Before you begin this exercise, you need to evaluate your Internet habits to determine what security options best suit your needs. You have the chance to set your personal preferences in the last step of this challenge.

Before you begin, launch the Internet Explorer browser. Remember that you can refer to the exercises if you need help with any of the steps.

1 Set the Content Advisor levels as follows: Language 2, Nudity 1, Sex 2, and Violence 2.

How do you change the supervisor password used by the Content Advisor?

How do you prevent people who use your computer from accessing Web sites that are not rated by a ratings service?

2 Add the Microsoft (www.microsoft.com) and IDG Books (www.idgbooks.com) home pages to your list of trusted Web sites.

3 On the Security tab of the Internet Options dialog box, select the Custom security level for the trusted sites zone. Change all of the options under the ActiveX Controls and Plug-ins section so that you are prompted before these controls can be downloaded.

4 Add your digital ID to the Profile Assistant. Open the Profile Assistant and click the Digital IDs tab. Select your e-mail address and the digital ID from the list.

How many different credit cards can you set up in Microsoft Wallet?

5 Add any additional credit cards you may want to use for online shopping to Microsoft Wallet.

Troubleshooting

6 Go back through steps 1, 2, and 3 in this exercise and change the settings so that they reflect your personal preferences.

TROUBLESHOOTING

Here are some common problems that users have encountered and suggested solutions.

Problem	Solution
I am upgrading to a new computer. I was able to find and transfer Outlook Express and my Windows Address Book to the new machine, but I am having problems transferring my personal certificate.	You must revoke your existing certificate and request a new one. A personal certificate is specific to both user and computer.
I'm trying to view a page on a Web site that is signed with a certificate from an authority not recognized by Internet Explorer 4. How can I add the certificate authority?	When you attempt to download content from a Web page, the Internet Explorer browser posts a Security Warning dialog box. At the bottom of the dialog box, check the box next to Always trust software from (manufacturer).
When I tried to download a software program, I received an Authenticode Security Technology Warning dialog box. Does this warning mean that the program I am attempting to download will damage my computer?	This warning does not mean that the software is unsafe; it only acts as a prompt. When you receive such a warning, you should check the digital certificate of the company or person that created the software. Click the publisher hyperlink found in the center of the certificate and then click the More Info button located at the bottom of the certificate. If you are reassured by the certificate information, you can download the program.

Wrap up ◀

Problem

Besides using Internet Explorer's security features, what else can I do to keep my computer safe and secure?

Solution

Make regular backups of all your important data files. Run an anti-virus utility in the background whenever your computer is operating and perform a thorough virus scan at least once a week. Approach downloads cautiously; before you download any content, verify the source. Stay informed on security issues; check Microsoft's Internet Explorer 4 site regularly for updated security information.

WRAP UP

In this lesson, you exercised the following skills:

- Using the Content Advisor to restrict access to the Internet
- Setting security levels to restrict access to your computer
- Obtaining a digital certificate
- Setting up the Profile Assistant to manage personal information
- Setting up Microsoft Wallet to manage shipping and financial information

In the next lesson, you explore the exciting possibilities of e-mail and the numerous features of Internet Explorer's Outlook Express mail program.

TRY OUT THE

INTERACTIVE TUTORIALS

ON YOUR CD!

9

Becoming Security Aware

PART IV

Communication Tools

Explore the phenomenal communications tools in Internet Explorer 4: e-mail, newsgroups, chat, and electronic conferencing. You can even create your own Web page and establish a presence on the World Wide Web. Talk to the world in the following lessons:

Using Outlook Express for E-mail

60 MINUTES

GOALS

In this lesson, you learn how to send, receive, and manage e-mail messages. This detailed lesson covers the following:

- Configuring Outlook Express
- Setting up multiple mail accounts
- Creating and sending a basic message
- Adding HTML formatting to a message
- Setting HTML formatting as the default
- Attaching a file to a message
- Creating a signature file
- Setting up contacts in the Windows Address Book
- Creating a distribution group
- Managing your messages with folders
- Retrieving and answering your e-mail messages
- Routing incoming mail automatically

Get ready

GET READY

To work your way through this lesson, you must first install Outlook Express (see Appendix A). Although you don't need to be connected to the Internet during the early part of the lesson, you'll need to connect during the exercises.

    When you finish working through this lesson, you will know how to compose and format an e-mail message. You'll also understand how to retrieve and manage your e-mail messages.

USING E-MAIL

Outlook Express allows you to send and receive private e-mail messages across the Internet. E-mail works by transmitting messages from one computer to another computer anywhere in the world over the phone lines. Sending an e-mail message is comparable to leaving a message on someone's answering machine. The recipient doesn't need to be at home or at work (or even connected to the Internet) when you send the message, because it's delivered directly to his or her mailbox.

    E-mail provides a great way to communicate with your friends or business associates. Remember playing phone tag? You place a telephone call to a business associate to find out some urgent information. Your call is picked up by an answering machine, and you leave a message. For the next few hours, you hang around your office waiting for the return call. At the very instant you leave your office to get a package of crackers, the return call comes in. Now you have a message on *your* answering machine instead of the information you need. Your return call is picked up by the answering machine again, and the process continues. If you'd used e-mail instead of the phone, your question could have been received, answered, and sent back to you in no time.

    Using e-mail has many advantages. For one thing, it's inexpensive. Aside from the cost of the call to your ISP (usually a local call covered by your monthly phone charges), you don't have to pay long-distance or connection fees. For another, files like business plans, invoices, and memos can be attached to e-mail messages. (The folks at IDG Books and I used e-mail to send all files

Configuring Outlook Express

for this book back and forth.) Another advantage is that you can send one message to all the names on a distribution group list instead of sending individual messages to each person. And, best of all, you can set up your e-mail contacts in the Windows Address Book so you don't have to type their e-mail addresses each time you send a message.

Configuring Outlook Express

In this exercise, you configure Outlook Express to send and receive messages. Before you begin the steps, make sure that you have the following information handy: your e-mail address, Post Office Protocol (POP) account name and password, the server names of both the incoming and outgoing mail servers, and whether the incoming server uses the POP3 or IMAP protocol. (You learn about these protocols later in this lesson.) If you're not sure about *any* of the information, call your ISP before you begin this exercise.

Unless you change ISPs or something else about your Internet account, you'll only have to perform these steps once.

1 Open Outlook Express by clicking the Launch Mail icon on the Quick Launch toolbar. If the toolbar isn't visible, display it by clicking the right mouse button on a blank spot on the Windows taskbar and selecting Toolbars ➢ Quick Launch from the pop-up menu.

2 Because this is the first time you've used Outlook Express, the Internet Connection Wizard dialog box appears. Make any necessary corrections to your name shown in the Display name text box.

3 Click Next.

TIP *Wizards are step-by-step instructions that guide you through Windows tasks such as setting up a particular feature or option. Many programs use wizards.*

4 The next dialog box requires you to enter your e-mail address. Make sure you type it correctly.

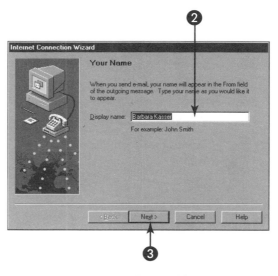

10

Using Outlook Express for E-mail

5 Click Next.

6 The third dialog box requires the names of your incoming and outgoing mail servers. These addresses usually look something like mail.ispname.net.

7 If your incoming server uses Internet Message Access Protocol (IMAP), click the drop-down arrow next to POP3 and choose IMAP. If your incoming server uses POP3, accept the default.

8 When you're ready to continue, click Next.

9 The next dialog box covers the information about your Internet Mail Logon. Unless your ISP requires you to use Secure Password Authentication to access your e-mail account, make sure the option button next to Log on using is selected.

10 Type your POP account name and password in the correct fields.

11 Click Next to continue.

NOTE

If your ISP requires you to use Secure Password Authentication to access your e-mail account, click the option button next to Log on using Secure Password Authentication and click Next. You are prompted to complete another screen with information provided by your ISP.

12 The fifth dialog box asks for a "friendly" name for the mail account. Outlook Express supplies a default name—the name of the mail server—and you can accept the default. Or you can click inside the Internet mail account name box and type a name you like. For example, I've named my mail account Barbara's Mail.

13 When you're ready to move along, click Next.

14 The sixth dialog box asks for information about the way you connect to the Internet:

- If you connect to the Internet through an ISP and a modem, click the option button next to Connect using my phone line.

- If you connect to the Internet through your company's local area network, choose the second option.

Click to select IMAP.

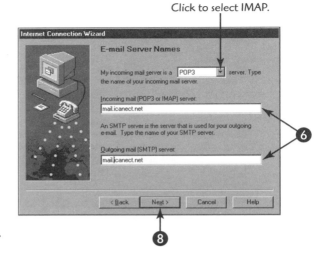

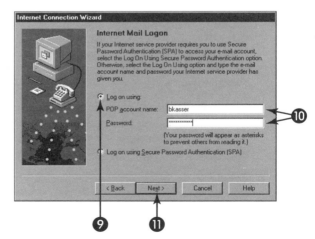

Setting up multiple mail accounts

- If you plan to use Outlook Express while you're traveling, click the option button next to I will establish my Internet connection manually.

⓫ Click Next to continue.

⓬ The next dialog box asks for information about your dial-up connection — the way you connect to the Internet:

- If you want to establish a new dial-up connection, click the option button next to Create a new dial-up connection. When you move to the next wizard screens, you are asked to fill in information like the ISP's phone number, your name and password, and other information in a series of Connection dialog boxes.

- If you already have a dial-up connection, the Internet Connection Wizard detects it and places the name in the existing dial-up connection box. Click the option button next to Use an existing dial-up connection and choose a connection from the list. If you have more than one dial-up connection, click the one that connects to your ISP.

⓮ Once you've selected either a new or existing dial-up connection, click Next.

⓯ The final dialog box offers congratulations and informs you that you've successfully entered all of the information needed to set up your account. Click Finish. The Outlook Express Quick Start page appears.

You're ready for e-mail! Later on, if you need to change any information about your mail account, select Tools ➢ Accounts ➢ Properties and make the necessary corrections.

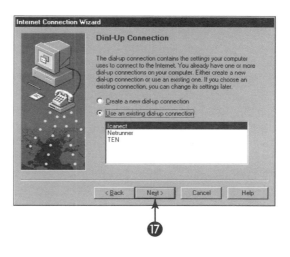

Setting up multiple mail accounts

Outlook Express understands that you might have more than one mail account. For example, maybe you have an account that you use for business and an account that you use for personal matters. If you have multiple mail accounts, Outlook Express can retrieve all of your mail — no matter what mail server it's coming from.

10

Using Outlook Express for E-mail

Setting up multiple mail accounts

1 From the Outlook Express screen, select Tools ➤ Accounts to display the Internet Accounts dialog box.

2 Click the Add button.

3 Choose Mail from the submenu. The Internet Connection Wizard dialog box appears.

4 Fill in each of the dialog boxes. (If you need help, refer to the steps in the previous exercise.) When you're finished, the Internet Accounts dialog box appears, showing the new account you set up.

5 Click Close to close the Internet Accounts box and return to Outlook Express.

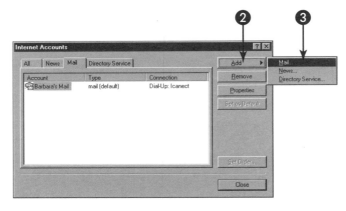

TIP

The first time you start Outlook Express, it connects to the mail server you specified, logs in to your account, and downloads your new messages into the Inbox.

A MAIL SERVER PRIMER

When you send mail through the regular postal service (now called *snail mail*), your letter is processed by several postal agents before it arrives at its final destination. Your e-mail messages are handled by electronic postal agents called mail servers. The mail servers send, sort, and process the messages for delivery.

Internet mail goes through SMTP gateways. You can think of SMTP (Simple Mail Transfer Protocol) as the official e-mail language of the Internet because it processes messages sent from one e-mail server to another. For example, your outgoing message is translated from Outlook Express to SMTP, sent over the Internet to your recipient's mail server, received at the second SMTP

gateway where it is automatically translated back into the correct format, and then delivered to your mail recipient.

POP3 and IMAP come into play during the processing of incoming messages. Your new mail is received at the incoming mail server and held until you retrieve it. If your ISP or company uses POP3 (shortened from Post Office Protocol 3), your messages are deleted from the mail server as soon as you retrieve them. IMAP, short for Internet Message Access Protocol, is the newest standard protocol for getting e-mail from the mail server. If your messages are received by an IMAP server, you might have other options, like viewing just the headings and the senders of mail messages before you decide to retrieve them.

Creating and sending a basic message

■ Exploring the Outlook Express window

The Outlook Express Quick Start page provides all the tools you need for online communication. Arranged for your convenience are the toolbar and a list of the folders you use to store your messages. In the center of the screen are a set of graphic commands that you can use to work with Outlook Express.

If you don't want to see the Quick Start page each time you open Outlook Express, check the box at the bottom left of the window to change the default so that Outlook Express opens to your Inbox. You can return to the Quick Start page at any time by clicking the Outlook Express icon at the top of the Folder list.

Now that Outlook Express is all set up and you're familiar with the Quick Start page, it's time to send some messages.

SENDING E-MAIL

With the message creation options in Outlook Express, the possibilities for personal expression are practically unlimited. You can write basic text messages and send them with or without attached files. You can liven up your communiqués with colors and special effects and send them to recipients with mail programs capable of reading messages formatted in the Hypertext Markup Language (HTML). You can even create a distinctive signature file to include at the bottom of each of your messages.

So fire up your creativity and get ready to communicate.

Creating and sending a basic message

In this exercise, you create and send an e-mail message. If you just want to practice, you can use the fictitious names shown in the steps. If you know the e-mail address of a friend or family member, you can use that. Otherwise, use your own e-mail address. (You'll be sure to get mail that way!) You don't have to be connected to the Internet to create messages.

① If it's not already open, launch Outlook Express by clicking the Launch Mail icon on the Quick Launch toolbar. The Outlook Express Quick Start page appears.

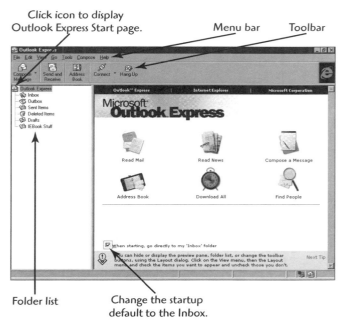

Click icon to display Outlook Express Start page. Menu bar Toolbar

Folder list Change the startup default to the Inbox.

10

Using Outlook Express for E-mail

Creating and sending a basic message

2 Click the Compose Message button on the toolbar. The New Message window appears.

3 Click the To line.

4 Type the recipient's e-mail address. As an example, type **bfranklin@history.com**. If you'd like to enter additional addresses, type a semicolon or comma between each address.

If you've set up entries in your Windows Address Book, you can open the Windows Address Book by clicking the card icon to the left of the To line. Later in this lesson, you learn how to set up contacts in the Windows Address Book.

5 An optional step is to send the message as a Cc, or carbon copy, which means that a copy of the message is sent to the recipient specified in the box. To send a copy of the message to another person, click the Cc line.

6 Type an e-mail address such as **barnold@traitors.net**.

NOTE

You can also specify a recipient to receive a Bcc—or blind carbon copy—of the message. Neither the original recipient nor any Cc recipients will know that a copy of the message was sent to the recipient specified on this line.

7 When you've finished adding addresses, click the Subject line.

8 Type a subject for your message like **Meeting of the Revolutionary War Club**. Notice that the name in the title bar changes to match the text in the Subject line.

TIP

Instead of using the mouse, you can also use the Tab key to move from line to line.

9 Advance to the message area by clicking inside the window or pressing the Tab key.

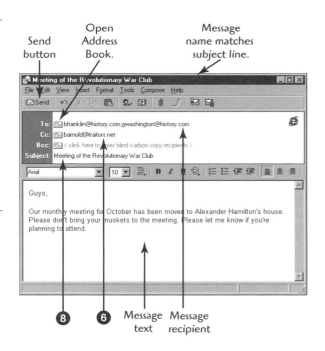

Send button

Open Address Book.

Message name matches subject line.

8   **6**   Message text   Message recipient

⑩ Type your message. Your message can be long or it can consist of only a few lines like the sample that's shown in the illustration: **Guys, Our monthly meeting for October has been moved to Alexander Hamilton's house. Please don't bring your muskets to the meeting. Please let me know if you're planning to attend.**

⑪ When you finish composing the message, select Tools ➤ Spelling to check your spelling. It's always a good idea to let Outlook Express check your work because spelling mistakes can trivialize the most important message. Look over the message once more for other mistakes before you send it.

⑫ Since you composed this message for a practice exercise, you probably won't want to send it, especially if you used the fictitious e-mail addresses for Benjamin Franklin and Benedict Arnold. However, when you write messages on your own and are ready to send them, here's how to do it:

- If you are not connected to the Internet, select File ➤ Send Later to place the message in the Outbox. Later, once you're connected, click the Send and Receive button on the Outlook Express toolbar. If you set up multiple mail accounts, you'll be asked to choose the account for sending the mail.

- If you are already connected to the Internet, click the Send button on the message window toolbar. A dialog box appears, showing the status of the message as it's sent. A copy of the message is placed in the Sent Items folder.

⑬ To delete the message you composed in this exercise, select File ➤ Close.

⑭ Click No in response to the query asking if you want to save changes to the message. The message is removed from the screen.

TIP

If you're composing several messages at once, save time by selecting File ➤ Send Later each time you complete a message. Click the Send and Receive button on the toolbar when you've finished composing your messages to send all of the messages at one time.

10

Using Outlook Express for E-mail

Creating and sending a basic message

The New Message Window

This illustration shows the New Message window and identifies the numerous options you can select as you compose e-mail messages.

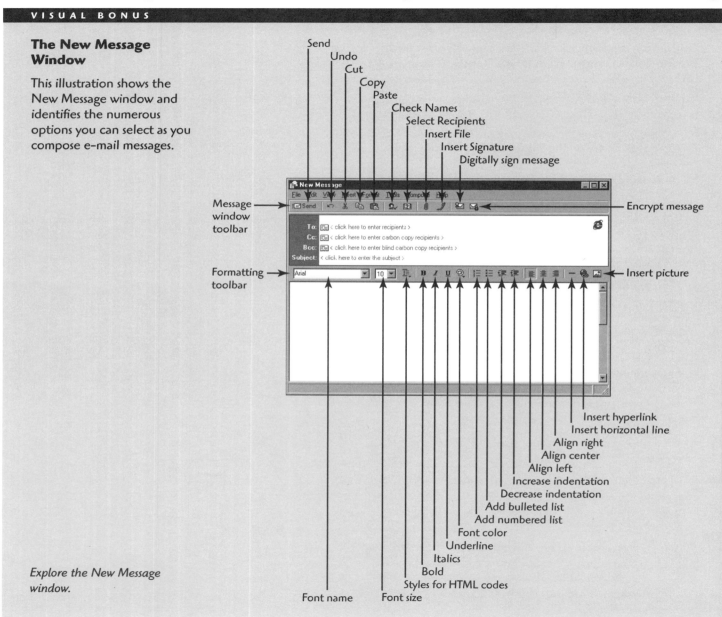

Send
Undo
Cut
Copy
Paste
Check Names
Select Recipients
Insert File
Insert Signature
Digitally sign message

Message window toolbar

Encrypt message

Formatting toolbar

Insert picture

Insert hyperlink
Insert horizontal line
Align right
Align center
Align left
Increase indentation
Decrease indentation
Add bulleted list
Add numbered list
Font color
Underline
Italics
Bold
Styles for HTML codes
Font name
Font size

Explore the New Message window.

Adding HTML formatting

■ Enhancing your e-mail messages with HTML

Now that you've composed and sent a basic e-mail message, you're ready to get creative and add some HTML formatting to a message. Hypertext Markup Language (HTML) is the language of the Internet. The Web pages you see with the Internet Explorer browser are written in HTML, in which underlying codes, called tags, are placed around text to specify how it displays. (You learn more about HTML formatting in Lesson 14.)

Outlook Express allows you to send HTML messages across the Internet—and you don't even have to learn HTML! Outlook Express has an easy-to-use Formatting toolbar that adds the tags for you. Adding HTML tags to your messages can make them look exciting and dramatic. But before you spend extra time making your messages more visually appealing, make sure that your recipients can receive messages in HTML format. Of course, anyone who's using Outlook Express will have no problem seeing the formatting, but some other mail packages, especially older programs or those used by many corporations, don't support HTML formatting tags and won't display them.

Since Outlook Express doesn't know which e-mail program will be used to read the message, it sends two files when you use HTML formatting. If the recipient's mail program can't read HTML, the message displays as plain text. The recipient can open and view the HTML copy with any Web browser.

Adding HTML formatting to a message

The steps in this exercise cover several formatting options. If you completed the preceding exercise, Outlook Express should be open and on the screen. If it's not, open Outlook Express before you begin the steps in this exercise.

1 If the Formatting toolbar isn't displayed, select Format ➤ Rich Text (HTML) to display it.

2 Click the down arrow next to the Compose Message button on the Outlook Express toolbar to display the names of some preformatted stationery.

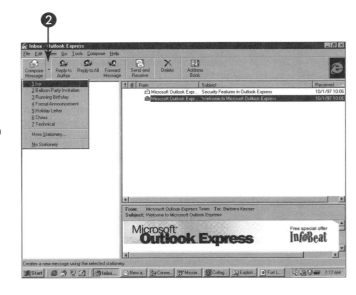

Adding HTML formatting

3 Choose Ivy from the list. The New Message window appears with an ivy border on the left side of the message.

4 Click the To line.

5 Type the recipient's e-mail address. If you want to make sure you receive mail, use your own address.

6 Advance to the Subject line by clicking it or pressing the Tab key.

7 Type **Options**.

8 Now you can add some HTML codes to the message. Advance to the message area by clicking inside the window or pressing the Tab key.

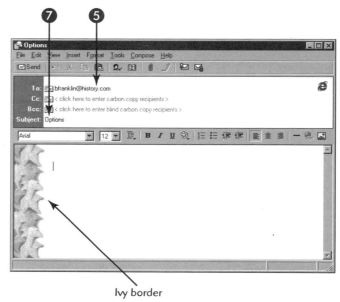

Ivy border

If your message window is too small to display all of the buttons on the Formatting toolbar, make the window bigger. First position the mouse on the right border of the window. When the pointer takes the shape of a double-headed arrow, click the mouse button and drag the border until all of the toolbar buttons are visible.

9 In the message area, type **Learning About Options**.

10 Select the text by dragging the mouse over it so it appears highlighted.

11 Click the Align Center button on the Formatting toolbar. The text moves to the center of the window and still appears highlighted.

Formatting the text of an e-mail message is similar to formatting text in your favorite word processing program. If you're familiar with Microsoft Word or WordPad, for example, you'll find many of the same text attributes and alignment options available in the Outlook Express Formatting toolbar.

⑫ Click the drop-down arrow next to the font size display box on the Formatting toolbar and choose 18. The text increases in size.

⑬ Press the right arrow key on your keyboard to deselect the text.

⑭ Press the Enter key twice to move down two lines.

⑮ Click the Align Left button on the Formatting toolbar to align the next text you type with the left margin.

⑯ Click the Add Numbered List button on the Formatting toolbar. The number 1 appears, followed by a period.

⑰ Type **Enhance the appearance of the text**.

⑱ Press Enter. A new number point—number 2—appears, waiting for you to add the second point.

⑲ Type **Include numbered or bulleted lists**.

⑳ Select Edit ➤ Select All or press Ctrl+A on the keyboard to highlight all of the text in the message area.

㉑ Click the Font Color button on the toolbar. A drop-down list appears, displaying the available colors.

㉒ Click a color for the text. The list closes and the text is colored.

㉓ Deselect the text by pressing the right arrow key.

㉔ To add some visual interest to the message, add a background color. Select Format ➤ Background ➤ Color.

㉕ Choose a color from the list. Your message should look similar to the one in the illustration.

Even though you've finished typing the message, leave it on the screen. You continue working with the message in a later exercise.

Setting HTML formatting as the default

When you use the Formatting toolbar, you're adding HTML codes to the message. To set HTML formatting as the Outlook Express default, follow these steps.

❶ Select Tools ➤ Options from the Outlook Express menu bar to display the Options dialog box.

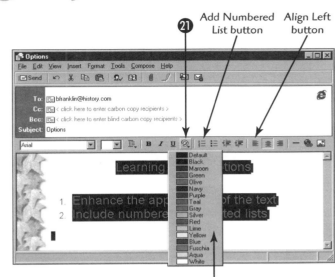

Add Numbered List button / Align Left button

Font color selections

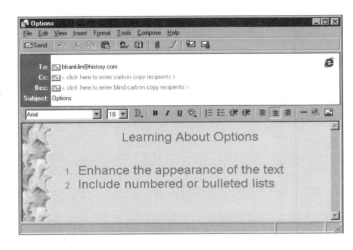

10

Using Outlook Express for E-mail

Attaching a file to a message

② Click the Send tab.

③ In the Mail sending format section of the dialog box, click the option button next to HTML.

④ Click OK to close the Options dialog box.

TIP

Although text attributes and color add excitement to messages, many e-mail packages do not display the added formatting. Don't spend time adding visual elements unless you're sure the recipient will be able to see them.

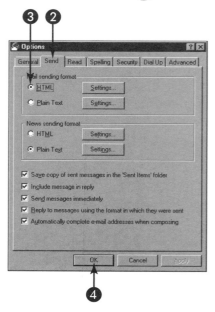

Attaching a file to a message

You can attach almost any type of electronic file to an e-mail message. For example, you can send memos, graphic images, tax returns, or even scanned images. As I've mentioned before, I sent most of the lessons in this book to IDG Books via e-mail.

There's a major headache with attaching files to e-mail messages. Unless the recipients have either the exact software program that was used to create the file (or a similar one), they may not be able to open the attachment. It's frustrating to receive a file created with Pagemaker when you don't have Pagemaker or other desktop publishing software installed on your computer.

TIP

Almost all current e-mail programs include an automatic process to decode sent files, so most of the time the attachments you send with Outlook Express will be readable when they reach their destination.
However, you might want to send a test attachment in advance — especially if the file is important.

❶ With the message you created in the previous exercise on the screen, click the Insert File button on the message window toolbar or select Insert ➢ File Attachment to display the Insert Attachment dialog box.

Creating a signature file

2 Move to the file you want to attach. If you're not sure which file to choose, browse to your Windows folder (usually C:\Windows) and choose the win.ini file.

3 Select the file.

4 Click the Attach button.

The Insert Attachment dialog box closes, and the message window appears. The message is now split into two frames, with the text in the top frame and the attached file name and icon displayed in the bottom frame.

5 Select File ➢ Send Later and, if applicable, choose which of your multiple accounts should be used to send the message. The Send Mail dialog box appears, advising you that the message will be placed in your Outbox and sent whenever you click the Send and Receive button.

6 If you don't want this message to display each time you choose to send a message later, click the checkbox next to Don't show me this message again.

7 Click OK to close the dialog box.

8 Open your Outbox folder and delete the message you created.

Creating a signature file

You can personalize your correspondence by creating a distinctive signature that can be attached to the end of your outgoing e-mail messages. Signature files can be used to show your name, title, phone number, or other pertinent business information. Signatures can also be clever, amusing snippets of text.

Actually, creating signature files has become an art form for many users, so expect funny and provocative sig files on many of the messages you receive. Some people take signature files too far and include vulgar or offensive language. What you include in your own signature file is a matter of taste; just be aware of who's reading your message and the likely reaction to your signature.

1 From within Outlook Express, select Tools ➢ Stationery. The Stationery dialog appears.

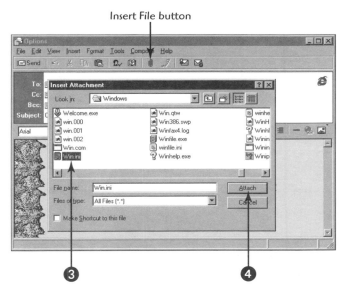

Insert File button

③ ④

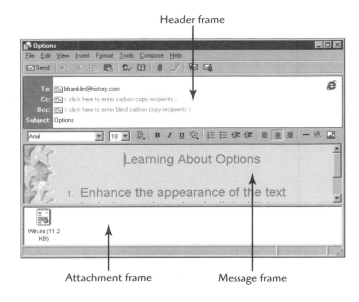

Header frame

Attachment frame   Message frame

Creating a signature file

2 Make sure that the Mail tab is selected.

3 Click the Signature button to display the Signature dialog box.

4 Click the option button next to Text.

5 Type your signature text in the box, pressing Enter to advance to a new line.

If you've already created a file that contains the text you want to use, click the File option button and type the folder path and filename.

6 If you want to include the signature file on all of your outgoing messages, click the corresponding checkbox.

7 By default, the signature file is not included on message replies and message forwards. To change the default and include your signature on replies and forwards, uncheck the box.

8 Click OK when you've finished creating the signature file and setting options for its use.

9 Click OK to close the Stationery dialog box.

10 If you chose the option to attach your signature to all outgoing messages, you don't need to do anything to include it. Otherwise, whenever you create a message on which you wish the signature to appear, click the Insert Signature button where you want the signature to show.

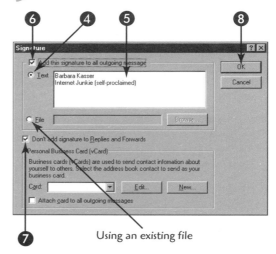

Using an existing file

MANAGING MAIL WITH THE WINDOWS ADDRESS BOOK AND FOLDERS

The Windows Address Book works as both an e-mail directory and a typical address book. Each contact is treated as a separate card, very much like the card file you may keep on your desk. You can make a contact card as simple or as detailed as you want since each one has seven information tabs—including Personal, Home, and Business—for you to fill in. Once you've established contacts in your Windows Address Book, you can set up distribution lists.

Setting up contacts

Managing e-mail information from the Windows Address Book makes good sense. After all, many e-mail addresses are complex combinations of user and domain names like hqle4gal@skisp.net. If you type even one wrong character, your e-mail message won't reach its recipient. Once you've entered the address in the Windows Address Book, you don't have to think about it again.

Folders are a great way to organize your messages. Message folders work just like the folders that hold the files on your computer. Although Outlook Express provides a few default folders for your convenience, you can create more. Your message filing system can be as elaborate or as simple as you choose.

Setting up contacts in the Windows Address Book

It's a snap to set up your contacts in the Windows Address Book.

① Click the Address Book button on the Outlook Express toolbar to display the Windows Address Book.

② Select File ➢ New Contact or click the New Contact button on the toolbar to display the Properties dialog box.

③ Enter the information for your new contact in the appropriate panel by selecting one of the six tabs along the top of the Properties dialog box: Personal, Home, Business, Other, NetMeeting, and Digital IDs.

The following table provides information about what data you might enter in each tab. Keep in mind that you don't need to fill out every field under every tab. These are your contacts; only fill in the information you need.

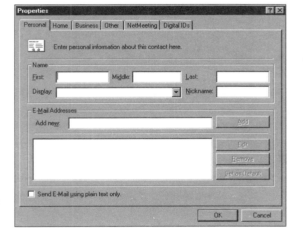

Tab	Information
Personal	Name, nickname, e-mail address
Home	Home address and phone numbers, URL of Web page
Business	Business address and phone numbers, job title, department
Other	Additional information about the contact

continued

Creating a distribution group

Tab	Information
NetMeeting	Servers and other information used for Microsoft NetMeeting (You learn about NetMeeting in Lesson 13.)
Digital IDs	Digital certificates the contact holds for enhanced e-mail security (You learned about digital IDs in Lesson 9.)

4 In the Personal tab, type the name and e-mail address of the contact. For this exercise, use your own name and address. Verify that the information doesn't contain any typos.

5 Click the Add button. The information is added to the Windows Address Book.

6 Click each tab and fill in as much information as you want.

7 Click OK to close the Properties dialog box when you have added all the information.

8 Repeat steps 1 through 7 to add additional contacts to your Windows Address Book.

TIP   *It's easy to make changes to information in the Windows Address Book. Open the Windows Address Book and click the right mouse button on the contact you want to change. Select Properties from the pop-up menu to open the Properties dialog box. Make the changes and click OK.*

Creating a distribution group

In this exercise, you learn how to organize the contacts in your Windows Address Book into distribution groups. The contacts in your Windows Address Book can be added to as many groups as you like. If you change any of the information for a contact in one group, the person's other group entries automatically update.

Groups make sending e-mail to multiple recipients as simple as sending one message. For example, you could send one message

Creating a distribution group

about the Revolutionary War Club to hundreds of people at one time, instead of addressing individual messages to each person.

1 If it's not already open, open the Windows Address Book by clicking the Address Book button on the Outlook Express toolbar. The Windows Address Book opens.

2 Click the New Group button on the Address Book toolbar.

3 On the resulting Properties dialog box, type a name for the group.

4 Click the Select Members button to display the Select Group Members dialog box.

5 In the list of names on the left, highlight the name of the first person you want to add to the group.

6 Click the Select button. The name appears in the members list on the right.

7 Repeat steps 5 and 6 to add each additional person to the distribution list.

8 When you finish adding names to the list, click OK to return to the Group Properties dialog box.

9 Review the distribution group and then click OK to display the Windows Address Book.

10 Scroll through the list of contacts to find the new distribution list.

NOTE *Distribution lists are shown in bold type, and the icon before the group name is a group of people instead of an index card.*

11 To add more members to the group, double-click the group name to display the Properties dialog box.

12 Click the Select Members button.

13 Follow steps 5 and 6 of this exercise.

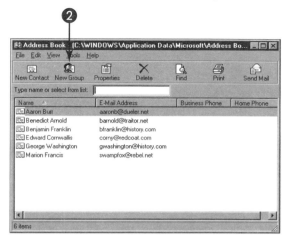

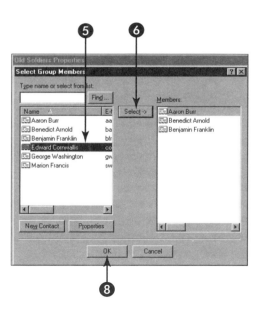

⑭ To remove members from the group, double-click the group name to display the Properties dialog box.

⑮ Highlight the name you want to remove.

⑯ Click the Remove button.

Managing your messages with folders

Outlook Express provides default folders for you to organize your messages. Unless you specify otherwise, new messages are automatically routed to the Inbox folder. When you compose a message and select the Send Later option, the message is stored in the Outbox until you choose to send it. Once you send a message, a copy is placed in the Sent Items folder where you can refer to it later. The last default folder, Deleted Items, works like the Recycle Bin on your Windows desktop. When you delete a message, it's placed in the Deleted Items folder. You need to empty the Deleted Items folder to completely remove the message from Outlook Express. The default folders can't be renamed or deleted.

You can create other folders that help you organize your messages. For example, I have a folder called IEBook Stuff for all the correspondence I receive regarding this book. You might want to call your folders something like Home and Work.

TIP *Your e-mail folders are also used by News to store newsgroup postings. You learn more about News in the next lesson.*

❶ If Outlook Express isn't open, launch it by clicking the Launch Mail button on the Quick Launch toolbar.

❷ Your default folders are listed in the folder list on the left side of the window in the Folder list pane. Click the Inbox folder to display its contents.

❸ The top frame of the Inbox folder, called the Header pane, displays message header information such as who sent the message, the subject of the message, and the date and time it was received. The bottom frame of the folder, called the

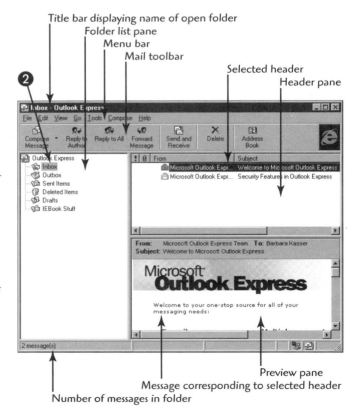

Title bar displaying name of open folder
Folder list pane
Menu bar
Mail toolbar
Selected header
Header pane

Number of messages in folder
Message corresponding to selected header
Preview pane

Preview pane, displays the contents of the message that's selected in the top frame.

4 To adjust the size of the frames, position the mouse pointer on the divider between the top and bottom frames.

5 When the vertical arrow appears, click and drag the mouse pointer in the direction you want to resize a frame. For example, if you want to make the Preview pane larger, drag the divider upward.

6 Release the mouse button, and the frames are resized.

7 If the Preview pane is still too small to display your messages, double-click a message header to display the message in a separate window.

8 Close the open message by clicking the Close button in the upper right corner of the title bar.

9 To create a new folder, right-click inside the Folder list pane.

10 Select New Folder on the pop-up menu. The Create Folder dialog box appears.

11 The folder you're creating will be a subfolder of the one that's highlighted in the dialog box. To make this new folder a top-level folder, click Outlook Express, the first item on the list in the Create Folder dialog box.

12 Type Junk Mail in the Folder name text box.

13 Click OK. The Create Folder dialog box closes, and the folder appears on the folder list.

14 If you have too many folders to fit inside the Folder list pane, click the up or down arrow at the top and bottom edges of the Folder list pane to scroll through the list.

15 It's easy to move messages into folders. First, click a message header to select it.

16 Drag the header into the Deleted Items folder.

17 Release the mouse button, and the message is moved to the Deleted Items folder.

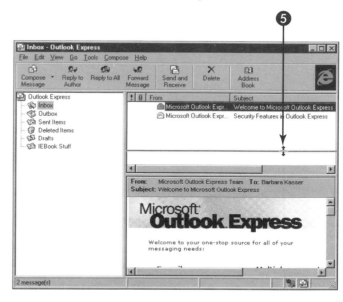

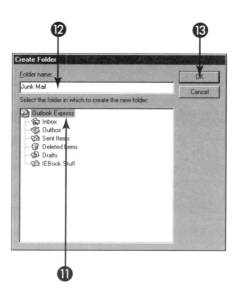

10

Using Outlook Express for E-mail

Retrieving and answering e-mail

18 To empty the Deleted Items folder, right–click the folder name.

19 Choose Empty Folder on the pop-on menu.

20 Click Yes in response to the prompt asking if you're sure.

RECEIVING E-MAIL

You've worked hard in this lesson. Now you're going to have some fun by receiving mail! Let's face it, everyone loves to get mail. Knowing that you might be getting a message from someone across the corridor or across the globe is exciting.

Retrieving and answering your e-mail messages

In this exercise, you retrieve the mail messages that people have sent you. If you don't have any new messages, don't worry; the world just hasn't found you yet. Once you share your address with a few folks and start sending e-mail, your Inbox will fill up. To work through the steps in this exercise, connect to the Internet and send yourself three or four messages for practice if you don't think you'll have any new messages. Review the send mail procedures earlier in this lesson if you need help.

1 If Outlook Express isn't open, click the Launch Mail icon on the Quick Launch toolbar.

2 Click the Send and Receive button on the Outlook Express toolbar. A status window appears, showing the status of the connection and the progress as the messages are received. When any messages you placed in the Outbox have been sent and your new messages are received, the window closes.

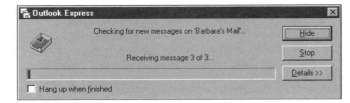

3 Read a message by clicking the message header to display the message in the Preview pane.

4 Drag a message (preferably one you sent to yourself) to the Junk Mail folder.

5 To print a message, click the message header to select it and then select File ➤ Print.

6 To answer a message, click the message header to select it and click one of the following buttons:

- **Reply to Author:** To reply to the person who sent you the message

- **Reply to All:** To reply to everyone who received the message

- **Forward Message:** To send the message to another person

TIP

Use Reply to All with care. Be sure that you really want your answer to go to everyone who received the message.

Routing incoming mail automatically

Use the Inbox Assistant in Outlook Express to automatically distribute incoming mail to special folders by specifying priorities and rules for mail sorting. Here are the steps for configuring the Inbox Assistant to automatically route your incoming mail.

1 From within Outlook Express, select Tools ➢ Inbox Assistant to display the Inbox Assistant dialog box.

2 Click the Add button to display the Properties dialog box. You use the Properties dialog box to specify the criteria for incoming messages and the associated routing or sorting action.

3 You may choose, for example, to route mail from a specific person to a specific folder you have set up in Outlook Express. In the From field, type the person's e-mail address or click the Address Book button to select a contact name.

4 Check the Move To box.

5 Click the Folder button to display a list of the folders you have set up in Outlook Express.

6 Highlight the destination folder.

7 Click OK to return to the Properties dialog box.

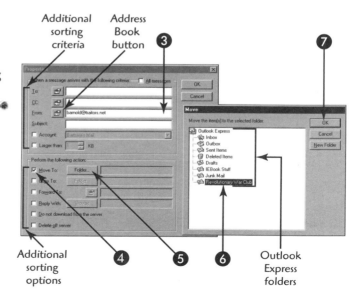

Additional sorting criteria

Address Book button

Additional sorting options

Outlook Express folders

8 Click OK to return to the Inbox Assistant. The criteria you specified are now listed in the Description window.

NOTE *If you want to temporarily disable a set of criteria without deleting it permanently in case you want to use it again, open the Inbox Assistant and uncheck the box next to the set of criteria.*

SKILLS CHALLENGE: CORRESPONDING WITH A FRIEND

You've done some great work in this lesson! Before you begin the final exercise, get up and walk around for a few minutes. You send mail to yourself in this exercise, but if you know the address of a business associate or friend, you can substitute that address for your own.

As you work through the steps, you practice everything you learned in this lesson while learning a few new tricks. If you need help with a particular step, feel free to go back through the material covered in the exercises. When you finish the Skills Challenge, you'll be well on your way to becoming a mail genius. In fact, don't be surprised if your friends start asking you for help.

1 If it's not already open, launch Outlook Express.

2 Compose a new message to yourself. Instead of typing the e-mail address, click the index card icon next to the To box and select your name from the Windows Address Book.

3 Advance to the message area.

4 Type a few lines of text about sending mail.

5 Add the following HTML formatting options to the text you typed:

- Add a text color
- Add a background color
- Change the font point size to 18

6 Attach a file to the message.

7 Check the spelling.

8 Send the message.

 If you choose the Send Later option, where does the message go?

9 When Outlook Express asks if you want to include a subject, click Yes and type a subject. Notice that if you forget to fill in the Subject line on an e-mail message, Outlook Express prompts you to enter one before sending the message.

10 Start composing a new message to yourself.

11 Instead of typing your address or looking at the Windows Address Book, type the first four letters of your last name and click the Check Names button on the toolbar. (Outlook Express supplies your name from the entries in the Windows Address Book. If more than one name matches the letters you typed, you can choose the correct name from a list.)

12 Fill in the Subject and type a brief message.

13 Check the spelling.

14 Send the message.

 How do you check the spelling of a message?

15 Create a new folder called Mail from Me.

16 Receive your new messages.

17 Move the first message to the Deleted Items folder.

18 Empty the Deleted Items folder.

19 Reply to the second message.

 What's the difference between Replying to Author and Replying to All?

20 Move the second message into the Mail from Me folder.

Troubleshooting

 Set up the Inbox Assistant to automatically route mail that you send yourself to the Mail from Me folder.

⭐ 4 *How do you temporarily disable routing criteria set in the Inbox Assistant?*

TROUBLESHOOTING

The following table lists possible problems that you might encounter as you use Outlook Express and offers some suggestions for dealing with them.

Problem	Solution
I sent a message in error and now I've changed my mind. Is there any way to get it back?	If the message you want to cancel is in the Outbox, delete it by opening the Outbox folder, clicking the message to select it, and clicking Delete. But if the message is in the Sent Items folder, it's gone! Like letters you drop in the mailbox, you can't get a message back once it has been sent through the Internet.
Someone sent me a file but I don't know how to open it.	Proceed with caution. With the vast number of computer viruses out in the world right now, you don't want to infect your computer. Play it safe; if the file attachment was unsolicited and you don't know the sender, drag the message into the Deleted Items folder. If you are sure of the sender, double-click the file. When the Opening Attachment Warning dialog box appears, choose whether to open the file now or save it to disk.

Problem	Solution
I emptied my Deleted Items folder and now I want to look at one of the messages that was in it.	Bad news. When you empty the Deleted Items folder, the messages are gone forever. Maybe you can ask the person who sent you the message to resend it.

WRAP UP

In this lesson, you covered a lot of new ground as you exercised the following skills:

- Sending and receiving mail with Outlook Express
- Composing mail messages that incorporate HTML formatting
- Managing your mail with the Windows Address Book, folders, and the Inbox Assistant

The next lesson explains how to use Outlook Express as a newsreader and introduces the multifaceted world of newsgroups.

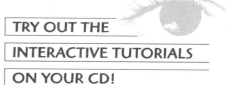

TRY OUT THE
INTERACTIVE TUTORIALS
ON YOUR CD!

10

Using Outlook Express for E-mail

Using Outlook Express for News

GOALS

In this lesson, you use Outlook Express to explore the world of newsgroups. No matter what your interests are, there's sure to be a special interest group just for you. You learn about:

40 MINUTES

- Setting up Outlook Express to read news

- Finding the right group

- Subscribing to a newsgroup

- Unsubscribing from a newsgroup

- Displaying new groups

- Reading new postings

- Posting messages

- Downloading new messages

- Setting up offline reading

- Downloading the postings to read offline

Get ready

GET READY

To complete this lesson, Outlook Express must be installed on your computer (see Appendix A). Additionally, you should be connected to the Internet before you begin the exercises. Since all the exercises in this lesson are related, try to work through all of them at one sitting.

When you complete this lesson, you will have set up Outlook Express as a newsreader and learned how to read and reply to newsgroup postings.

GETTING STARTED WITH NEWSGROUPS

Newsgroups are one of the most popular features on the Internet. Think of newsgroups as computerized discussion groups. Each day, millions of people from all over the world read messages and post responses to more than 30,000 of these newsgroups. With so many groups available, the topics cover just about every subject you can imagine.

Most newsgroups are actually part of the Internet's Usenet News, short for User's Network. Other groups can be formed in a company, an ISP, or an online service like CompuServe or America Online. Your ISP determines which groups are available to you.

Some groups are *moderated*, which means that a designated person decides which postings to allow or to remove. However, most of the groups are unmoderated. In an unmoderated group, you can post just about anything, as long as the subject of your posting, called a *thread*, pertains to the newsgroup topic.

Unlike a discussion group at your local library or community center, you don't need to make a reservation to join a newsgroup. You don't need to pay dues. You can subscribe to a newsgroup and become an active participant, or you can *lurk*—hang back and read the postings without posting a response of your own.

To read the postings of Internet newsgroups, you need a program called a *newsreader*. Outlook Express is designed to work as a newsreader, as well as the program you use to send and receive e-mail. Since you became familiar with Outlook Express in Lesson 10, you don't need to learn a whole set of new commands to look at newsgroup postings.

Setting up Outlook Express

Setting up Outlook Express to read news

In this exercise, you configure Outlook Express as a newsreader. Just as you did when you set up your mail in the previous lesson, you need information before you begin this exercise. You need your e-mail address and the name of the Network News Transfer Protocol (NNTP) server your Internet service provider uses for news. You also need to know if your ISP requires a logon name and password and an authentication code to log on to the news server. If you're not sure about *any* of the information, call your ISP before you begin this exercise.

Unless you change ISPs or something else about your Internet account, you'll only have to perform these steps once.

1 Open Outlook Express by clicking the Launch Mail icon on the Quick Launch toolbar. If the toolbar isn't visible, display it by clicking the right mouse button on the Windows taskbar and selecting Toolbars ➤ Quick Launch from the pop-up menu.

2 Select Tools ➤ Accounts to display the Internet Accounts dialog box.

3 Click the Add button.

4 Choose News from the submenu to bring up the Internet Connection Wizard.

5 In the first dialog box, titled Name, verify that your name appears correctly. If you need to change any information in this or any other dialog boxes, click inside the box and make the necessary corrections.

6 Click Next.

TIP

The name you type will appear on the postings you make to a newsgroup. If you're shy or reluctant to reveal your identity to strangers, you can enter a pseudonym in place of your real name. You can always run the Internet Connection Wizard later and replace the phony name with your real one.

Setting up Outlook Express

7 In the next dialog box, verify that your e-mail address is shown correctly.

8 Click Next.

9 The third dialog box requires the name of your Internet news server (NNTP). Type the name your ISP has provided (usually something like news.myserver.net).

10 If you don't need a password to log on, click Next.

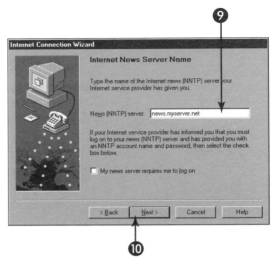

NOTE *If your ISP requires you to log on to the news server and has given you a logon name and password, check the box next to My news server requires me to log on. Click Next. In the next dialog box that appears, type your news account name and password. Click the Secure Password Authentication option box if your ISP requires SPA to log on and complete the subsequent screen with information from your ISP. Click Next to continue.*

11 The next dialog box asks for a "friendly" name for the news account. Outlook Express supplies a default name—the name of the news server—and you can accept the default. Or you can click inside the Internet news account name box and type a name you like. For example, I've named my news account Barbara's News.

12 When you're ready to move along, click Next.

13 The next dialog box asks for information about the way you connect to the Internet:

- If you connect to the Internet through an ISP and a modem, click the option button next to Connect using my phone line.

- If you're connecting to the Internet through your company's local area network, choose the second option.

- If you're planning to use Outlook Express while you're traveling, click the option button next to I will establish my Internet connection manually.

14 Click Next to continue.

⑮ The next dialog box asks for information about your dial-up connection — the way you connect to the Internet:

- If you want to establish a new dial-up connection, click the option button next to Create a new dial-up connection. When you move to the next wizard screen, you are asked to fill in information like the ISP's phone number, your name and password, and other information in a series of Connection dialog boxes.

- If you already have a dial-up connection, the Internet Connection Wizard detects it and places the name in the existing dial-up connection box. Click the option button next to Use an existing dial-up connection and choose the connection from the list. If you have more than one dial-up connection, click the one that connects to your ISP.

⑯ Once you've selected either a new or existing dial-up connection, click Next.

⑰ The final dialog box offers congratulations and informs you that you've successfully entered all of the information needed to set up your account. Click Finish.

TIP *Just like mail, you can have multiple news accounts. If you need to set up additional news accounts, repeat steps 2 through 17.*

⑱ The first time you set up a news account, Outlook Express asks if you'd like to download the newsgroups from the news server you added. Click Yes.

The Downloading Newsgroups dialog box appears and tracks the progress of the total number of groups downloaded. When the download is complete, the Downloading Newsgroups dialog box closes. The list of newsgroups from your news server appears in the Newsgroups dialog box.

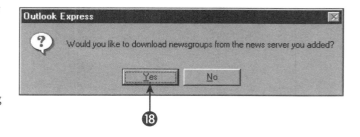

Setting up Outlook Express

If you ever need to change any information about your news account, select Tools ➣ Accounts ➣ Properties from the Outlook Express Newsgroups window and make the necessary corrections.

■ Deciphering newsgroup names

When you first look at them, newsgroup names can appear to be made up of secret code. Actually, the names follow a simple naming convention. Newsgroup names are read from left to right, and contain words separated by periods, such as `alt.internet.access`. The first word describes the main category of the newsgroup, the second word is a subcategory of the first, and so on. Table 11-1 explains some of the most common newsgroup categories.

TABLE 11-1 COMMON NEWSGROUP CATEGORIES

Abbreviation	Description
alt	Alternative topics that may be controversial or offensive (but aren't always)
bit	Newsgroups that provide mailing list digests
biz	Business topics
comp	Topics relating to computers, including hardware and software
k12	Topics related to elementary and secondary education
misc	Miscellaneous topics
news	Topics having to do with Usenet News and related issues
rec	Recreational topics of all sorts, including hobbies, sports, and TV
sci	Science-related topics
soc	Topics of a social nature
talk	Hot topics that lead to debate and heated discussions

Finding the right group

Category names are usually descriptive. When you look at the `alt.internet.access` group name, it's easy to see that the group is an alternative group about the Internet that discusses access issues.

Finding the right group

With so many newsgroups to choose from, it's hard to find the groups that interest you. Fortunately, you can pick a group name that looks promising and read some of its postings before you subscribe.

1 The Newsgroups dialog box should be on the screen from the last exercise. If it's not, open Outlook Express (if it's not already open) and select Go ➢ News. Then click the News groups button on the Newsgroup toolbar.

2 Scroll down the list of newsgroup names using the vertical scroll bar. Notice how the names change as you scroll.

3 Click inside the text box beneath the words Display newsgroups which contain.

4 Type **elvis**. As you type, the list changes to match the letters you've typed.

When you finish typing, the list is shortened and displays only the groups with titles containing the word elvis. The title of the first group on the list appears highlighted.

5 If you want to find group titles that contain other words, click inside the text box and type the new keywords. The list changes to match the words you type. To display the entire list, simply clear the contents of the box. However, for this exercise, make sure that **elvis** appears in the text box labeled Display newsgroups which contain.

NOTE *Depending on the newsgroups that your ISP subscribes to, your list may contain more or fewer groups than the one in the illustration.*

6 Click the first elvis group name on the list.

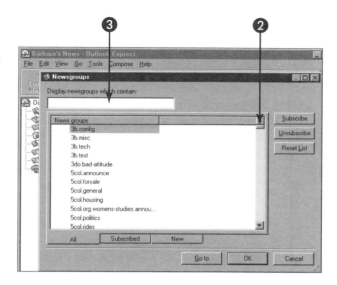

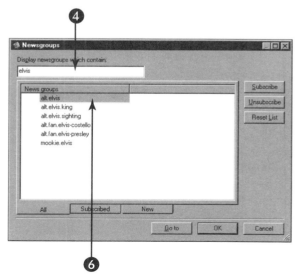

Subscribing to a newsgroup

➐ Click the Go to button. The Newsgroups dialog box closes, and the postings of the elvis group you selected are displayed in Outlook Express, in essentially the same way that your e-mail messages are displayed.

The first time you view a newsgroup, don't be surprised if it takes several minutes for the messages to download. The next time you view that newsgroup, the postings will appear much faster because Outlook Express downloads only the new messages.

NOTE *If you don't see any postings, the group isn't active and doesn't have any messages. Click the News groups button on the toolbar to access the list of all the groups. Type **elvis** in the text box labeled Display newsgroups which contain, click another group on the list, and then click Go to.*

▶ Subscribing to a newsgroup

Once you find a group that you like, you can subscribe to it. When you subscribe to a newsgroup, a subfolder for it is placed in your news server folder in the Outlook Express Folder list pane. Anytime you're using Outlook Express, all you have to do is click the news server folder and then click the specific newsgroup subfolder to read that newsgroup's postings.

In this exercise, you learn two different ways to subscribe to a newsgroup.

❶ You can subscribe while you're viewing a group. Since you're currently looking at postings from one of the elvis groups (you opened it in the previous exercise), select Tools ➣ Subscribe to this newsgroup.

❷ To verify the subscription, click the news server folder in the Folder list pane. The folder opens and the newsgroup name is displayed.

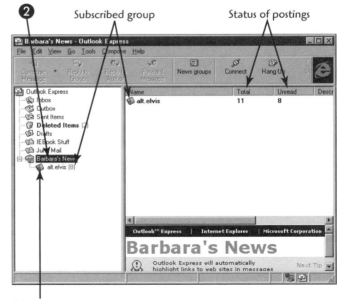

Subscribed group   Status of postings

Subscription icon

Subscribing to a newsgroup

VISUAL BONUS

Looking at the Newsgroups Window

This illustration shows the arrangement of the Outlook Express Newsgroups window.

Folder list pane

News server folder

Subscribed newsgroups

Selected newsgroup

The newsgroup window shows a list of the postings.

Status of postings

Title bar displaying open newsgroup name

Menu bar

News toolbar

Selected header

Header pane

Preview pane

Threads

Posting corresponding to selected header

❸ You can also subscribe to a group directly from the Newsgroups dialog box. Click the News groups button on the Newsgroup toolbar. The Newsgroups dialog box appears. If you've set up multiple news servers, click the one you want to access.

❹ Type **newbie** in the text box below Display newsgroups which contain. *Newbie* is an Internet term for a new user. In a moment, all of the groups appear that contain the word newbie in their titles.

TIP

If you want to find a special discussion group or conduct a comprehensive search of all discussion groups, visit http://sunsite.unc.edu:80/usenet-i/groups-html/ *on the Web for a*

Unsubscribing from a newsgroup

master list of existing newsgroups. You'll find each group listed with a brief description.

5 Highlight a group name from the list (preferably `alt.newbie`) and click Subscribe. A subscription icon appears next to the group name to let you know that you're subscribed to the group.

Unsubscribing from a newsgroup

Let's face it, tastes change. The group that seemed so interesting last week can seem pretty boring today! Or you can feel overwhelmed by the volume of messages posted to each of your subscribed groups. For example, I belonged to a group of technical writers, a group of people interested in Mongolian cooking, and a group that loved a popular Thursday night sitcom—all at the same time. When I got too busy to keep up with the postings of all three groups, I unsubscribed from the group that wasn't quite as scintillating as the other two.

Unsubscribing from a group is simple. Best of all, if you change your mind later, you can subscribe to the group again.

1 Outlook Express must be open for you to unsubscribe from a newsgroup. If Outlook Express isn't open, click the Launch Mail button on the Quick Launch toolbar.

2 Click the news server folder in the Folder list pane. The folder opens and displays the names of all the newsgroups to which you're subscribed.

3 Right-click the group `alt.newbie`.

4 Choose Unsubscribe from this newsgroup on the pop-up menu.

5 You can also unsubscribe from a newsgroup from the Newsgroups dialog box. To access the box, click the News groups button on the Newsgroup toolbar.

6 If you've set up more than one news server, select the one you want from the left frame.

7 When the Newsgroups dialog box opens, click the Subscribed tab at the bottom of the window. A list displays, showing the names of the groups you've subscribed to. A subscription icon appears to the left of each newsgroup name.

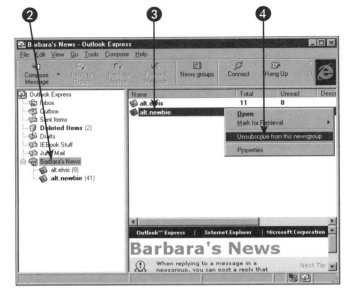

8 Click the name of the group you want to remove.

9 Click the Unsubscribe button. The group name remains in the box, but the subscription icon is removed. The next time you check your subscribed newsgroups, the one you unsubscribed from will not be displayed. (Since I've subscribed to a few more newsgroups, your screen may look a little different than mine.)

10 Click OK. The Newsgroups dialog box closes, and you're returned to the Outlook Express Newsgroups window.

Displaying new groups

Your ISP adds new groups to the list often. So that you don't need to look through the entire list of newsgroups for the newest entries, you can display the new groups in their own list.

1 From within Outlook Express, click the News groups button on the Newsgroup toolbar. The Newsgroups dialog box displays.

2 If you've set up more than one news server, select the one you want to check for new newsgroups.

3 Click the New tab at the bottom of the window to display a list of the new newsgroups. You can scroll through the list or search it by typing a keyword.

4 To view the postings of a new group, first click the group name to select it.

5 Click the Go to button.

6 To subscribe to the group, first click the group name to select it.

7 Click the Subscribe button.

8 Click OK to close the Newsgroups dialog box and return to the Outlook Express Newsgroups window.

Subscription icon removed

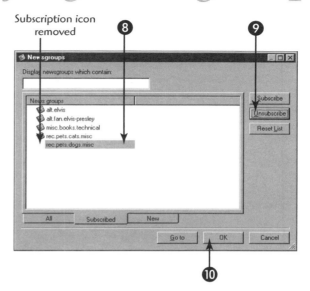

Using Outlook Express for News

11

Reading news postings

WORKING WITH NEWSGROUP POSTINGS

Newsgroup postings (also called articles) are displayed as headers on the Outlook Express Newsgroups window. Headers contain the sender, subject, date and time, and size of the posting. When you click a header, the body of the posting (the actual message) is displayed in the Preview pane below. Just like you did with your e-mail messages, you can drag any posting into one of the folders you've set up for mail. You can even set up new folders to hold postings or to hold postings and mail.

Reading news postings

Now that you've subscribed to a newsgroup, it's time to read the postings.

❶ If you're following the exercises in order, the Outlook Express Newsgroups window should be open on the screen. If it's not, click the Launch Mail button on the Quick Launch toolbar to open Outlook Express. When the program opens, select Go ➤ News.

❷ Click the news server folder in the Folder list pane. The folder opens and a list of all the groups to which you've subscribed appears.

❸ Double-click the group whose postings you want to view. The headers appear in the Header pane. A closed envelope icon indicates that the posting is unread.

❹ Scroll through the list and find a header that sounds interesting.

❺ Read the message by clicking the message header in the Header pane. The message is displayed in the Preview pane. When you read a message, the closed envelope icon changes to a letter icon.

❻ Double-click a header to display it in its own message window. If the posting is lengthy, opening it in a window makes it easier to read.

❼ Close the message window by clicking the Close button at the top right corner.

Envelope icon identifies unread postings.　　Expanded thread　　Letter icon identifies read postings.　　Click a column head to sort postings.

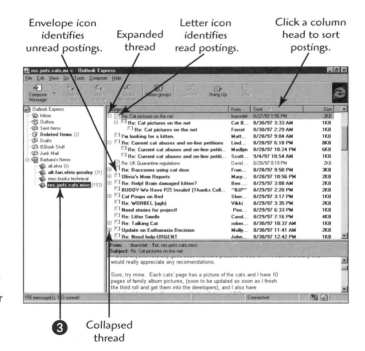

❸ Collapsed thread

8 A + (plus) sign next to a header indicates that the message header you're viewing is the most recent in a *thread*, or series of messages about the same subject and based on the same original message. Click the + sign to expand the thread and display the other messages.

9 When a thread is expanded, the + sign changes to a – (minus) sign. Click the – sign to collapse the thread.

10 If you want to sort the newsgroup headers in the window by column, click the column heading you want to sort by.

11 To switch between ascending and descending order, click the column header again.

12 Postings that you read will not be displayed the next time you view the postings of the group. Often you are able to determine from the header if you want to read a particular posting and may identify several that you don't want to read. To mark an individual posting that you don't want to look it as read so that it won't display the next time you open the newsgroup, right-click the header.

13 Choose Mark as Read on the pop-up menu.

14 If the posting is part of a thread that you don't want to read, choose Mark Thread as Read on the pop-up menu.

15 If you don't have the time to read all the postings or simply want to mark them all as read, select Edit ➤ Mark All as Read. The next time you open the newsgroup, those postings won't appear.

13 **14**

```
Open
Combine and Decode
Print

Mark as Read
Mark Thread as Read
Mark as Unread

Reply to Newsgroup
Reply to Author
Forward by Mail
Forward as Attachment
Cancel

Mark Message for Download

Properties
```

11

Using Outlook Express for News

Posting messages

Newsgroups have a set of rules and their own unique phrases. For example, newsgroup postings should never be typed in all uppercase letters. All caps is considered to be shouting and in very poor taste. (I FOUND OUT THAT RULE THE HARD WAY.) If you don't know the rules and violate the code, you may get *flamed*, or lambasted publicly in newsgroup postings.

Fortunately, most of the rules you need to know are just good common sense. For example, you wouldn't post a list of dog food recipes to a list of technical writers. Nor would you monopolize a newsgroup with your personal views and opinions, over and over again. These and other rules fall into a class of manners called *Netiquette*. If you want to look at some Web pages that contain great information about posting to newsgroups, A Primer on How to Work with the Usenet Community at `www.cis.ohio-state.edu/hypertext/faq/usenet/usenet/primer/part1/faq.html` and Rules for Posting to Usenet at `www.cis.ohio-state.edu/hypertext/faq/usenet/usenet/posting-rules/part1/faq.html` are great sites to visit.

In addition to using good Netiquette, you need to learn some new terms. An impromptu language has sprung up in newsgroup postings. The following list is a composite of some common abbreviations used in newsgroups (and in e-mail and chat) with their translations.

Phrase	What it Means
BTW	By the Way
FYI	For Your Information
IMHO	In My Humble Opinion
TIA	Thanks in Advance (also sometimes written advTHANKSance)
RTFM	Read the Friendly Manual (The word *manual* here refers to any documentation.)
LOL	[I] Laughed Out Loud [at what you wrote]
ROTFL	[I am] Rolling on the Floor Laughing [at what you wrote]
RSN	Real Soon Now

Use some of these terms in your newsgroup postings. Have fun!

Posting messages

You can make two types of newsgroup postings. The first is a reply you send in response to an existing posting. Replying to a newsgroup posting is a lot like sending an e-mail message, except you generally send the message to the group instead of to an individual. (You can reply to the author if you want to, but doing so defeats the purpose of using the newsgroup as a public forum.) You can also reply to the newsgroup and the author.

The other type of posting is a new message you create. When you post a new message, your posting may start a new thread.

1 To send a reply that will appear as a posting on the newsgroup, first click the header of the posting you want to answer.

2 Click the Reply to Group button on the Newsgroup toolbar. A new window opens with the text of the original posting displayed.

3 Type your response.

4 Click the Post button on the message window toolbar to send the posting.

TIP

When you send a posting to a newsgroup, it takes a while to show up on the list. Unlike e-mail, which is delivered instantly, your posting must go through a series of computer systems to reach the list. It may take up to a couple of hours to appear. If you reply to a moderated group, your posting will be evaluated and may never appear.

5 To reply just to the author of a posting, click the header of the posting.

6 Click the Reply to Author button on the Newsgroup toolbar.

7 Type your response in the message window that appears.

8 Click the Post button on the message window toolbar to send the posting.

9 To reply to both the newsgroup and the author, click the header of the posting.

10 Select Compose ➤ Reply to Newsgroup and Author.

11 Type your reply in the message window.

12 Click the Post button on the message window toolbar to send the posting.

13 To forward a newsgroup posting to another person, click the header of the posting.

4 Message will be posted to this newsgroup

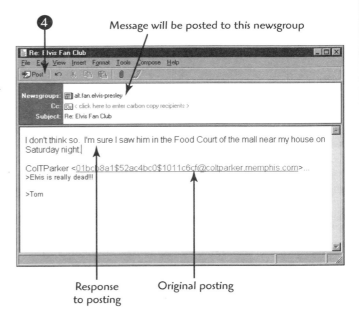

Response to posting   Original posting

Downloading new messages

⑭ Click the Forward Message button on the Newsgroup toolbar to bring up a message window.

⑮ Enter the e-mail address of recipient.

⑯ Click the Post button on the message window toolbar to forward the posting.

NOTE *If you're replying to the author of a message or forwarding it to someone else, you can treat it like regular e-mail. If you need help with sending e-mail messages, refer to Lesson 10.*

⑰ To write a new posting for a newsgroup, make sure that the newsgroup is open on your screen.

⑱ Click the Compose Message button on the Newsgroup toolbar. A message window appears with the newsgroup's address entered on the Newsgroups line.

⑲ Type the subject of your posting on the Subject line.

⑳ Type the text of your posting in the message area.

㉑ Once you've checked it for accuracy and are satisfied with the posting, click the Post button on the message window toolbar.

Downloading new messages

While you're looking at newsgroup postings, you may want to check for the newest ones.

❶ Select Tools ➤ Download this Newsgroup. The Download Newsgroup dialog box appears.

❷ Check the box next to Get the following items.

❸ Click the option button next to New messages (headers and bodies).

❹ Click OK. Outlook Express connects to the news server, retrieves the new messages, and displays them in the Header pane.

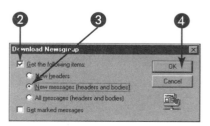

WORKING OFFLINE

Outlook Express enables you to work offline. If you only have one phone line or if you're traveling, working offline makes good sense. You can briefly connect to the Internet, download the headers of a newsgroup to which you've subscribed, and disconnect. While you're offline, you can mark the headers of the postings that look interesting and then connect to the Internet and download the complete posting later. Considering that some newsgroups have about 500 postings a day, working offline in this way can save you a lot of valuable connect time.

Setting up offline reading

In this exercise, you make changes to the properties of a newsgroup so that you can work offline.

1 From within Outlook Express, double-click the news server folder on the Folder list pane that contains the newsgroup you want to set up for offline viewing. The list of subscribed newsgroups appears.

2 Right-click the name of the newsgroup for which you want to download headers.

3 Choose Properties on the pop-up menu to display the Properties dialog box.

4 Click the Download tab.

5 Check the box next to When downloading this newsgroup, retrieve.

6 Click the option button next to New headers.

7 Click OK. The Properties dialog box closes.

8 Repeat steps 2 through 7 for any other newsgroups you wish to include in the download.

9 When you're ready to download the headers, you must be connected to the Internet. Select Tools ➢ Download All. Outlook Express connects to your ISP's news server and

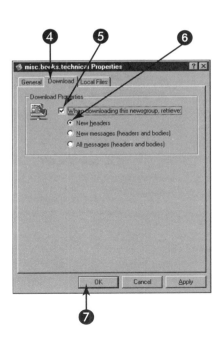

Downloading the postings

downloads the headers of the messages in the newsgroups you specified.

10 Disconnect from the Internet.

When you finish this exercise, immediately move to the next exercise.

Downloading the postings to read offline

In this exercise, you look through the downloaded headers and select the postings you want to see. Then you connect to the Internet to retrieve the postings.

1 Display the downloaded headers for a newsgroup by first double-clicking the news server folder in the Folder list pane.

2 Click the name of the newsgroup for which you downloaded the headers.

3 Look through the headers. If a header sounds interesting and you want to download the complete posting when you connect to the Internet later, right-click the header.

4 Click Mark Message for Download on the pop-up menu.

5 Repeat steps 3 and 4 for each posting you want to download.

6 If you've downloaded headers for additional newsgroups, click the next newsgroup you want to open. Repeat steps 3 and 4 for each posting you want to download.

7 When you've marked the headers, minimize Outlook Express.

8 Reconnect to the Internet in the normal manner.

9 Switch back to Outlook Express by clicking the Outlook Express button on the Windows taskbar.

10 Select Tools ➤ Download All. Once again, Outlook Express connects to your ISP's news server, and this time, downloads the bodies of the postings you specified.

11 Disconnect from the Internet. You can now read the postings at your convenience.

SKILLS CHALLENGE: JOINING THE WORLD OF NEWSGROUPS

You've covered a lot of ground in this lesson! Just think, a short while ago, you probably didn't know much about newsgroups. This challenge tests your knowledge of the material covered in this lesson, including finding and subscribing to a newsgroup and replying to a posting. Feel free to substitute a keyword for a group that interests you if the one in the challenge isn't something you find interesting.

1 Open Outlook Express if it is not open already.

 What are newsgroups?

2 Display a list of the newsgroups from your news server.

3 Find a group that contains the abbreviation UFO in its title.

4 Subscribe to one of the UFO groups.

2 *Can you read the postings of a newsgroup if you haven't subscribed?*

5 Open the new UFO group you just joined.

6 Read the first message.

7 Display the body of the second message in its own window.

8 Close the message window when you've finished reading the posting.

9 Choose a message and send a reply to the newsgroup.

10 After you've read a few more postings, mark all of the messages as read.

11 Unsubscribe from the group.

3 *Can you subscribe to and unsubscribe from any newsgroup as often as you wish?*

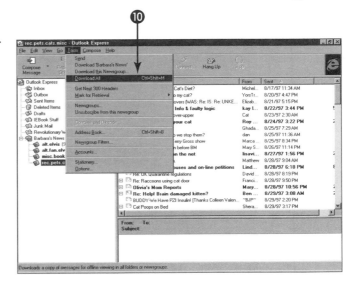

Troubleshooting

TROUBLESHOOTING

As you work with newsgroups, you might have a few questions. The following table shows some of the common questions that newbies ask about newsgroups.

Problem	Solution
I'm so overwhelmed by the number of groups. How do I find the ones I want?	Use the search field (the text box labeled Display newsgroups which contain) on the Newsgroups dialog box to look for group names that contain the keywords you want. Or you can always cruise to the Web and go to the Master List at `sunsite.unc.edu:80/usenet-i/groups-html/` for a list of groups and descriptions. As a third alternative, take a few minutes and just scroll the list of group names and look for ones that interest you.
Now that I've subscribed to a newsgroup, I feel too shy to post a message but I don't want the group members to think I'm rude.	Don't worry; they don't even know you're a member of the group. It's a good idea to hang back for a bit after you've joined a new group and follow the message threads for a while before you speak up (this practice is called lurking). When you're ready to post, let everyone know you're a newbie. Or if you decide you're really not interested in the group's topic, unsubscribe from the group.

Problem	Solution
If I open Outlook Express and then switch to another program on my computer, I sometimes see an error message that I need to refresh the screen when I switch back to Outlook Express. Why?	When Outlook Express doesn't detect any action for a while, it displays that message. As long as you're still connected to the Internet, select View ➢ Refresh on the Outlook Express menu bar.

WRAP UP

In this lesson, you exercised the following skills:

- Configuring Outlook Express as a newsreader
- Finding and looking at newsgroups
- Subscribing to and unsubscribing from newsgroups
- Working offline

In the next lesson, you learn about Microsoft Chat, a fun way to keep in touch with your friends.

TRY OUT THE

INTERACTIVE TUTORIALS

ON YOUR CD!

Using Microsoft Chat

45 MINUTES

GOALS

This lesson shows you how to use Microsoft Chat to participate in online conversations with people across the Internet. Unlike the conversations in discussion groups that you learned about in the last lesson, chat conversations occur in real time and can be viewed as comic strips or plain text. In this lesson, you complete the following exercises:

- Using Chat for the first time
- Personalizing Chat
- Conversing in a chat room
- Saying it in different ways
- Changing rooms
- Creating a new room
- Inviting users
- Using Whisper Boxes
- Changing to text view

Get ready

GET READY

Before you begin this lesson, you must have Internet Explorer installed (see Appendix A) and be connected to the Internet. You're going to have fun working through the exercises as you communicate with people across the Internet. When you complete the lesson, you'll be able to participate in textual chat conversations.

TRY OUT THE
INTERACTIVE TUTORIALS
ON YOUR CD!

WHAT IS MICROSOFT CHAT?

Microsoft Chat is a component of Internet Explorer that allows people to have real-time text conversations over the Internet with others from all over the world. Chatting on the Internet is similar to attending an international convention at a big convention center. A convention center usually has many different rooms, each hosting a group that's talking about a different topic. In each of these rooms, people discuss issues as a group, while individuals whisper to one another at the same time.

On the Internet, instead of going to a convention center, you go to a *chat server,* a computer that houses chat rooms. Once you connect to a chat server, you see a list of individual chat rooms. A chat room is a virtual meeting room, where people come together to discuss different topics. Just like in a convention center, some rooms are open to the public and others are private rooms that require an invitation to enter.

In a chat room, you type your conversation instead of speaking it. However, Microsoft Chat enables you to express emotions, send thoughts, and whisper private messages. Since not everyone who appears in your chat room is using Microsoft Chat, some options may not be available during your conversation.

Microsoft Chat is just one of many different types of Internet Relay Chat (IRC) programs available on the Internet. Microsoft Chat is different from these other chat programs because, in addition to viewing plain-text conversations line by line, you can view your conversations in comic strip form. In fact, the earlier version of the program was named Comic Chat, and the new version, Microsoft Chat, is still often called Comic Chat by most people.

Using Chat for the first time

CONFIGURING CHAT

In order to use Chat, you need to answer a few questions before you jump into a conversation. First, you need to tell Chat your nickname, the name you'll be identified by while you're chatting. You can use your real name or a bogus one, as long as no one else is using it during the current Chat session. If the nickname you want has been claimed by another chatter, Chat asks you to choose a new one. When you start Chat for the first time, you'll be prompted for your nickname. Chat saves your nickname for future sessions, but you're free to change it whenever you want.

Chat also needs the name of the chat server you want to use. If you don't know the name of any chat servers to log on to, don't sweat it. When you open Chat, a default Microsoft chat server is selected for you. You also specify the name of the room you want to chat in. The first time you use Chat, you're given the option of entering the Comic Chat room or entering a different one. When you open Chat in future sessions, you can return to the room you last chatted in, or you can view a list of all the available rooms and make a new selection.

Using Chat for the first time

❶ Click the Start button on the Windows taskbar.

❷ Select Programs ➢ Microsoft Chat. The program opens in its own window with the Enter New Nickname dialog box asking for your nickname.

❸ Type your desired nickname in the Nickname box.

> **TIP**
>
> *Your chat room nickname is called a* nick. *Most people use the same nick every time they chat, but you can change it anytime. You can even change your nick during a chat session.*

❹ Click OK to close the Enter New Nickname dialog box.

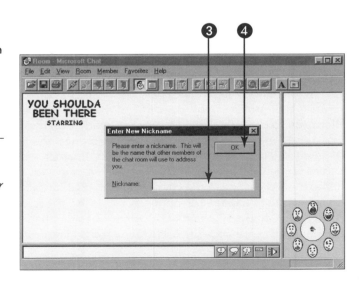

Personalizing Chat

5 The Connect dialog box appears and prompts you for more information. Since you haven't chatted before, the Favorites box is blank. Unless you know a specific chat server you'd like to connect to, accept the default server of `comicsrv.microsoft.com`.

6 Make sure the Go to chat room option is selected and that the #Comic_Chat room name is displayed. (The #Comic_Chat room is specifically designed for people using Microsoft Chat and its earlier version, Comic Chat.)

7 Click OK to close the Connect dialog box.

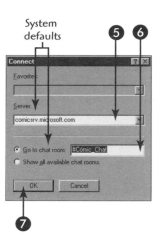

You are now in the #Comic_Chat room, ready to begin your conversation. In order to observe proper *Chatiquette* (Chat etiquette), it's a good idea for you to just observe any ongoing conversations for a few minutes before letting everyone know what you have to say.

TIP

Even if you don't actively engage in the ongoing conversation, the people in the chat room know you are there. Don't be surprised if someone says hello to you.

Personalizing Chat

When you're using Chat, you can allow people to know as much or as little about you as you please by completing a profile. You can include your real name (or some other of your choosing), your e-mail address, the URL of your home page, and a brief description of yourself. Your profile can be viewed by other chatters. Chat also allows you to control how you interact with other chatters.

Some fun options include the ability to change how you appear to others and how the chat session appears on your screen. Once you enter a room, Chat assigns a cartoon character, or *avatar*, named Anna to appear as you in the comic strip conversation. However, if Anna's not quite *you*, use the option available in Chat to easily change your character to one of the other 11 comic characters. In addition, you can change the background scene and the number of

Personalizing Chat ◀

comic panels that display in the comic strip version of the chat session on your computer.

1 Chat should be open and on the screen from the previous exercise. If it's not, open Chat now by selecting Start ➤ Programs ➤ Microsoft Chat.

2 Select View ➤ Options. The Microsoft Chat Options dialog box appears with six tabs across the top.

3 Click the Personal Info tab. You use this panel to record the personal information that you want to include in your Chat profile. Other chatters can access your profile to learn more about you.

4 Fill in as much information about yourself as you want by clicking inside the boxes and typing the information. Your nickname, or *nick*, is the only mandatory field that needs to contain information. The optional fields include your real name, your e-mail address, your home page, and a brief description. (If you don't want to list your real information, you don't have to. I use my dog's name instead of my own!)

5 Click the Comics View tab to change the layout of the comic strip.

6 Click the down arrow in the Page Layout section of the box and choose the 3 Panels Wide option from the drop-down list. Setting this option causes the comic strip rendering of your conversation to be displayed in three panels across instead of the default two.

TIP

Maximize Chat by using a three-panel comic strip. You'll enjoy your session more if you have an unobstructed view of the conversation.

7 Click the Background tab. Three backgrounds are available for your comic strip.

8 Click each of the backgrounds to see how they appear in the Preview box.

Only
mandatory field
3   **5**

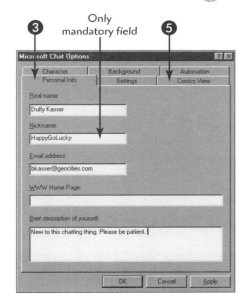

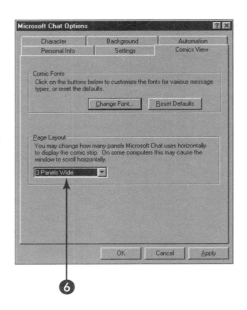

6

12

Using Microsoft Chat

Personalizing Chat

9 Click your favorite background to select it.

10 Click the Character tab. A list of available comic character names appears.

11 Click each name to see the character associated with it in the Preview box.

12 Choose the one that you like best or that most resembles you.

13 Click each facial expression below the sample character to change the character's expression and body position. Since the character is a representation of you, choose carefully!

14 Click OK to close the Microsoft Chat Options dialog box and return to the chat screen. All the changes you made are now in effect. You're ready to talk!

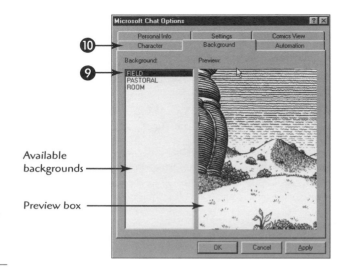

Available backgrounds

Preview box

NOTE

Changing the background and the number of panels affects how the conversation looks on your computer monitor only. Since all the chatters in the room can set up their computers any way they like, the conversation can look different to each of the participants.

HAVING CONVERSATIONS

Now that you've set up your options, it's time to share your opinions with the world. When you chat, your words appear in a bubble over your character's head, just like in a comic strip. You can manually change your character's facial expression or let the program change it for you. Microsoft Chat changes your expression randomly each time you make a statement unless you use a word or expression that is preprogrammed to invoke a particular expression. For example, if you type the word laugh, your character appears to be laughing. While you're in a chat room, you can think aloud, perform an action, and even whisper privately to someone else.

Available characters

Preview

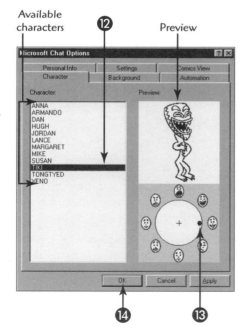

The Microsoft Chat Window

When you chat in comic mode, the Microsoft Chat window displays the conversation, gives you information about your current character, and provides a way to change your character's expression. The Chat window also includes an area for you to type text for the conversation and buttons to change the way the text is presented to others.

The Microsoft Chat window during a conversation in comic mode

Menu bar
Create Room button
Title of chat
Text View button
Chat Room List button
User List button
Compose box
Status bar showing room name

Whisper Box button
Member List pane
View pane
Your character
Say
Think
Whisper
Action
Sounds
Emotion wheel
Number of characters in room

12

Using Microsoft Chat

Conversing in a chat room

In this exercise, you chat with others in the Comic Chat room you entered earlier. You also change your character's facial expression to match the conversation. If you're not already in a chat room, reopen Chat and enter the #Comic_Chat room.

TIP

If the #Comic_Chat room is full, Microsoft Chat will attempt to put you into a similar room, such as #Comic_Chat1.

Conversing in a chat room

1 Make sure that your cursor (a flashing vertical line) appears in the empty Compose box. If it doesn't, click inside the Compose box.

2 Type **Hi room!** or another greeting of your choice.

3 Click the first button to the right of the box called the Say button. Alternatively, you can press Ctrl+Y to enter your comment. Your message appears on the screen in a bubble over your character's head. Since chatters are a vocal group, wait a moment and someone will respond to you.

TIP *Don't be confused if what you see at first doesn't make sense. What may appear to be random statements from other chatters are probably comments of an ongoing conversation. Remember that you may be entering in the middle of a heated argument or droll discussion.*

4 The response to your comment appears on the screen in a comic pane. Type your response in the Compose box and click the Say button. All typed conversation appears in a bubble over the speaker's head. If another chatter begins a statement with your name, your character appears in the comic pane with the speaker, even if you haven't said anything.

5 Make your character smile by clicking the happy face in the Emotion wheel at the right of the chat screen.

6 Type a message in the Compose box and click Say. Alternatively, you can press Enter to register your comment. Your character appears on the screen smiling, and your text is in a bubble.

7 Along with providing this manual control for facial expressions, Chat automatically associates some words and phrases with a particular expression. For example, if someone in the room says something funny, type **LOL** (laughed out loud).

8 Click Say or press Enter. Your character automatically appears to be laughing.

9 Type some text followed by three or more exclamation points in the Compose box. If you can't think of anything else, type **I'm**

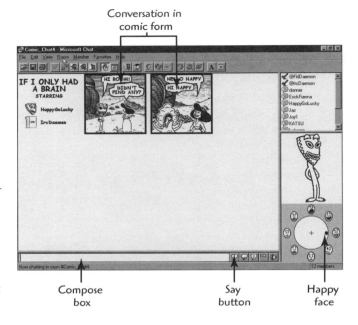

Conversation in comic form

Compose box

Say button

Happy face

Laughing

so happy to be here!!! Be sure to include the exclamation marks.

🔟 Press Enter or click Say to send the text to the others in the room. Your character appears on the screen screaming your text.

Since conversational cues like body language and tone of voice are unavailable in chat sessions, chatters have developed some conventions to say things quickly and to express emotions. They use abbreviations and *emoticons,* or pictures drawn from keyboard characters. Here are some common shortcuts.

Shortcut	Meaning
BRB	Be Right Back
GMTA	Great Minds Think Alike
HHIS	Hanging Head in Shame
IMHO	In My Humble Opinion
L8R	Later
L8R G8R	Later 'Gator
LMSO	Laughing My Socks Off
OIC	Oh, I See
TTYL	Talk To You Later
:-{}	Blowing a kiss
\-o	Bored
:-c	Bummed out
(((((name))))	Hug (cyber hug)
@[_]~~	Mug of hot coffee or tea

TIP *Since Microsoft Chat has a limited number of available characters, it's likely that more than one person in a room will have the same character. If you get confused about who's who, hold your mouse on a character in the View pane. The nickname of the person controlling that character appears in a screen tip.*

Saying it in different ways

Saying it in different ways

In addition to using facial expressions to get your point across, you can also vary the way you say something. In Microsoft Chat, you can perform an action, such as handing someone a soda have a thought, or whisper privately to someone else in the same room. When you perform an action, whatever you type appears in a box above your character's head with the statement preceded by your nickname. Actions are limited only by your imagination. Thoughts appear above your character's head in a thought bubble. Whispers appear in a dashed bubble that only those whispering back and forth can see.

If you're not already in a chat room, reopen Chat and enter the #Comic_Chat room.

1. When you meet someone you like in a chat room, you might want to give the person a drink or perform some other action. Make sure that your cursor is inside the Compose box. If it isn't, click inside the box.

2. In Chat, you perform actions textually. Type your action in the box exactly as you want it to appear. Type **Hands everyone in the room a root beer**.

3. Click the Action button (the fourth button to the right of the Compose box) or press Ctrl+I. The action appears on the screen in a box over your character's head with your nickname before it.

4. You can express a thought without speaking to anyone in particular. First, click inside the Compose box.

5. Type your thought. If you can't think of a meaningful thought, type **I wonder where I am?**

6. Click the Think button (the second button to the right of the Compose box) or press Ctrl+T. Your thought appears in a thought bubble above your character's head.

7. If you meet someone in a chat room that you want to engage in private conversation, you can whisper your comments. In the Member List pane, click the name of the person you want to whisper to.

> **TIP**
>
> *If you want to learn more about a person, right-click the name in the Member List pane and then click Get Profile. The chatter's profile is displayed in a comic strip in the View pane. If Get Profile is not available*

on the menu, it means that the chatter is not using Microsoft Chat.

8 Whisper to your new friend. Type the text you want to whisper in the Compose box.

9 Click the Whisper button (the third button to the right of the Compose box). The text appears in a dashed bubble above your character's head. Even though it appears in a regular comic frame, only you and the person you are whispering to can see the whisper.

Don't close Chat yet! You explore many more Chat options in the next few exercises.

FINDING NEW PLACES AND PEOPLE

In your exploration of chat rooms, you sometimes come across a room that is empty or one that is full of people you think are dull or uninteresting. You also discover rooms that have freewheeling, uncensored discussions. The people you chat with range from intelligent, reasonable adults to stupid, foul-mouthed children (not to mention intelligent, reasonable children and stupid, foul-mouthed adults!). When the conversation in the room begins to turn you off or bore you, change rooms. At any given time of the day or night, hundreds of rooms are usually available on any server. If you don't find any rooms you like, you can create your own. You can even invite other people to join you in your room.

Changing rooms

In this exercise, you leave your current chat room and explore some others that are available on the server. The chat session from the previous exercise should still be active. If not, open Chat and follow the prompts to enter a room and begin a conversation.

Whispered (private) conversations

Regular conversations

Creating a new room

1 Select Room ➤ Room List or click the Chat Room List button on the toolbar. The Chat Room List dialog box appears.

2 The Chat Room List dialog box lists all the chat rooms available on the server and the number of members in each room. Some rooms have topics associated with them as well. Scroll through the list to see all your chat room choices.

3 Double-click the name of a room that interests you. A new room appears with its title displayed in both the title bar and the status bar. The Member List pane now contains the nicknames of all of the people in this new room.

4 If you don't want to scroll through the entire list looking for a particular topic, narrow the list by searching for the topic of your choice. Select Room ➤ Room List to redisplay the Chat Room List dialog box.

5 Click inside the box labeled Display chat rooms that contain.

6 Type **Comic**. As you type the word, the list of rooms in the window narrows to include only rooms that contain the word comic in their name. These are the rooms devoted to general Comic Chat discussion.

7 Double-click the name of a room on the Chat Room List. In a moment, the new room appears. You can now chat in the selected room.

List of available chat rooms

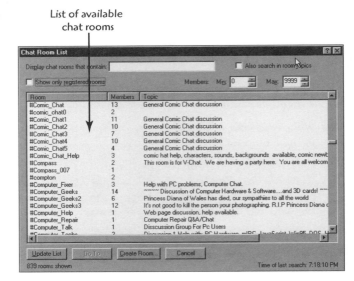

TIP *One of the rooms that appears in your list is the Comic_Chat_Help room which is one of the best places to go if you have any questions about how to use Chat. The chatters in Comic_Chat_Help are very willing and able to assist you in using the program.*

Creating a new room

Sometimes no rooms are available on the server that meet your needs, or all the good rooms are already full. That's no problem—you can create your own chat room! The biggest bonus of creating your own room is that you have control over many of the room's features. You should still have Chat open from the last exercise when you begin this one.

① Select Room ➢ Create Room or click the Create Room button on the toolbar. The Create Chat Room dialog box appears.

② Click inside the Chat room name box and type the name of your new room. If you're at a loss for words, type **mynewroom**. The name must be one word since spaces aren't allowed.

③ Click inside the Topic box and type a conversational topic. For this exercise, type **Come in and say Hello**.

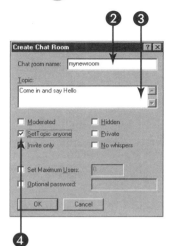

| TIP |

When you create a room, you become the room host, the person in charge of the room. The host of a room is granted special privileges, like the ability to throw others out of the room, set the room topic, and even make other people cohosts. Hosts are labeled by a gavel next to their name in the Member List pane.

④ The next step is to select options that define the nature of the room. You can select more than one, but for this exercise, only click the checkbox labeled SetTopic anyone. Here's what these options mean:

Option	What It Does
Moderated	Restricts chatting. In a moderated room, only a room host or someone designated by the host can speak. All others are spectators.
Hidden	Keeps the room off of the Chat Room List. Users must know it exists to visit the room. Creating a hidden room is great if you want to set up a family chat, for example.
SetTopic anyone	Permits anyone to change the room topic. If this option is not checked, only room hosts can set the topic.

continued

Inviting users

Option	What It Does
Private	Specifies if information about who is in the room is available to others outside the room.
Invite only	Allows only participants who have been invited to enter the room. (You learn how to invite chat participants in the next exercise.)
No whispers	Prevents private conversations in the room.
Set Maximum Users	Sets an upper limit on the number of people in a room.
Optional password	Designates a password that a user must know to enter the room.

5 Click OK. You are now in your own chat room.

Don't exit the program yet. You need to invite people in to chat in your newly created chat room!

Inviting users

Now that you've created your own room, it's time to get some people inside and chatting. If you wait long enough, chatters are likely to come by, but you can also invite them. In this exercise, you access a list of all chatters on your server and invite some of them to come to your room. For this exercise, it's a good idea to have a few friends who are also chatting if you're shy about extending invitations to strangers.

1 Select Member ➤ User List on the menu bar or click the User List button on the toolbar. The User List dialog box appears.

2 Make sure that the option button next to All users is selected in the Search for box.

3 Click the Update List button to get a current list of users on the server. The list includes the users' nicknames as well as some information about the users' computer names and ISPs or their identities.

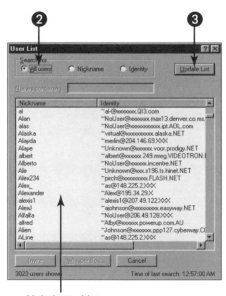

Alphabetical list
of users on the server

If you want to find a particular user, choose the Nickname option and type the nickname of the chatter in the Names containing box. Click the Update List button to show only users that match the name you typed. If the chatter you are looking for is currently logged on to the same server as you are, the nickname appears on the list.

4 Scroll through the list and click the nickname of a chatter you want to invite to your room. The name and identity appear highlighted.

5 Click the Invite button. A box appears, confirming that you invited the person to your room.

6 Click OK to close the box. You return to the User List dialog box.

7 Repeat steps 4, 5, and 6 to invite others into the room.

8 Close the User List dialog box by clicking its Close button in the top right corner.

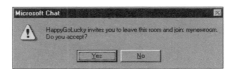

The users you invite see an alert box on their screens, letting them know that you would enjoy the pleasure of their company. They can accept the invitation by clicking Yes or decline it by clicking No. When a chatter joins your room, the person's nickname appears in the Member List pane. You are not directly notified if the chatter declines your generous offer.

With all the people in your room now, you should be having a wonderful time!

COMMUNICATING IN DIFFERENT WAYS

Now it's time to add even more functionality to your chat sessions by learning about two additional communication options: Whisper Boxes and text–mode chat.

As you develop more online friends, it becomes harder to meet them all in the same room. Sometimes you and your friends are participating in chat discussions in different rooms but still want to talk to each other. With Chat, you can whisper to people in other

Using Whisper Boxes

rooms on the same server by using a Whisper Box. The Whisper Box works like the whispers you sent earlier in this lesson since only the chatters who are whispering can see them. However, the Whisper Box can cut across chat rooms.

The ability to display conversation in comic strip form makes Microsoft Chat a fun and enjoyable program to use. However, with only 12 characters to choose from, more than one person is bound to have the same character as another. Trying to keep track of which Armando character is talking can detract from the conversation. For the times when comic view becomes difficult to follow, Microsoft Chat allows you to view your conversations as text.

The exercises in this section show you how to use these two Microsoft Chat enhancements.

Using Whisper Boxes

In this exercise, you have a Whisper Box conversation with someone. Before you begin the exercise, you might want to call a friend and perform the steps together. Otherwise, consider telling the chat room participants that you're practicing your Whisper Box technique so you don't give other chatters the wrong idea.

1. If it's not already open, click the Start button and select Programs ➢ Microsoft Chat. When the program opens, the Connect box appears.

2. Click OK to return to the last room you visited.

3. Open the User List dialog box by clicking the User List button on the Chat toolbar.

4. Scroll through the list to find someone you would like to whisper to and click that person's name.

5. Click the Whisper Box button. A Whisper Box appears in front of your Chat window with a tab for the person you chose.

6. Type your message in the Compose box at the bottom of the Whisper Box.

7. Click the Whisper button to send your message. Your message and any responses appear in the top part of the box. Messages are presented as text only, with no comic characters.

8 While you are whispering, you can also chat with others in the room you're in. Click anywhere in the Chat window to return to the actual program.

9 Return to the Whisper Box by clicking the Whisper Box button on the Windows taskbar at the bottom of your screen.

10 When the private conversation is complete, close the Whisper Box by clicking the Close button. You return to the Chat window.

Leave Chat open for the next exercise.

Changing to text view

In text view, all the messages typed by users are presented as straight text. Thoughts, actions, whispers, and regular conversation are presented in different colors. By default, statements made by the host are displayed in bold. The View pane shows new room members in green text and room departures in red text.

In this exercise, you change from comic view to text view. Before you begin this exercise, Chat should be open from the last exercise with a few panes of conversation visible.

1 Select View ➤ Text View or click the Text View button on the Chat toolbar. The screen changes from comic view to text view, and the entire conversation is presented as text.

2 Type **Here I am saying something!** in the Compose box.

3 Press Enter. The text appears in black within the View pane and is preceded by your nickname and the word "says" in blue.

4 Click the nickname of a fellow chatter you would like to whisper to in the Member List pane.

5 Type **Here I am whispering to someone else** in the Compose box.

6 Click the Whisper button or press Ctrl+W. The text appears in black within the View pane and is preceded by your nickname, the nickname of the person you're whispering to, and the word "whispers" in brown.

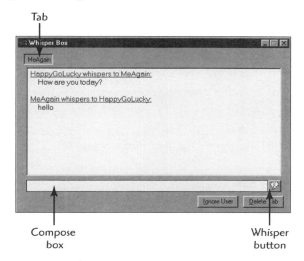

Tab

Compose box

Whisper button

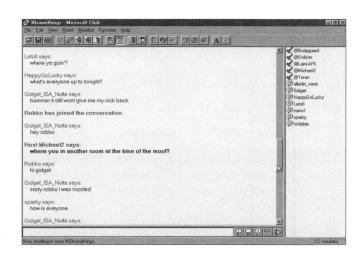

Changing to text view

7 Type **Hmm. So this is what thinking looks like** in the Compose box.

8 Click the Think button or press Ctrl+T. Your text appears in the View pane preceded by your nickname and the word "thinks."

9 Perform an action. Type **I'm typing in an action and this is what it looks like!** in the Compose box.

10 Click the Action button or press Ctrl+I. Your text appears with your nickname before it. The entire action line is purple and in italics.

11 If you're ready to exit, close Microsoft Chat by clicking the Close button to the right of the title bar. Click No in response to the query that asks if you'd like to save the Chat session.

Chatting is such fun that you may decide to wait a while before you sign off!

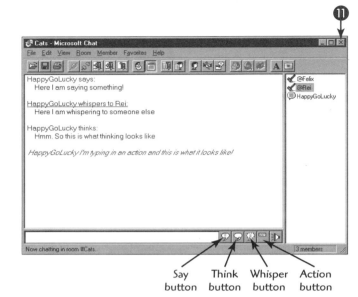

Say   Think   Whisper Action
button button button   button

SKILLS CHALLENGE: USING MICROSOFT CHAT

This Skills Challenge helps you review what you learned about Microsoft Chat. The exercise directs you to begin a chat session, so if you're the shy type, now is a good time to call a friend who also has Chat. Or you can just jump into the chat world the same way most others do—head first! You must be connected to the Internet to complete the steps in this challenge.

1 Open Microsoft Chat.

2 Enter the default chat room.

3 Change your character and emotion.

 How many characters are available to choose from in Microsoft Chat?

4 Begin a conversation.

5 Change your facial expression by clicking a new one from the wheel.

2 *Why do people use abbreviations and emoticons for chatting?*

6 Change your facial expression by changing your text.

7 Change the background image and number of panes.

 3 *Do the changes you make to the Chat screen affect other computers?*

8 Display a list of chat rooms.

9 Enter a different room.

10 Create a new chat room.

11 Invite another user to your new room.

 4 *How do you obtain a fellow chatter's profile?*

12 Whisper to your new friend.

13 Use a Whisper Box to whisper to a user who is not in the same room as you are.

14 Switch to text mode (if you really want to).

15 Continue chatting. When you're ready to exit, make sure you say goodbye to everyone!

Wrap up

TROUBLESHOOTING

The questions in the following table are often asked by new users.

Problem	Solution
When I call up the list of available rooms, the first ones look like gibberish and the conversations in those rooms do as well. What's wrong?	Nothing is wrong! People in those rooms are speaking a different language. The odd–looking characters appear as letters to Chat users who have their computers set for that language.
Sometimes what people say is only partly understandable. Some of the words appear normal, but they have weird characters around them. Is my eyesight going?	Microsoft Chat has features not available in other chat programs, and other chat programs have features not available in Chat. However, people using different programs can join conversations in the same chat rooms. These weird symbols are Chat's attempt to understand the unique features of the other programs.
I keep trying to whisper to someone but somebody else keeps answering me. Why?	You must select the person you want to whisper to first. Click the recipient's name in the Member List pane.

WRAP UP

In this lesson, you exercised the following skills:

- Configuring Microsoft Chat
- Having an online conversation
- Creating a new chat room
- Using comic and text views

In the next lesson, you explore Microsoft NetMeeting, another application for communicating with people across the Internet.

TRY OUT THE
INTERACTIVE TUTORIALS
ON YOUR CD!

Using Microsoft NetMeeting

45 MINUTES

GOALS

This lesson shows you how to use Microsoft NetMeeting to talk with people across the Internet. With NetMeeting, both voice transmissions and voice and video transmissions are possible, and the application includes several collaborative tools. You work through the following exercises:

- Setting up NetMeeting for the first time
- Selecting another directory server
- Starting a conference from a directory
- Starting a conference using an IP address
- Accepting a NetMeeting call
- Using Chat
- Using the Whiteboard
- Sending and receiving files
- Sharing applications

Get ready

GET READY

To complete this lesson, NetMeeting must be installed on your computer (see Appendix A). Additionally, you should be connected to the Internet before you begin the exercises, and you must know your modem speed. For audio conferencing, your computer must have a sound card, microphone, and speakers. Check that your microphone is plugged in and operational.

When you complete this lesson, you will know how to conduct a conference with another NetMeeting user across the Internet.

UNDERSTANDING NETMEETING

Microsoft NetMeeting is an exciting component of Internet Explorer 4 that uses international communication standards to connect computers. Although you don't need to run the Internet Explorer browser when you use NetMeeting, you need to be connected to the Internet. With NetMeeting, you attach your computer to one or more computers also running NetMeeting. The computers can be across the room from one another or thousands of miles apart. Once you're connected, your NetMeeting conference is ready to begin.

NetMeeting enables you to avoid expensive telephone charges by using a technology called Internet telephony to enable voice transmissions between colleagues or friends over the Internet. Instead of speaking into a telephone receiver, you talk into a microphone that's attached to the sound card in your computer. NetMeeting sends your voice across the Internet to the computers that are attached to yours. Speakers amplify the conversation.

Also included with NetMeeting are Chat, a program that enables you to text-chat with other NetMeeting participants, and the Whiteboard, a program that works like a chalkboard. In addition, during a NetMeeting, an application installed on one computer can be shared by other NetMeeting participants, and files can be transferred between the connected computers. If you don't have any audio equipment in your computer, you can still participate in a NetMeeting conference by using these other tools.

One of NetMeeting's most dramatic features is its ability to enable video conferencing. Setting up a video conference requires some technical knowledge and fairly expensive, specialized equipment. To use the video features of NetMeeting, you need either a video-capture card and camera or a video camera that connects to your computer's parallel port. Additionally, your machine must have a Pentium-equivalent processor. Video transmissions appear in boxes on the NetMeeting screen.

NetMeeting supports meetings of as many as 32 participants. However, during your NetMeeting you can be connected to only one other person with audio or video at a time. No matter how many people are participating in a meeting, only three people at a time can share applications running on their computers.

CONFIGURING NETMEETING

Before you can connect to others with NetMeeting, you need to spend a few minutes setting it up. You can always make changes to the configuration later if you upgrade to a new sound card or a faster modem.

Setting up NetMeeting for the first time

Before you use NetMeeting for the first time, you need to provide personal data and specify some sound and communications information so that the program can take full advantage of your computer equipment. If you performed a full install when you installed Internet Explorer, NetMeeting should already be set up on your computer.

When you finish this exercise, immediately progress to the next exercise.

1 In a previous lesson, you set up the NetMeeting icon on your Quick Launch toolbar. Click the NetMeeting icon one time to start NetMeeting.

2 Alternatively, click the Start button on the Windows taskbar and select Programs ➤ Internet Explorer ➤ Microsoft NetMeeting. Either way, the Microsoft NetMeeting setup wizard displays a dialog box that contains information about the program.

3 After you've read the information, click Next.

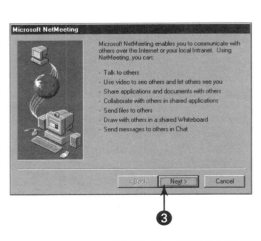

4 The second dialog box asks if you would like to be listed in a directory when you use NetMeeting. A directory server lists the names of all of the people who are connected and available for conferencing. Unless you know the name of a specific directory server that you'd like to connect to, accept the default by clicking Next.

5 The third dialog box asks for information about you. The information you enter on this screen will appear on the directory listing. The name and e-mail fields are mandatory, but you don't have to use real information. If you want to remain anonymous, you can type a *handle* for yourself. (I sometimes use my dog's name in place of my own.) Type your name and e-mail address in the appropriate fields.

6 The remaining fields on the screen are optional. Enter your location information and a comment if you wish.

7 Click Next.

8 The fourth dialog box asks if you'd like the information you provided in the last step to be categorized for personal use, for business use, or for adults only. Click an option button next to your choice.

9 Click Next.

10 The Audio Tuning Wizard is the next dialog box that appears. Since you don't need to answer any questions or provide information, click Next.

In the next few dialog boxes, you'll be asked to confirm the speed of your Internet connection and read aloud into your microphone so NetMeeting can match its settings to the sound equipment installed inside your computer.

11 The sixth dialog box asks you to confirm the speed of your Internet connection: 14,400 bps modem, 28,800 bps or higher modem, ISDN, or LAN (local area network). Check the option button next to the choice that matches your connection.

12 Click Next.

Default server

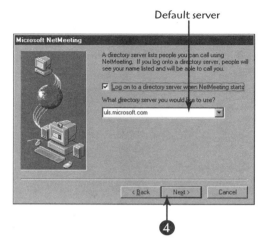

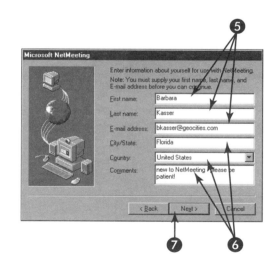

13 The seventh dialog box asks you to read aloud into the microphone attached to your computer to verify your audio settings. Click the Start Recording button and record for up to 9 seconds. As you speak, a meter tracks your progress.

14 When you finish recording, click Next.

15 The last dialog box advises that you've successfully set up NetMeeting. Click Finish to end the setup wizard and start NetMeeting.

TIP

If you need to make changes to your sound settings later, select Tools ➤ Audio Tuning Wizard and go through the dialog boxes again, making the appropriate changes.

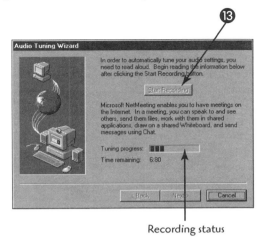

13

Recording status

IP, ILS, AND NETMEETING

Much of the language that's used on the Internet isn't made up of words, but instead consists of acronyms and abbreviations. Learning some of the common Internet terms will help as you use NetMeeting—not to mention amaze your friends!

First, there's IP. Every computer that's connected to the Internet has a unique Internet Protocol number, IP for short. If you're connected to the Internet through an ISP (Internet service provider), your provider assigns you a number each time you connect. For the period you're connected, the assigned IP address identifies your computer. As soon as you disconnect, the number goes back into the rotation and is assigned as someone else's Internet address.

ILS servers are the Microsoft directories that NetMeeting uses to identify users. Previous versions of NetMeeting used the ULS, or User Location Server. However, with the newest version of NetMeeting, the one you're using now, Microsoft uses the ILS, or Internet Locator Server. As soon as you open NetMeeting, you're registered with the server you specified during the configuration. Each of these servers functions as NetMeeting phone books for users who are logged on at a particular time. But instead of keeping track of phone numbers, the directory servers maintain the current IP numbers of NetMeeting users' computers.

Selecting another directory server

▶ *Selecting another directory server*

When you start NetMeeting, it tries to connect to the user location server you specified when you set up the program. This procedure can take a few minutes, so don't get impatient. If after a while you see an error message that you were unable to connect to the default directory server, you need to select another server. Otherwise, your name won't appear in the list of users. You'll be able to make calls, but no one will be able to call you without knowing your Internet Protocol (IP) number.

There are many reasons why you might not be able to log on to the default server, and you don't have control over any them! Too many people may already be logged on, for example, or there may be a problem with the phone lines and data transmission. Fortunately, you can log on to another server by following the steps shown here:

❶ From within NetMeeting, select Call ➢ Change My Information. The Options dialog box appears.

❷ Click the Calling tab.

❸ In the directory section of the window, click the drop-down arrow next to Server name.

❹ Choose another server from the list.

❺ Click OK to close the dialog box. Another dialog box appears.

❻ Click Yes to log on to the server you selected in step 4.

The NetMeeting screen appears. As you connect to the directory server, the status bar displays the message, Logging on to ils (...). In a few moments, the list of names of the people currently logged on to the server appears on the screen.

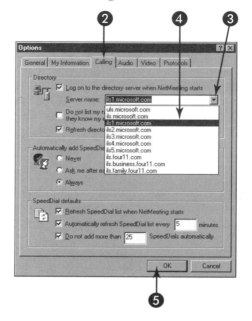

The NetMeeting Window

The NetMeeting window changes when a call is active. The window shown in the illustration displays the current connection information.

This NetMeeting window provides information about the current connection.

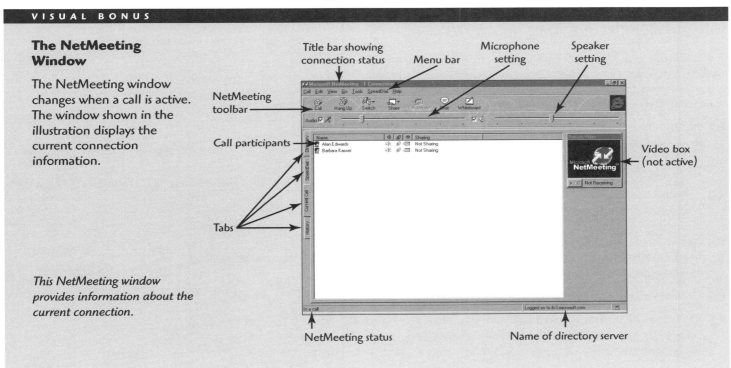

Title bar showing connection status — Menu bar — Microphone setting — Speaker setting

NetMeeting toolbar

Call participants

Tabs

Video box (not active)

NetMeeting status

Name of directory server

13

Using Microsoft NetMeeting

MAKING AND RECEIVING CALLS

After NetMeeting is set up properly, you're ready to begin placing and receiving calls. Be careful though, because using NetMeeting can be addicting.

If you haven't used NetMeeting before, you're in for a treat! It's amazing to sit at your computer and talk to someone through the Internet. However, don't expect the audio transmission to be as clear as you're used to on a telephone call. The voices may sound tinny, or you may hear static or an echo.

Starting a conference from a directory

▶ Starting a conference from a directory

In this exercise, you place a call over the Internet. Your computer must be equipped with a sound card, speakers, and a microphone. If you're reluctant to speak with strangers, try to arrange for a friend to connect at the same time and log on to the same directory server.

1 NetMeeting should be open from the previous exercises. If it isn't, open it by clicking the NetMeeting icon on the Quick Launch toolbar. If necessary, log on to another server by following the steps in the preceding exercise.

2 Scroll down the list of people logged on to the server and select the person you'd like to call. The names on the list are sorted alphabetically by e-mail address. Keep in mind that some of the names may be fictitious. For example, you probably won't reach President Abraham Lincoln, Madonna, or Mickey Mouse, although their names appeared on the list the day I wrote this lesson!

3 Click the name one time to select it.

4 Click the Call button on the NetMeeting toolbar. The New Call Dialog box appears, showing information about the person you're calling.

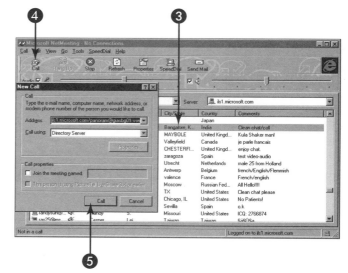

5 Click the Call button on the New Call dialog box. NetMeeting attempts to make the connection. In a few moments, you receive one of the following messages:

Response	Next Step
Your invitation has been accepted.	You will be connected shortly.
Your invitation has been declined.	Select another name from the list and try again.
The person could not be located.	Although the name appeared on the directory, the person probably closed NetMeeting a short while ago. Select another name from the list and try again.
You're asked to join an existing conference.	Click Yes or No.

6 If your invitation is accepted, NetMeeting connects the computers and updates the screen to reflect the names of the people participating in the call.

7 Speak slowly into the microphone.

8 If necessary, adjust the audio and microphone settings with the slider bars under the NetMeeting toolbar.

9 If someone else wants to join your call, a box appears at the bottom of the screen, asking if that person may join. Click Accept or Ignore.

If you click Accept, the new arrival's name is added to the list of participants on the main NetMeeting screen.

TIP

Although as many as 32 people can participate in a call, you can only exchange audio and video with one other participant at a time.

10 If you want to add another person to the call, repeat steps 2 through 5.

11 When your call is finished, click the Hang Up button on the NetMeeting toolbar. The connection is broken. In a few moments, you're free to place another call.

Starting a conference using an IP address

Every computer attached to the Internet has its own unique number. If you want to set up a NetMeeting call with specific people, you might want to have NetMeeting find them by their IP addresses instead of trying to find them on a directory. One excellent reason for using the IP address method is that you're sure to connect. Because so many people are logging on to the various ILS sites, you may not be able to connect to the directory you specified in your configuration. Think how frustrating it would be to connect to the Internet with NetMeeting open, only to have people unable to find you on a directory list.

Names of conference participants

Video is not active.

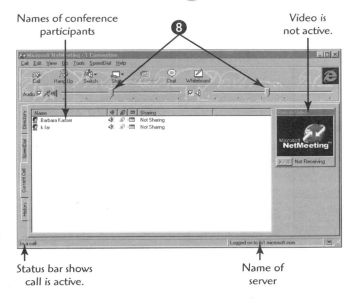

Status bar shows call is active.

Name of server

13

Using Microsoft NetMeeting

Starting a conference using an IP

Setting up a call with IP numbers takes some preparation. All potential participants must find the IP numbers assigned to their computers.

1 Find the IP address of your computer by selecting Start ➤ Run. The Run dialog box appears.

2 Click inside the Open text box.

3 Type **winipcfg**.

4 Click OK. The IP Configuration dialog box opens and displays your unique IP address.

5 Write the number down carefully.

6 Click OK to close the IP Configuration dialog box.

7 Obtain the IP addresses of the other participants. You may need to walk them through steps 1through 4 in this exercise.

(Since you're placing the call in this exercise, you don't need your IP address. However, you can e-mail it to a friend or colleague and have the person call you in the next exercise.)

8 Click the Call button on the NetMeeting toolbar to display the New Call dialog box.

9 Type the IP address of the person you're calling in the Address box.

10 Click the drop-down arrow next to Call Using to open a list of NetMeeting call types.

11 Select Network (TCP/IP) from the list.

12 Click the Call button. As the call is placed, several messages showing the progress of the connection appear in the status bar.

13 When NetMeeting locates the specified IP address on the Internet, the person receives an invitation to join the call. From that point, the call proceeds normally.

14 If you wish to call other people, repeat steps 8 through 12 of this exercise.

IP address display

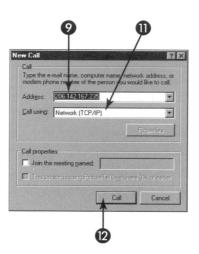

⑮ Click the Hang Up button on the NetMeeting toolbar when the call is over.

TIP

The names of the people who call you are automatically added to SpeedDial. Click the SpeedDial tab (on the far left of the NetMeeting window) to display a list of names and to determine if they're logged on. If the person you want to call is logged on, click the name once to select it and then click the Call button. NetMeeting places the call for you.

Accepting a NetMeeting call

This exercise is easy!

❶ If you're not already connected to the Internet, connect now.

❷ Open NetMeeting by clicking the NetMeeting icon on the Quick Launch toolbar if it's not already open.

When NetMeeting opens, make sure that you're logged on to a directory server. If not, follow the steps in the second exercise of this lesson to log on to another directory.

❸ Sit back and wait! So many people use NetMeeting that you're bound to be called before too long. In a short while, you'll hear a ringing phone sound, and a dialog box will appear at the lower right corner of your screen showing the name of the person who's calling you.

❹ If you want to participate in the call, click Accept. The call will proceed normally. If you don't want to accept the call, click Ignore.

❺ Set the Do Not Disturb option if you don't want to accept any more calls. Select Call ➤ Do Not Disturb to prevent any new calls from coming through.

❻ When you're ready to receive more calls, repeat step 5 to remove the option and enable calls.

Using Chat

USING OTHER NETMEETING TOOLS

NetMeeting offers other options in addition to providing the ability to speak with someone over the Internet. Even if you don't have a sound card and speakers, these other tools allow you to participate in real-time Internet conferencing—without sound. Chat enables you to communicate by writing words instead of speaking. The Whiteboard allows you to share images. The File Transfer tool makes it easy to transfer a file from your hard drive to the connected computer. You can even collaborate with other NetMeeting participants by allowing the other conference members to work on a program that's installed on your computer. NetMeeting must be open to access any of the tools discussed in the following exercises.

Using Chat

When the audio is garbled or one of the participants doesn't have a PC microphone, Chat is a great way to communicate. Chat is a separate program and opens in its own window, complete with its own menu and toolbar. When Chat is opened by one of the conference participants, it's opened on all the computers participating in the conference as well.

1 After your computer is connected to another computer in NetMeeting, open Chat by clicking the Chat button on the NetMeeting toolbar. The Chat program opens in its own window.

2 Type your comments in the Message box located near the bottom of the screen.

3 When you're finished typing, click the Send button or press the Enter key.

TIP *Remember to send the text after you type it. If you forget to click the Send button, the person on the other end won't see what you typed.*

4 Each person's comments are preceded by the person's name. Type as many comments as you want.

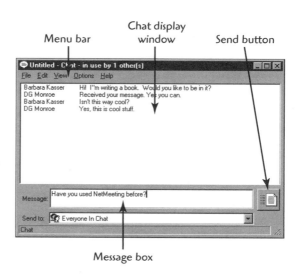

Menu bar / Chat display window / Send button

Message box

Using the Whiteboard

5 If you want to send a private message to one person rather than posting a message to the group, click the drop-down arrow next to Send to and select the person's name from the list. Until you change it back, only that person sees what you type.

6 If you want to change the information display or the message format, select Options ➤ Chat Format to open the Chat Format dialog box.

7 Select the options you want.

8 Click OK to close the box when you've made your selections. The text reflects your changes.

9 If you want to change the font in which the typed chat messages are displayed, select Options ➤ Font.

10 Choose a font from the resulting dialog box.

11 Click OK to return to Chat.

12 Close Chat by selecting File ➤ Exit.

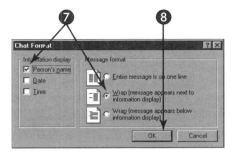

Using the Whiteboard

The Whiteboard looks very similar to the Windows Paint program. It can be used as a doodle pad or as a way to share images captured from files on your computer. After a participant places an image on the board, each person in the conference can draw pointers to parts of the screen or even collaborate on a drawing.

1 While a conference is active, click the Whiteboard button on the NetMeeting toolbar to open the Whiteboard. The Whiteboard appears on the computer(s) you're connected to.

The Whiteboard contains a palette of drawing tools on the left side, as well as a menu bar.

2 If you want to draw a freehand picture, click the Pen tool.

3 Move the mouse pointer onto the Whiteboard area. The mouse pointer takes the shape of a pen.

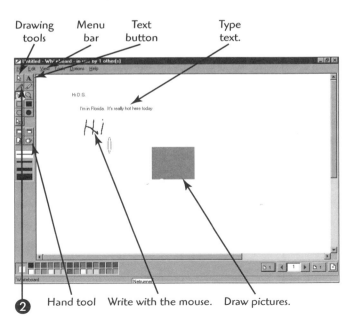

Drawing tools   Menu bar   Text button   Type text.

Hand tool   Write with the mouse.   Draw pictures.

Using the Whiteboard

4 Hold the left mouse button down and drag the mouse pointer on the screen, as if you were using a pen. Draw any shape you like. The other people in the conference can draw as well. Each person's efforts appear on the picture.

5 You can type on the Whiteboard too. First click the Text button.

6 Click the Whiteboard. A box appears.

7 Type your text inside the box.

8 You can paste the image of a file that is already open on your computer to the Whiteboard. First, switch to the program window that contains the file you want to capture (such as an Excel spreadsheet or a Word memo, by clicking the program's button on the taskbar.

9 When the program appears, click its title bar located at the top of the window. The title bar shows both the name of the program, such as Microsoft Word, and the name of the open file.

10 Highlight the area or range you want to copy to the Whiteboard and select Edit ➤ Copy.

11 Switch back to the Whiteboard by clicking the Whiteboard button on the taskbar.

12 Click the top right corner of the white area.

13 Select Edit ➤ Paste. The image of the file you copied from the other window appears.

14 You can emphasize something on the Whiteboard by adding a pointing hand. Select the Hand tool from the tool palette.

15 Position the mouse pointer and click inside the white area.

16 When the hand appears, drag it wherever you'd like on the screen.

17 Print the image on the Whiteboard by selecting File ➤ Print.

18 Select File ➤ Close to close the Whiteboard. Closing the Whiteboard does not close NetMeeting.

Text pasted from another application

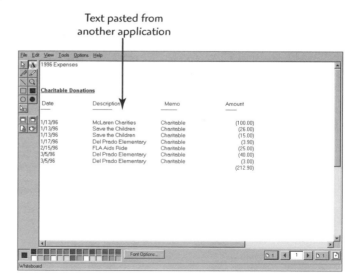

▶ Sending and receiving files

All conference participants can transfer files among computers.

1 To transfer a file, select Tools ➤ File Transfer ➤ Send File. The Select a File to Send dialog box appears.

2 Browse the dialog box and select the file you want to send.

3 Click Send to begin the file transfer. When the file transfer is completed successfully, a confirmation message is displayed.

4 When you are receiving a transferred file, a dialog box shows the status of the transfer. The bottom of the dialog box has three buttons: Close, Open, and Delete:

- If you choose Close, the file is saved on your computer in the C:\ProgramFiles\NetMeeting\Received Files folder.

- If you choose Open, the file opens in the associated application (if you have it installed on your computer).

- If you choose Delete, the process terminates and the file is not transferred to your computer.

TIP

To change the directory where NetMeeting saves transferred files, select Tools ➤ Options, click the General tab, and click the Change Folder button. Browse to the folder you want to use and click it one time to select it. Click OK to close the Browse Folder dialog box, and then click OK to close the Options dialog box

5 To view transferred files, select Tools ➤ File Transfer ➤ Open Received Files Folder. A window displays the files you received during a NetMeeting file transfer.

6 Double-click a file to open it.

Sharing applications

Sharing applications

You can share any program that's currently running on your computer with conference participants. The program window from your computer screen will appear on their computers. Unless you allow conference participants to collaborate, only you can make changes to the file. If you grant access to someone, you can always take back the controls.

1 During an active conference, select Tools ➢ Share Application.

2 Chose from the list of programs running on your computer.

3 Click OK on the Microsoft NetMeeting dialog box informing you that you'll be sharing files. The application then appears on the screen of every computer connected to the conference. Additionally, the words In Control appear in the Sharing section of the window on the line with your name.

4 Work with the application normally. The conference users can see the changes you make and discuss them with you.

5 To give conference users access to make changes to your file, click the Collaborate button on the NetMeeting toolbar.

6 Carefully read the information in the resulting dialog box.

7 Click OK. The Collaborate button toggles to a Work Alone button.

8 Make changes to the file. Conference participants cannot make changes at the same time; control of the file passes to the person who's making the changes.

9 When you finish working on the file or you want to regain sole control, click the Collaborate/Work Alone button again.

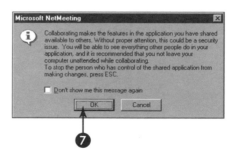

TIP

Be cautious about letting someone share a file on your computer. Never have My Computer or Windows Explorer open during a collaborative effort, since someone could easily gain access to your files on your computer.

SKILLS CHALLENGE: CONDUCTING A NETMEETING CONFERENCE

You'll initiate a NetMeeting conference in this Skills Challenge, so if possible, prearrange a conference time with a friend or coworker. Alternatively, choose a name from the list of participants on a directory server. You must be connected to the Internet for this challenge.

1 Open NetMeeting.

2 After you're connected, log on to a different directory server.

3 Invite someone to join your NetMeeting conference.

4 Repeat step 3 and invite an additional person to join.

> *How many people can participate in a Microsoft NetMeeting conference?*

5 Optionally, use the IP addresses of friends or business associates to call and invite them to the conference.

> *What is an IP address?*

6 Open the Whiteboard.

7 Draw a picture with the Pen tool and invite your conference partners to help.

8 Close the Whiteboard.

9 Open Chat.

10 Type a comment and send it.

11 Send a follow-up reply to the comment you receive.

12 Close Chat.

13 Prevent others from calling you.

> *How do you prevent other people from calling you?*

Wrap up

14 Continue with your NetMeeting conference. When you're ready, politely break the connection.

TROUBLESHOOTING

These questions are commonly asked by new NetMeeting users.

Problem	Solution
My business associate had different options in the audio phase of the setup phase as she was configuring NetMeeting. Why?	The Audio Tuning Wizard determines what sound card is installed in your computer and presents its options accordingly.
Can I erase the image that's currently showing in the Whiteboard?	To erase the image, select Edit ➢ Clear Page.
How will I know if someone in the NetMeeting conference is using Chat?	By default, if another member of the conference opens Chat, the chat program opens in an active window on your computer.
I tried to use NetMeeting at work, but I got a message about a firewall error. Why?	Many business networks limit incoming and outgoing Internet access. Contact your network administrator for help.

WRAP UP

In this lesson, you exercised the following skills:

- Configuring NetMeeting software
- Logging on to a directory server
- Participating in a NetMeeting conference
- Using NetMeeting's other tools during a conference

In the next lesson, you begin to explore Microsoft FrontPage Express, an application for designing your own Web page.

TRY OUT THE
INTERACTIVE TUTORIALS
ON YOUR CD!

Using FrontPage Express

45 MINUTES

GOALS

FrontPage Express is an easy-to-use Web page design tool with some powerful features. In this lesson, you create a basic Web page and master the following skills:

- Inserting and formatting text
- Adding a background
- Inserting hyperlinks
- Adding graphics
- Adding sound
- Adding video
- Adding a scrolling marquee
- Adding a timestamp WebBot
- Editing Web pages

Get ready

GET READY

To complete this lesson, you must install FrontPage Express (see Appendix A). When you finish this lesson, you will know how to create a simple Web page containing text, graphics, and hyperlinks). You will also know how to add other Web page elements such as scrolling marquees.

TRY OUT THE

INTERACTIVE TUTORIALS

ON YOUR CD!

CREATING A BASIC WEB PAGE

The Hypertext Markup Language (HTML) is the basis for creating Web pages. HTML is not a page layout program, but a standardized method of identifying text formatting, links to other Web pages, and graphics so that these elements can be transmitted across the Internet and interpreted by Web browsers. You can create Web pages in three ways. You can write the HTML code yourself using a text editor such as Notepad. You can convert an existing document to HTML using an HTML conversion program. Or—and most people find this method easiest—you can use an HTML editor such as FrontPage Express that adds the HTML tags to the text, hyperlink, and graphic elements on your Web page. If you use an HTML editor, you do not need to learn HTML.

Along with being easy to use, FrontPage Express also makes it easy for you to see how your Web page will look on the Web. FrontPage Express displays your work just as if you were looking at it in a Web browser. The possibilities for Web pages created with FrontPage Express are limited only by how much time and creativity you want to invest. The exercises in this section walk you through the steps for creating a simple Web page.

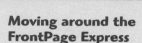

Get ready

VISUAL BONUS

Moving around the FrontPage Express Screen

These illustrations show the numerous options available in FrontPage Express and how the application helps to make Web page creation almost as easy as clicking a few buttons.

The FrontPage Express screen

Format toolbar →

Standard toolbar →

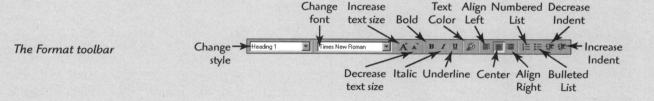

14

Using FrontPage Express

The Format toolbar

Change style →

Change font — Increase text size — Bold — Text Color — Align Left — Numbered List — Decrease Indent

Decrease text size — Italic — Underline — Center — Align Right — Bulleted List — Increase Indent

The Standard toolbar

New Page →

Open a File — Print — Cut — Paste — Undo — Insert WebBot component — Create or Edit hyperlink — Back — Refresh — Help

Save a File — Print Preview — Copy — Redo — Insert Table — Insert Image — Forward — Stop — Show/Hide Formatting marks

Inserting and formatting text

The Hypertext Markup Language was developed so that documents that contain text formatting, hyperlinks to other documents, pictures, sounds, and other multimedia elements could be transmitted and displayed across the Internet.

A Web page consists of a text file that contains HTML tags (or programming codes) that define the different elements on the page such as headings, paragraphs, lists, and graphic images. HTML does not define the format or layout of a Web page. It only defines the specific elements that make up the page. The Web browser that is used to view the Web page controls how the page appears in the browser window.

For example, if a text element is defined as being a level 1 heading by the HTML tag, it may display as 24-point Times New Roman in one Web browser and 18-point Courier in another Web browser. Display depends on the Web browser and how it is configured. Because of these differences, you may want to view your Web page using the popular Web browsers (Microsoft Internet Explorer, Netscape Navigator, and NCSA Mosaic) while you are creating it.

Several Web sites contain information—both basic and advanced—about HTML. If you are interested in learning more about this special language, the following sites will get you going:

- Beginner's Guide to HTML at `www.ncsa.uiuc.edu/General/Internet/WWW/HTMLPrimer.html`

- The Library of Congress Internet Resources Web Page at `lcweb.loc.gov/global/internet/html.html`

- Microsoft HTML Reference at `www.microsoft.com/workshop/author/newhtml/htmlr018.htm`

- The HTML Writers Guild list of HTML resources at `www.hwg.org/resources/html/`

Inserting and formatting text

Text is the major element in any Web page. If you are familiar with word processing, you will find this exercise very similar to working with your favorite word processing program. This exercise shows you how to add and format text on a Web page.

1. Select Start ➤ Programs ➤ Internet Explorer ➤ FrontPage Express. This action opens FrontPage Express with a blank page.

2. Type the following text exactly as it appears. Press the Enter key once at the end of each paragraph. When you're finished, the screen should look like the illustration.

Craig's Personal Web Page

About me

About my birds

About my publisher

About Me

Hi! Here is where you find out a little about me. I was born on Halloween the year they dropped the bombs on Hiroshima and Nagasaki. I have been fascinated with computers since reading science fiction in my childhood introduced me to "thinking machines." I write about computers and software (and other things technical and non-technical) and I wouldn't trade jobs with anyone. I live happily with my wife Coletta in a nice house in Hawaii.

About My Birds

I have a collection of hundreds of wild birds that I feed twice a day from my lanai. I have quite an assortment: Java Rice Finches, California House Finches, Saffron Finches, and Brazilian Cardinals. Want to learn more about finches?

About My Publisher

I have published several books with IDG Books. From their home page, type "Witherspoon" in the search field and a list of my books will appear.

 NOTE

You do not have to press Enter at the end of each line. Just like a word processing program, FrontPage Express automatically wraps the lines when the text reaches the right margin.

3 Position the cursor in the first line of text that reads Craig's Personal Web Page.

14

Using FrontPage Express

Adding a background

④ Select Heading 1 from the Change Style drop-down list. The text becomes larger and bold.

⑤ With the cursor still positioned in the first line of text, click the Center button to center the line on the page.

⑥ Highlight the next three lines of text.

⑦ Click the Bulleted List button.

⑧ Place the cursor in the next line of text that says About Me.

⑨ Use the Change Style drop-down list to select Heading 2.

⑩ Repeat step 9 for the next two lines that read About My Birds and About My Publisher. Your Web page should look like the illustration.

⑪ Now is a good time to save your work. Click the Save button. The Save As dialog box appears.

⑫ In the Page Title text box, type **Practice Web Page**.

⑬ Click the Save As File button. The Save As File dialog box appears.

⑭ Click the down arrow next to the Save in drop-down list and select the folder where you want to save the file.

⑮ Click inside the File name text box.

⑯ Type **Craig1.htm**.

⑰ Click the Save button. The Web page is now saved on your computer under the name Craig1.

Adding a background

Well-chosen backgrounds add appeal to your Web page. Experiment with different backgrounds and select one that enhances the text and images on the page. The background should never overpower or obscure the other page elements.

① With the Web page from the previous exercise displayed on the monitor, select Format ➤ Background to display the Page Properties dialog box.

Save button   Change style drop-down list   ⑤   ⑦

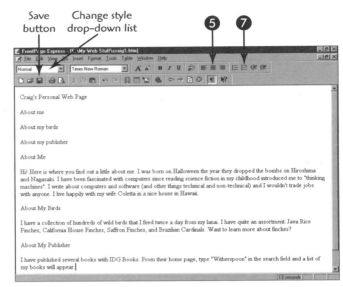

Bulleted list   Heading 1

⑪

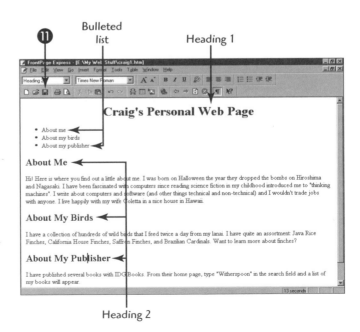

Heading 2

② On the Background tab, click the checkbox next to Background Image.

③ Click the Browse button to display the Select Background Image dialog box.

④ Click the Other Location tab.

⑤ Select the From File button, and then click Browse.

⑥ Click the Look in drop-down arrow.

⑦ Select the CD-ROM drive and double-click to select the Exercise file.

⑧ Select Backgr1.gif.

⑨ Click OK to return to the Page Properties dialog box.

⑩ Click OK again to add the background to your Web page.

Inserting hyperlinks

Hyperlinks are the basic tool used by Web surfers to move from Web page to Web page. Hyperlinks add personality and interest to your Web page by giving visitors choices of other sites to visit or other areas of your page to view. Hyperlinks can be either text or graphics. Clicking a hyperlink can take you to another location on the same Web page (these links are called bookmarks), to another Web page at the same Web site (these are called internal hyperlinks), or to a different Web site (these are external hyperlinks). This exercise shows you how to create a bookmark and an external hyperlink. The Web page from the previous exercise should still be displayed on the monitor.

❶ To create a bookmark, first highlight the Heading 2 text that reads About Me.

❷ Select Edit➢Bookmark to display the Bookmark dialog box.

❸ FrontPage Express displays a suggested name for the bookmark in the Bookmark Name field. You can either accept the default

Inserting hyperlinks

or assign a different name to the bookmark. For this example, accept the default.

4 Click OK. The Heading 2 title is still highlighted and is underlined with a dotted line. The dotted line means that the underlined text is a bookmark and ready for a hyperlink.

5 Bookmark the last two Heading 2 titles by selecting the text and repeating steps 2, 3, and 4.

6 Now that the bookmarks (or the targets) for the hyperlinks have been set, it is time to create the hyperlinks. Highlight the first bullet item, About me.

7 Click the Create or Edit Hyperlink button. The Create Hyperlink dialog box appears.

8 Make sure the Open Pages tab is displayed.

9 In the Open Pages window, make sure that the page that you are working on is selected.

10 In the Bookmark field, select About Me from the drop-down list.

11 Click OK. The first bullet list item is underlined with a solid line.

12 Repeat steps 6 through 11 for the next two bullet list items, linking the bullet list item with the matching heading.

13 The next task is to add an external hyperlink to another Web site. In the last sentence on the Web page, highlight the words IDG Books.

14 Click the Create or Edit Hyperlink button to display the Create Hyperlink dialog box.

15 Click the World Wide Web tab.

16 Click the URL field and type `http://www.idgbooks.com`.

17 Click OK. You have created an external hyperlink to the IDG Books home page.

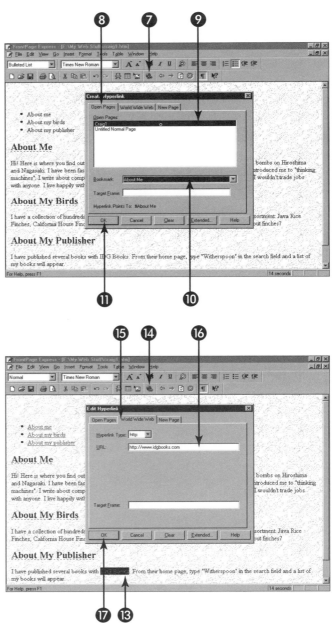

Adding graphics

Graphic elements are another way to add personality to a Web page. You can separate a Web page into sections with graphic lines, use icons to call attention to bulleted lists, and even scan your favorite photographs and add them to Web pages. This exercise shows how to insert a graphic line on a Web page. You can use the instructions in this exercise to add other types of images to a Web page.

❶ Place the cursor before the first Heading 2 that reads About Me.

❷ Press Enter to create a space to place a horizontal line.

❸ Press the up arrow key to move the cursor to the blank line.

USING GRAPHICS ON YOUR WEB PAGE

Graphic images are extensively used on Web pages as an integral part of the design. You can create your own graphics for your Web page or you can use free clip art that is available on the Internet. Each Web site that provides free clip art posts the terms and conditions for its use. Before you use a piece of clip art, you must read and accept the terms and conditions. Here are a few sites to get you started: Swedish University Network at `ftp.sunet.se/pub/pictures`, Yahoo! at `www.yahoo.com/Computers_and_Internet/Multimedia/Pictures/Clip_Art/`, and Over the Rainbow at `www.geocities.com/SiliconValley/Heights/1272/rainbow.html`.

If you want to create your own images or if you want to make changes to an image you already have, you need a software program such as Adobe Photoshop or Microsoft Photo Editor. These programs contain tools and filters to manipulate images and covert images to different file formats.

The two types of images most widely used on Web pages are GIF and JPEG images. GIF (which stands for Graphics Interchange Format) is used for images that are created using a drawing program. This format works best on images that contain large areas of the same color and do not contain much detail.

The JPEG (which stands for Joint Photographic Experts Group) format is used when an image, such as a scanned image of a photograph, contains many colors and a high level of detail.

Here are a few helpful hints for using images on a Web page:

- Image resolution should be 72 dots per inch (dpi). This resolution is adequate for most monitors but makes a poor copy if it is printed.

- Image file size should be 100K or less. Images of this size or smaller do not require long download times.

- Image screen size should be 4 x 5 inches or less. This size provides a good viewing image for most monitors.

Adding sound

④ Select Insert ➤ Image or click the Insert Image button to display the Image dialog box.

⑤ Click the Other Location tab.

⑥ Select the From File button, and then click Browse.

⑦ From the Look in window, choose Line2.gif.

⑧ Click OK. You now have a colorful break between sections of your Web page.

⑨ Click the Center button. The horizontal line appears centered on the page.

ADDING MULTIMEDIA COMPONENTS

Another way to enhance your Web page is to add multimedia components such as sound and video. FrontPage Express simplifies the task of adding multimedia components to your page. These exercises explain how.

Centered graphic line

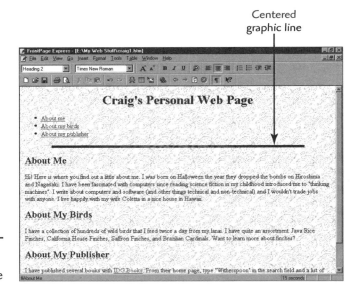

Adding sound

Sound is the simplest multimedia element that you can add to your Web page, but you want to select a sound file format that is compatible with most Web browsers. One of the most popular sound file formats used on the Internet is the Musical Instrument Digital Interface (MIDI). FrontPage Express does not include a sound library, but you can find public-domain sound files on the Internet that are available for personal use.

To perform this exercise, you must have the Web page you created in the previous exercises open on the screen.

NOTE
For visitors to your Web page to hear sounds, their computers must be equipped with a sound card and speakers.

① Select Insert ➤ Background Sound to display the Background Sound dialog box.

2 Select the From File option button.

3 Click the Browse button.

4 Click the down arrow next to the Files of type drop-down list and select Midi Sequencer (*.mid) from the list.

5 Click the CD-ROM drive and select the Exercise folder.

6 When you find the .mid file, click it. Click 1812.ovt.mid.

7 Click Open. This action adds the sound to your Web page.

8 Save your Web page again by clicking the Save button. The Data to File dialog box appears.

9 Click Yes to save the sound file in the same folder as the Web page.

At this point, you might be curious about how your Web page looks and sounds when it is viewed in the browser. To find out, launch the Internet Explorer browser. On the browser menu, select File ➤ Open and click the Browse button. From the Open dialog box, select the Web page file and click Open. Click OK on the File Open dialog box. Your Web page appears in the browser.

Adding video

A short video or movie file can be a real addition to a page. FrontPage Express does not include a video library, but you can either create your own video file or find a public-domain video file on the Internet. Before you add any video file to your Web page, though, make sure you have permission and that you are not infringing on anyone's copyright. Since one of the most common video file formats is the AVI format, this exercise shows how to add an AVI video to your Web page.

Before you begin this exercise, the Web page you've been working on throughout this lesson must be open and displayed on the screen.

Adding a scrolling marquee

1 Place the cursor at the bottom of the page.

2 Select Insert ➤ Video to display the Video dialog box.

3 Select the From File option button.

4 Click the Browse button.

5 Select the CD-ROM drive and then the Exercise folder.

6 Click Gulls.avi.

7 Click Open. You are returned to the Video dialog box.

8 Click OK. The first frame of the video is displayed in the layout area.

9 Click the video image.

10 Click the Align Right button to position the video in the lower right corner.

ADDING OTHER COMPONENTS AND EDITING EXISTING PAGES

Other components are available that you can add to your page. Marquees allow you to display text that moves from side to side across the page. You can also add a timestamp that shows visitors when you last updated the page. The exercises in this section show you how to add these additional touches to your presentation.

Adding a scrolling marquee

This scrolling marquee is an eye-catching enhancement to any page, and the steps in this exercise show you how to add one to yours.

1 With the Web page you've been working on displayed on the screen, place the cursor at the end of the title Craig's Personal Web Page.

2 Press Enter. This action adds a blank line to the Web page.

Adding a scrolling marquee

3 To position the marquee under the title, make sure the cursor is located on the blank line and select Insert ➤ Marquee to display the Marquee Properties dialog box.

4 In the Text box, type **Aloha! Welcome to my page.**

5 Select the Left option from the Direction section so the marquee moves across the Web page from the right to the left.

6 In the Repeat section, check the Continuously box. Selecting this option causes the marquee to move continuously across the Web page as long as the page is displayed.

7 In the Background Color section, select Fuchsia from the drop-down list to set the color of the marquee background.

8 Click OK. A scrolling marquee appears below the title of the Web page.

9 Click the marquee to select it. With the marquee selected, you can add formatting to the text.

10 Click the Increase Text Size button and select a point size. The font size increases, and the height of the marquee increases to accommodate the text. The largest size available is 36 points.

11 Click the Bold button to make the text easier to read.

12 Click the Italic button to add emphasis to the text.

TIP

If you want to try different settings for your marquee, right-click the marquee and select Marquee Properties to display the dialog box. Make whatever changes you want.

Adding a timestamp WebBot

WebBots are small programs that can perform a variety of functions such as handling forms and performing searches. This exercise shows how to add a timestamp WebBot to your Web page. The timestamp WebBot identifies the date that your Web page was updated. It is an

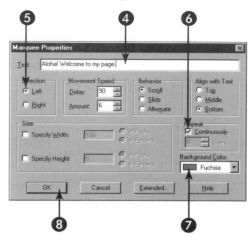

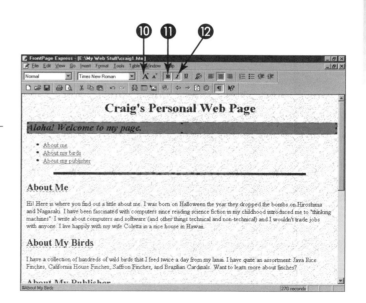

Adding a timestamp WebBot

easy component to add and gives you some incentive for keeping your Web content fresh and up to date.

1 With the Web page you've been working on displayed on the screen, place the cursor at the end of the page and to the left of the video image.

2 Type This page was last updated.

3 Press Shift+Enter to eliminate the extra paragraph space between the text you just typed and the timestamp you insert in the next steps.

4 Select Insert ➤ WebBot Component to display the Insert WebBot Component dialog box.

5 Select the Timestamp component.

6 Click OK to display the WebBot Timestamp Component Properties dialog box.

7 In the Display section, select the Date this page was last edited option. The date displayed by the WebBot shows the date that you last made changes to the Web page.

8 Click the down arrow next to the Date Format drop-down list and select the way you'd like the date to appear on the Web page.

9 Click the down arrow next to the Time Format drop-down list and select the way you'd like the time to appear on the Web page.

10 Click OK to complete the process and add the timestamp WebBot. Visitors to your site can tell from the date if you have changed your site since their last visit.

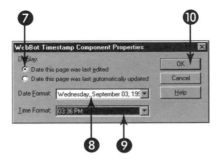

NOTE

When you are finished with your Web page, you are ready to publish it on your ISP's Web server. Your ISP can provide detailed uploading instructions and information on the amount of space available for your Web page. For details, check your ISP's Web page or call their technical support help desk.

Timestamp
WebBot

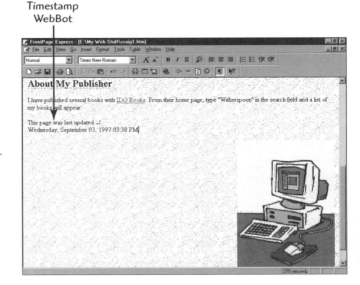

■ Using an existing Web page as a template

So far in this lesson, you have learned how to create a Web page from scratch and add graphics, multimedia components, and other enhancements. But you can also use an existing Web page as a template for building your own.

Editing Web pages

This exercise shows you how to edit a Web page to produce an entirely new one.

1 Open the Internet Explorer browser by clicking the Launch Internet Explorer Browser icon on the Quick Launch toolbar.

2 In the Address bar, type `www.yahoo.com/Health/Diseases_and_Conditions/Diabetes/`. The browser displays a page from Yahoo that lists hyperlinks to sites about diabetes.

3 Select Edit ➤ Page. FrontPage Express opens with the Yahoo Web page displayed in the layout window.

4 Delete everything on the Web page except the list of diabetes links and their descriptions:

- To delete a single graphic image, click it and press Delete.

- To delete a series of elements, click in the space before the first item you want to delete, press and hold the Shift key, click in the space after the last item you want to delete, and press Delete.

5 Add a title to the page. First, place the cursor at the top of the page.

6 Press Enter to create a blank line.

7 Press the up arrow key to move the cursor to the blank line.

8 Type **Diabetes Links**.

9 Select Heading 1 from the Change Style drop-down list.

10 Press Enter to create a new blank line.

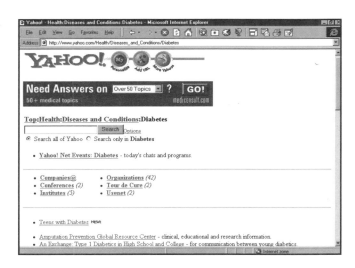

Skills challenge

⑪ Select Insert ➤ Image to add a graphic line to separate the title of the Web page from the rest of the text.

You have constructed a new Web page from an existing one.

⑫ Select the From File button and select Browse.

⑬ Select the CD-ROM drive and then the Exercise folder.

⑭ Select line2.gif and select Open.

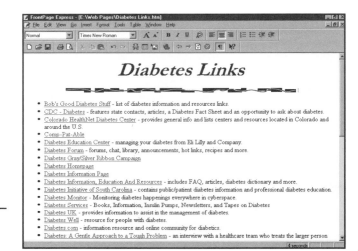

SKILLS CHALLENGE: CREATING YOUR OWN WEB PAGE

Now that you know the basics of designing Web pages, it's time to create your own. To complete this challenge, you must have a personal space allocation on your ISP's server and the instructions for uploading your page to the server.

❶ Open the Web page file you created earlier in this lesson and save it under a different filename.

❷ Replace the existing text. Rewrite the text to describe your hobbies, your job, sports you play, organizations you support, and knowledge that you want to share.

❸ Create a bookmark hyperlink and an external hyperlink.

 If you add a second page to your Web site, how do you link the second page to the first page?

❹ Choose a different background.

 If you don't have any graphics stored on your computer, you can search the Internet for Web graphics that are free for personal use. What search terms would give you good search results?

❺ Change the text contained in the marquee.

❻ Change the scroll direction and background color for the marquee.

3 *How many different directions can the marquee move across the Web page?*

7 Find some public-domain clip art on the Internet that you would like to add to your page. Add the image(s) to your Web page.

8 Experiment with your Web page until you are satisfied with it. When you are ready to publish, follow the Web publishing instructions from your ISP.

TROUBLESHOOTING

This section identifies some common problems and their solutions.

Problem	Solution
How do I add a screen tip to an image so that it displays when a visitor to my Web page holds the cursor over a graphic image?	Right-click the image and select Image Properties. With the General tab selected, type the text that you want to appear in the screen tip in the Text box found in the Alternative Representation section.
I typed the wrong URL address for a hyperlink. How do I fix the URL so that visitors to my Web page can access the link?	Right-click the hyperlink and select Hyperlink Properties from the menu. Type the correct URL address in the URL box.

Wrap up

WRAP UP

In this lesson, you exercised the following skills:

- Creating and editing Web pages
- Choosing options for your page
- Selecting and adding multimedia components to your page
- Adding marquees and WebBot components

TRY OUT THE

INTERACTIVE TUTORIALS

ON YOUR CD!

Installing Internet Explorer 4

The process of getting software "up and running" has changed dramatically. As recently as a couple of years ago, the new user struggling with software installation had to determine a lot of custom settings and assemble various and vaguely compatible supporting and helper applications. This painful process could range from being merely tedious to completely exasperating. The proliferation of nontechnical users, brought about in a significant way by the popularity of the Internet, forced software developers to provide more simplified setup and configuration procedures for their products. As a result, the process of installing, configuring, and even operating new software has become much more user friendly. In the case of Internet Explorer 4, ease of setup is achieved with the Active Setup wizard.

SYSTEM REQUIREMENTS

Having enough computer power—processor speed and memory resources—is imperative if you want to have a good time while you're surfing the Web. The Internet Explorer browser and the other programs in the suite will use a good share of your computer's resources, and navigating the Web claims its fair share too. The following table shows the minimum computer configuration that you need in order to run the Internet Explorer suite programs.

Installing Internet Explorer 4

	Windows 95	Windows NT 4.0	Windows 3.x
MINIMUM SYSTEM REQUIREMENTS FOR INTERNET EXPLORER			
Processor	486/66	486/66	486/33
Minimum Memory	8 MB RAM	16 MB RAM	12 MB RAM
Free Disk Space*	86 MB	86 MB	32 MB

* The disk space required includes disk space needed by the Internet Explorer setup and installation files.

The configurations shown in this table are the minimum system requirements recommended by Microsoft. You may be able to run the Internet Explorer programs on these minimum system configurations, but expect the computer to be sluggish at times. To enjoy better performance from Internet Explorer, you may want to consider a computer with a Pentium 100 or Pentium 120 processor, 24 MB RAM, and 200 MB of free disk space.

USING THE COMPLETE SUITE

The lessons in this book cover the entire suite of Internet Explorer programs. The suite is an integrated set of tools—all with a similar look and feel—that enables you to maximize your Internet experience.

You don't have to look beyond Internet Explorer for the features you need. Internet Explorer provides an excellent e-mail facility, file transfer, a newsreader for newsgroups, Internet telephone and conferencing capability, chat, enhanced security and facilities for electronic commerce, an HTML editor for designing Web pages, and built-in sound, graphics, and video viewers. Internet Explorer offers tools that more than measure up to the exciting range of possibilities waiting for you on the Internet.

INSTALLING THE SOFTWARE

Before you can use the software contained on the CD-ROM, you must install it on your computer. The installation process is

automated by the Active Setup wizard that guides you through the
steps needed to load Internet Explorer 4 on your machine.

*If Internet Explorer Preview Release 1 or Preview
Release 2 is installed on your computer, you must first
uninstall the Preview Release before you install this
version of Internet Explorer 4.*

1 Close all open programs before you begin the installation of
Internet Explorer 4.

2 Place the CD-ROM into your computer's CD-ROM drive.

3 Select Start ➤ Programs ➤ Windows Explorer. Windows Explorer
opens.

4 Click the Plus sign next to the drive letter for your CD-ROM
drive. The list of folders contained on the CD-ROM appears.

5 Click the Msie folder. The contents of the folder appear in the
right pane.

6 Double-click the ie.exe file. Then click the Install Internet
Explorer 4 button. The Internet Explorer 4.0 Active Setup wizard
opens.

*You can close Windows Explorer anytime during the
setup process by clicking the Close button located at
the top right of the Windows Explorer window.*

7 Click Next. The License Agreement page of the wizard appears.

8 Read the license agreement. When you are finished, click the
option button labeled I accept the agreement.

9 Click Next. The Installation Option page of the wizard appears.

10 Click the down arrow for the installation drop-down list and
select Full Installation. By choosing this option, you direct the
Active Setup wizard to install the entire Internet Explorer suite
on your computer.

⑪ Click Next. The Windows Desktop Update page of the wizard appears.

⑫ Click the Yes option. By choosing this option, you direct the Active Setup wizard to install the Active Desktop on your computer.

⑬ Click Next. The Active Channel Selection page appears. Click Next. The Destination Folder page of the wizard appears.

⑭ The Active Setup wizard suggests a default folder for installing Internet Explorer. Accept the default by clicking Next. The Active Setup wizard has gathered all the information it needs from you and begins the installation process. A status screen shows the progress of the installation.

⑮ When the Active Setup is complete, a dialog box appears telling you that the setup is finished. Click OK. The Active Setup then reconfigures your computer as part of the installation process.

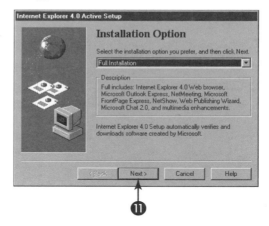

 NOTE

You may receive a dialog box informing you that setup was unable to close all programs automatically. If you have any programs open, close them and then click OK.

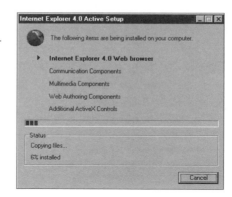

⑯ When Active Setup has finished reconfiguring your computer, another dialog box appears, informing you that Active Setup needs to restart your computer. Click OK. Your computer restarts.

⑰ After your computer restarts, you see a setup dialog box that shows the Internet Explorer program being installed on your computer. Once the dialog box disappears and after a few minutes, a series of Personalized Settings dialog boxes appear on the screen. When setup finishes with these settings, the setup is complete and the Active Desktop replaces your previous Windows wallpaper.

The Internet Explorer browser and the other programs in the Internet Explorer suite are now ready to use.

INSTALLING ADDITIONAL COMPONENTS

When you installed Internet Explorer, some add-on components (such as the NetShow On-Demand Player) were included in the installation. Additional add-on components developed by Microsoft and other software publishers are available for download from the Microsoft Internet Explorer Download site. Once you install them, these add-on components become a part of the browser and automatically load when you access a file that needs the add-on component in order to display.

Once you select the components you want to install from the Microsoft Internet Explorer Download site, Microsoft's Active Setup wizard does the rest for you.

These instructions guide you through the download and installation of the Microsoft VRML 2.0 Viewer, an add-on that lets you view interactive, three-dimensional images created with the Virtual Reality Modeling Language. You can use these instructions to download any of the components available at the download site.

Because Microsoft may develop additional components that can be installed to work with Internet Explorer, the Web pages shown here may look different from what you see in the browser window.

1 With the Internet Explorer browser open and displayed on the screen, click inside the Address bar.

2 Type www.microsoft.com/ie/ie40/.

3 Press Enter. The Internet Explorer 4.0 Web page appears in the browser window.

4 Click the Download link. A separate window appears.

5 Click the Internet Explorer 4.0 Components link. Another Web page appears that describes the add-on components.

6 Click the add-on component link that corresponds with your operating system. The Components Download page appears along with a dialog box asking you if it is OK for the Active Setup wizard to determine what components are already installed on your computer.

7 Click Yes. The Active Setup wizard searches your computer for components that have already been installed and displays the

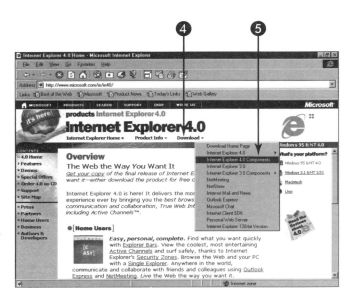

Components Download page after the search. The Status column at the far right of the page shows if a component has been installed or not and may also include information about available upgrades.

8 Click the red right-pointing arrow next to the Microsoft VRML 2.0 Viewer component. A description of the component appears. After you have read the description, click the red arrow again to hide the description.

9 Click the box next to the Microsoft VRML 2.0 Viewer component to select it for download. The size of the file and the estimated amount of time it will take to download appear at the bottom of the Web page.

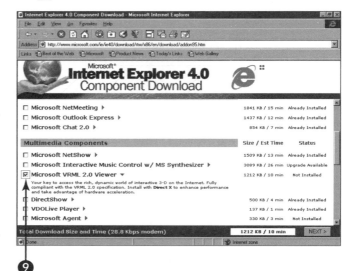

NOTE *If you want to download and install more than one component, you can select all the components at once to download one after the other.*

10 Click the Next button. Another download page appears.

11 Click the down arrow next to the Please Select a Download Site drop-down list. A list of sites offering the Microsoft VRML 2.0 Viewer for download appears.

12 Click the site that is nearest to your geographic location and click the Install Now button. A download dialog box appears. The VRML Viewer add-on is automatically downloaded and installed.

NOTE *Depending upon the components you select, you may receive a Security Warning dialog box during the download process. Click Yes to install the component.*

13 When the download and installation are complete, the browser closes automatically and a window appears showing the Internet Explorer components that are installed on your computer. Click the Close button at the top right of the window to close it.

The components are installed and ready to use.

TROUBLESHOOTING

If you have problems with Internet Explorer, one of the best places to get help is from the Microsoft Internet Explorer Technical Support Web page located at `www.microsoft.com/support/`. This Web page contains links to frequently asked questions about Internet Explorer, how-to articles on using Internet Explorer, troubleshooting wizards that walk you through problems and suggest possible solutions, Microsoft newsgroups where you can correspond with other Internet Explorer users, and the Microsoft Knowledge Base, a searchable technical support database containing solutions to problems found by other users.

To access and search the Microsoft Internet Explorer Technical Support Web site, follow these steps:

1 From any Internet Explorer suite program, select Help ➢ Online Support. The Internet Explorer browser opens, and a registration page appears.

2 Before you can use the support pages, you must register with Microsoft by supplying your e-mail address and designating a password. Once you complete the registration process, the Microsoft Technical Support page appears.

3 In the Search text box located in the middle of the Web page, type a few words that describe the problem you are having and click Find. A list of search results appears.

4 Scroll through the list of search results and click the title that looks like it may contain the solution to your problem.

5 If you do not find the answer to your question in the search results, click one of the links for Microsoft's other support options (FAQs, Knowledge Base, newsgroups) and continue looking for a solution.

Projects for Practice

Congratulations on making it through this book and learning all the skills you need to become proficient at surfing the Internet with Internet Explorer. But your journey has just begun. You have much to explore on the Internet and will find many ways to become involved with people from all over the world. The possibilities for learning, for teaching, for sharing ideas, for expressing opinions, and for working together are endless. And the only way for you to become a part of this exciting world is to dive in and splash about in the waves until you find a place for yourself.

In order to get comfortable surfing the Internet, you need to spend some time each day online. Find some time during the day to take care of your e-mail correspondence, check your favorite newsgroups, and visit a new Web site or two. As time passes, you may find yourself spending more time in front of your computer than in front of the TV. That may not seem like much of a change, but you can organize your online time to be more rewarding and productive.

This book showed you how to use the Internet Explorer 4 tools to explore the Internet and gave you glimpses of what you can do on the Internet. It's now time for you to put these tools to use. This appendix contains a list of projects to help you get started on your journey, along with the URLs of some interesting Web sites. Remember that the Internet changes daily, so some of these sites may not be available when you try to visit them. Enjoy the surf. Aloha!

Projects for practice

■ Find long-lost family and friends

Do you have a cousin that you haven't seen since you were a kid that you'd like to locate? Or maybe you'd like to find out what some of your high school pals are doing now. Search the various Internet directories for the e-mail addresses of the people you want to contact. Then send them e-mail messages and wait for their replies.

You can find several directory services by accessing Internet Explorer's Find People feature (select Start ➤ Find ➤ People). Here are a few useful directories:

- Four 11 at `http://www.four11.com/`
- InfoSpace at `http://www.infospace.com/`
- Bigfoot at `http://www.bigfoot.com/`

■ Organize a Friday night chat party

Ask your friends (by e-mail, of course) if they want to get together on a Friday night and have a different kind of party. Use Microsoft chat to set up a private chat room on one of the chat servers. You and your friends can gather at the appointed time. The rest of the party is up to you!

Here are a few Web sites that offer help with Microsoft Chat:

- Dave Central at `http://www.davecentral.com/563.html`
- The Unofficial MS Chat Add-on Site at `http://www.dido.com/chat/`
- Microsoft at `http://www.microsoft.com/ie/chat`

■ Send electronic greeting cards

Surprise your friends and relatives with a virtual greeting card or a virtual flower bouquet. Some of the sites that offer these greeting cards also sell and ship flowers, candy, and other gift items.

Projects for practice

Here are a few places that offer attractive cards and flowers:

- **Postcards From Hawaii** at `http://www.postcards-hawaii.com/pc_send.shtml`

- **Virtual Flowers** at `http://www.virtualflowers.com/`

- **A Card A Day** at `http://www2.info168.com/virtualcard/`

■ Browse the online magazine rack

Many popular magazines and newspapers now publish their full editions (or sometimes only a partial edition) on the Web. Many of these publications can be accessed at no charge, although some require you to register before you can enter the site. The publications that only publish a few articles from their current editions may require the payment of a subscription fee in exchange for full online access. Still, the Web is loaded with free magazines on every imaginable topic.

Try these publications for starters:

- **The New York Times** at `http://www.nytimes.com/yr/mo/day/index.html`

- **Microsoft Personal Computing Magazine** at `http://www.microsoft.com/magazine/`

- **PC World** at `http://www.pcworld.com/`

■ Experiment with shareware

Do you enjoy doodling and want to express your drawing abilities on the computer? Are you looking for an inexpensive software program for maintaining your checkbook? Or are you interested in finding an assortment of computer games? Shareware is your answer. You can try shareware for free and if you like the program, pay only a nominal registration fee to the program's developer.

These sites offer about every kind of shareware available:

- **SHAREWARE.COM** at `http://www.shareware.com`

B

Projects for Practice

Projects for practice

- The Jumbo! Download Network at `http://www.jumbo.com/`

- Shareware Links at `http://www.navicom.com/~bps/sharewre.html`

■ Create your own Web page

If your ISP offers space to publish a Web page as part of your monthly fee, take advantage of it. Your Web page can contain anything you like (well, anything that conforms to your ISP's rules). Use your Web page to explain your hobbies, offer dating advice, or display samples of your writing or artwork.

Here are a few Web sites to help you get started:

- Web Review at `http://www.webreview.com/`

- Laurie McCanna's Free Art Page at `http://www.mccannas.com/free/freeart.htm`

- HTML 101 at `http://www.compusmart.ab.ca/banderso/html1.htm`

■ Keep up with the rich and famous

Not all of us can be rich and famous, but we can live vicariously. See if you can find deep, dark secrets about your favorite celebrity—from the past or present. Or maybe look for similarities that you share with famous personalities. You never know; you may be star material.

The road to fame begins here:

- The Secret Diary of Bill Gates at `http://www.tiac.net/users/billg40/main/`

- Famous Birthdays at `http://oeonline.com/~edog/bday.html`

- A&E Biography at `http://www.biography.com/find/find.html`

■ Hold a family meeting

Use NetMeeting to keep in touch with family. But before you start that conference call, scan your photographs of the kids and the dog so you can share your images with grandma.

Here's where you can find more help for using NetMeeting:

- Microsoft NetMeeting home page at `http://www.microsoft.com/netmeeting`

- The NetMeeting Place at `http://www.netmeet.net/`

■ Keep your finances in order

It's a big job trying to save for a new car, a new home, the kid's college, and retirement. Use the resources on the Web to help you devise a budget and a financial plan, manage your money, and track your progress toward your goals.

Here's a sample of the financial information available on the Web:

- The IRS at `http://www.irs.ustreas.gov/prod/`

- The NASDAQ Stock Market home page at `http://www.nasdaq.com/`

- American Consumer Credit Counseling at `http://www.consumercredit.com/`

■ Live a healthy lifestyle

Staying healthy is an important factor in staying happy, and health is a hot topic on the Web. Learn about the measures you can take to avoid disease and illness, find support groups, and explore alternative treatments. The doctor is always in on the Web.

Here are a few sites that offer health-related information :

- The American Diabetes Association at `http://www.diabetes.org/default.html`

- Condom Country at `http://www.condom.com/`

Projects for practice

- Alcoholics Anonymous at `http://www.alcoholics-anonymous.org/`

■ Travel back through time

History offers many lessons. By looking at how people lived, how they dealt with conflict and adversity, and how events affected the future, we can make better choices and decisions in the present.

See how the events of the past have shaped the world we live in:

- Vietnam Veterans Home Page at `http://www.vietvet.org/`

- The History Net at `http://www.thehistorynet.com/`

- The History Channel at `http://www.historychannel.com`

■ Visit an online library

The library has always been one of my favorite places to hang out. I just love to browse the stacks until a book catches my eye. My only problem is that I can never remember to return the books to the library on time.

Check out these libraries and don't worry about being fined for overdue books:

- The Internet Public Library at `http://ipl.sils.umich.edu/ref/`

- The Library of Congress at `http://lcweb.loc.gov/`

- The On-line Books Page at `http://www.cs.cmu.edu/books.html`

Bonus Questions and Answers

Here are the answers to the questions that appear in the Skills Challenge section of each lesson. The questions are included for easy reference.

LESSON 2

Question	Answer
1. Where, during the Add Scheduled Task Wizard process, do you tell the wizard that you want to define additional settings for the scheduled task? What kinds of additional settings are available?	On the last screen of the Add Scheduled Task Wizard, check the box next to Open advanced properties of the task and click Finish. The Properties dialog box for the task opens. You can add parameters to the command line of the task that tell the task how it should operate. You can also add additional schedules to the task.
2. How do you change the size of the icons in a toolbar?	From Internet Explorer, select View ➢ Internet Options and click the Advanced tab. Scroll to the bottom of the list and find the Toolbar section. Select the option for Small Icons.
3. How do you hide toolbar titles and the descriptive text for toolbar buttons?	To hide toolbar titles, right-click the toolbar and deselect Show Titles from the pop-up menu. To hide the descriptive text, right-click the toolbar and deselect Show Text from the pop-up menu.

Bonus questions and answers

LESSON 3

1. Name the technology that's used to transmit new content to channels.	The technology is called push.
2. Is there a pay-per-view charge to subscribe to a channel?	No. Channel subscriptions are free.
3. Can you turn off the Active Desktop feature after you've set it up?	Yes, you can turn the Active Desktop feature off and on.
4. Where can you find help with Internet Explorer questions?	You can find help by clicking Help Contents and Index and searching through the list of available topics and keywords. If you can't find what you're looking for, you can visit the Microsoft Internet Explorer Support Home Page that contains a searchable index and links to other Microsoft Help sites.

LESSON 4

1. How do you know when your mouse passes over a hyperlink?	The mouse pointer takes the shape of a hand.
2. What is a URL?	The URL, short for Uniform Resource Locator, is the unique address of each page on the World Wide Web.
3. What happens when you click the Back button?	The Back button takes you backward (one page at a time) through the Web pages that you have accessed during your current Internet Explorer session.
4. Why do only some of the URLs of sites you've visited appear on the list when you click the down arrow to the right of the Address bar?	Only the URLs of the sites you've typed in the Address bar appear in the list.

Bonus questions and answers

LESSON 4

5. What are frames?	Frames are separate windows within a Web page.

LESSON 5

1. How does Autoscan work?	Autoscan, an exclusive Internet Explorer feature, searches for Web addresses that are close to the one you've typed in the Address bar.
2. Is it necessary to enclose search phrases in double quotes?	Whether or not you need to use double quotes to set off phrases is determined by the individual search engine, but it's a good idea to routinely use double quotes.
3. What's the difference between a search engine and a site directory?	Search engines send electronic rovers through the Web to find and reference new sites. Search directories add pages to their indexes when a Webmaster or sponsor registers the site. Search engines and search directories generally produce different search results even when you use the same keywords.

LESSON 6

1. Can you change the Web page that the Internet Explorer browser displays when it launches?	Yes, you can change the page to any site on the World Wide Web.
2. Describe two ways to add a site to your Favorites list.	Move to the page you wish to set as a Favorite. Select Favorites ➤ Add To Favorites. When the Add Favorite dialog box appears on the screen, with the title of the current site highlighted, click OK. An alternate

continued

Bonus questions and answers

method of adding a Web page to your list of Favorites is to right-click an empty area of the Web page and select Add to Favorites from the pop-up menu.

3. What is the advantage of placing Favorites in folders?

Using folders organizes your Favorites and makes them easy to find and use.

1. Which type of file (execution or zipped) requires the use of an additional application in order to run the program setup procedure?

Zipped files require a compression/decompression utility such as WinZip.

2. Where can you find information about the files located at an FTP site?

The main directory of an FTP site contains a readme or index file that will help you navigate the FTP site easier and find what you need.

3. How do you know if an add-on component is installed in Internet Explorer?

At the Add-on Component Download page, the status column for the component contains the words Already Installed.

1. How many font size choices do you have in Internet Explorer?

You can choose from five font sizes: Largest, Larger, Medium, Smaller, and Smallest.

2. How many different ways can you add a link to the Links toolbar?

You can add a link to the Links toolbar in three ways: from the Address bar, from a hyperlink, and from the Favorites menu.

Bonus questions and answers

LESSON 9

1. How do you change the supervisor password used by the Content Advisor?	Select View ➢ Internet Options. The Internet Options dialog box appears. Click the Content tab. Click the Settings button. A Password dialog box appears. Enter your password twice and click OK. The Content Advisor dialog box appears. Click the General tab. Click the Change Password button and enter the new password.
2. How do you prevent people who use your computer from accessing Web sites that are not rated by a ratings service?	In the Content Advisor dialog box, click the General tab. Make sure that the option labeled Users can see sites that have no rating is not checked.
3. How many different credit cards can you set up in Microsoft Wallet?	You can set up four different credit cards: Visa, MasterCard, American Express, and Discover.

LESSON 10

1. If you choose the Send Later option, where does the message go?	Messages queued to be sent later are moved to the Outbox. When you click Send and Receive, the message is moved to the Sent Items folder.
2. How do you check the spelling of a message?	Select Tools ➢ Check Spelling.
3. What's the difference between Replying to Author and Replying to All?	When you reply to the author, only the person who composed the message receives your reply. When you reply to all, everyone who received the message is sent a copy of your reply.

continued

Bonus questions and answers

LESSON 10

4. How do you temporarily disable routing criteria set in the Inbox Assistant?

If you want to temporarily disable a set of criteria without deleting it permanently in case you want to use it again, open the Inbox Assistant and uncheck the box next to the set of criteria.

LESSON 11

1. What are newsgroups?

Newsgroups are worldwide discussion groups that are conducted via computer networks in which people read messages and post responses.

2. Can you read the postings of a newsgroup if you haven't subscribed?

Yes. However, if you don't subscribe to a newsgroup, you'll have to take extra steps to display it each time you want to look at its postings.

3. Can you subscribe to and unsubscribe from any newsgroup as often as you wish?

You can subscribe to and unsubscribe from any newsgroup as many times and whenever you want.

LESSON 12

1. How many characters are available to choose from in Microsoft Chat?

By default, Microsoft Chat comes with 12 available characters.

2. Why do people use abbreviations and emoticons for chatting?

People use abbreviations, such as BRB (be right back), to save typing time. Emoticons are used to express emotions.

3. Do the changes you make to the Chat screen affect other computers?

No. Changing the background and the number of comic panes affects the view in your computer only.

LESSON 12

| 4. How do you get a fellow chatter's profile? | Right-click the chatter's name in the Member List pane and choose Get profile. Remember that you can only access profiles for chatters using Microsoft Chat. |

LESSON 13

1. How many people can participate in a Microsoft NetMeeting conference?	Microsoft NetMeeting supports meetings of as many as 32 participants. However, you can be connected to only one other person with audio or video at a time, and only three people at a time can share applications running on their computers.
2. What is an IP address?	An Internet Protocol (IP) address is the unique number that's assigned to your computer when it's connected to the Internet.
3. How do you prevent other people from calling you?	To prevent any new, incoming calls, select Call ➤ Do Not Disturb.

LESSON 14

| 1. If you add a second page to your Web site, how do you link the second page to the first page? | Type text to serve as the link to the second page. Highlight the text. Select Insert ➤ Hyperlink. Click the New Page tab. |
| 2. If you don't have any graphics stored on your computer, you can search the Internet for Web graphics that are free for personal use. What search terms would give you good search results? | Good search terms include free Web graphics, Web page art, and Web page design. |

continued

Bonus questions and answers

3. How many different directions can the marquee move across the Web page?

The marquee can move in two directions. It can scroll from right to left or from left to right.

What's on the CD-ROM

The CD-ROM in the back of the book includes the exclusive *One Step at a Time On-Demand* software. This interactive software coaches you through the exercises in the book's lessons while you work on a computer at your own pace. The CD-ROM also includes the full version of Internet Explorer 4 and two handy utilities: WinZip and WS_FTP LE.

USING THE ONE STEP AT A TIME ON-DEMAND INTERACTIVE SOFTWARE

One Step at a Time On-Demand software includes the exercises in the book so that you can search for information about how to perform a function or complete a task. You can run the software alone or in combination with the book. The software consists of three modes: Demo, Teacher and Concurrent. In addition, the Concept option provides an overview of each exercise.

What's on the CD-ROM

- **Demo** mode provides a movie-style demonstration of the same steps that are presented in the book's exercises.

- **Teacher** mode simulates the software environment and permits you to interactively follow the exercises in the book's lessons.

- **Concurrent** mode enables you to you the *One Step at a Time On-Demand* features while you work within the actual Internet Explorer environment. This unique interactive mode provides audio instructions, and direct you to take the correct actions as you work through the exercises. (Concurrent mode may not be available for all exercises.)

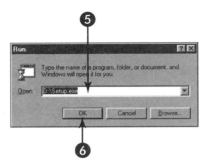

If you run the On-Demand Interactive Learning™ *software in Windows 98, we recommend you don't work in Teacher or Concurrent mode unless you turn off the Active Desktop feature. However, Teacher or Concurrent mode may not work properly at all in Windows 98. At the time of the writing of this book, the final release of Windows 98 wasn't available, and we couldn't test all the topics in Teacher or Concurrent mode.*

■ Installing the software

The *One Step at a Time On-Demand* software can be installed on Windows 95 and Windows NT 4.0. To install the interactive software on your computer, follow these steps:

1 Place the *Internet Explorer 4 One Step at a Time* CD-ROM in your CD-ROM drive.

2 Launch Windows *(if you haven't already).*

3 Click the Start menu.

4 Select Run. The Run dialog box appears.

5 Type **D:\Setup.exe** (where D is your CD-ROM drive) in the Run dialog box.

6 Click OK to run the setup procedure. The On-Demand Installation dialog box appears.

7 Click Continue. The On-Demand Installation Options dialog box appears.

8 Click the Full/Network radio button (if this option is not already selected).

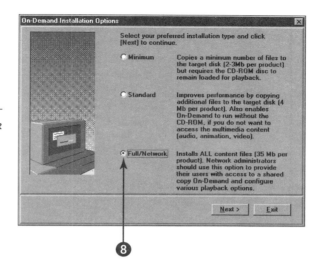

NOTE *Full/Network installation requires 150MB of hard disk space. If you don't have enough hard disk space, click the Standard radio button to choose Standard installation. If you choose standard installation, you should always insert the CD-ROM when you start the software to hear sound.*

9 Click Next. The Determine Installation Drive and Directory dialog box appears.

10 Choose the default drive and directory that appears, or click Change to choose a different drive and directory.

11 Click Next. The Product Selection dialog box appears, which enables you to verify the software you want to install.

12 Click Finish to complete the installation. The On-Demand Installation dialog box displays the progress of the installation. After the installation, the Multiuser Pack Registration dialog box appears.

13 Enter information in the Multiuser Pack Registration dialog box.

14 Click OK. The On-Demand Installation dialog box appears.

15 Click OK to confirm the installation has been successfully completed.

■ Running the software

Once you've installed the software, you can view the text of the book and follow interactively the steps in each exercise. To run Demo, Teacher or Concurrent mode, follow these steps:

1 From the Windows desktop, click the Start menu.

What's on the CD-ROM

2 Select Programs ➤ IDG Books ➤ Internet Explorer 4 One Step. A small On–Demand toolbar appears in the upper-right corner of your screen.

3 The On–Demand Reminder dialog box appears, telling you that the On–Demand software is active. If you don't want to display the dialog box, deselect the Show Reminder check box. Then, click OK.

4 Click the icon of the professor. The Interactive Training—Lesson Selection dialog box appears.

5 Select the Contents tab, if it isn't selected already. A list of the lessons appears, divided into four modules.

6 Click the plus icon next to the lessons you want to explore, or click the Lessons radio button. A list of the lessons appears.

7 Click the plus icon next to the lesson you want to explore. A list of topics appears.

8 Double-click a topic of your choice. A menu appears.

9 Select Demo, Teacher or Concurrent (if available).

10 Follow the onscreen prompts to use the interactive software and work through the steps.

In Demo mode, you only need to perform actions that appear in red. Otherwise, the software automatically demonstrates the actions for you. All you need to do is read the information that appears on screen.
(Holding down the Shift key pauses the program; releasing the Shift key activates the program.) In Teacher mode, you need to follow the directions and perform the actions that appear on screen.

■ Getting the most out of the One Step at a Time software

It is strongly recommended that you read the topics in the book as you are using the software. In those instances where the onscreen instructions don't match the book's instructions exactly, or the software appears to stop before completing a task, the book will provide the instructions necessary for you to continue.

■ Stopping the program

To stop running the program at any time, press Esc to return to the Interactive Training—Lesson Selection dialog box. (To re-start the software, double-click a topic of your choice and select a mode.)

■ Exiting the program

Press Esc when the Interactive Training—Lesson Selection dialog box appears to exit the program. The On-Demand toolbar appears in the upper right corner of your screen. Click the icon that displays the lightning bolt image. A menu appears. Choose Exit. The On-Demand —Exit dialog box appears. Click Yes to exit On-Demand.

■ Copying exercise files to your hard drive

Generally, your computer works more efficiently with files located on the hard drive, rather than a floppy disk or CD-ROM. To make your work in this book easier, copy the exercise files into a folder on your hard drive. You can then open and work with the files when instructed to do so from that location.

1 Double-click the My Computer icon on your desktop.

2 Double-click the hard drive C.

3 Select File ➢ New, and then choose Folder from the submenu that appears. A new folder appears, with the name New Folder.

4 Type One Step to name the folder.

5 Press Enter.

6 Close the My Computer window.

7 Place the Internet Explorer 4 One Step at a Time CD-ROM into the disc drive.

What's on the CD-ROM

⑧ Double-click the My Computer icon again and, in the My Computer window, double-click the CD-ROM icon to open the drive where you inserted the disc.

⑨ Click the folder named Exercise.

⑩ Copy the selected folder by pressing Ctrl+C.

⑪ Close the CD-ROM window.

⑫ Double-click the My Computer icon on your desktop.

⑬ In the My Computer window, double-click the hard drive C.

⑭ Double-click the One Step folder.

⑮ Paste the Exercise folder into the One Step folder by pressing Ctrl+V. The exercise files are now located within this folder on your hard drive.

■ Using the exercise files

You need to make sure you have removed the Read-only attribute from any files you copy to the hard drive before you start using them. Otherwise, you will not be able to save changes to the files. To remove the Read-only attribute, open the Exercise folder on your hard drive and press Ctrl+A to select all the files in the folder. From the File menu, select Properties. The Properties dialog box appears. Click the Read-only attribute to remove the check from the checkbox.

■ Installing additional modules

You may install additional modules of the *On-Demand Interactive Learning*™ software and find out more about PTS Learning Systems, the company behind the software, by using a file on the CD-ROM included with this book. Follow these steps:

❶ Start your browser.

❷ Select File from the menu.

❸ Select Open.

④ Type **D:\info\welcome.htm**, where D is your CD-ROM drive.

⑤ Click OK to view the contents.

USING INTERNET EXPLORER 4

The full version of Microsoft Internet Explorer 4 is on this CD-ROM, and the Favorites folder has been customized with links to some of the best sites referenced in this book. To install Internet Explorer, use My Computer or Windows Explorer to open the Msie folder on the CD-ROM. Then locate and double-click the ie.exe file and follow the on-screen instructions.

If you don't have an Internet connection yet, Internet Explorer can help. After you install the program, select Start ➤ Programs ➤ Internet Explorer ➤ Connection Wizard. You'll see a wizard that enables you to determine which national Internet service providers (if any) have local telephone connections in your area. If there's a local connection, you can sign up for Internet access immediately, using your credit card.

If you already have an Internet connection, you can use Microsoft Internet Explorer with any service provider.

Full installation instructions for Internet Explorer 4 are included in Appendix A.

USING WINZIP

A popular method for distributing and storing files is to zip the files into a compressed archive. A zipped file can contain one or more files that are compressed to take up less storage space. Using zipped files keeps related files together in a group and takes less time to transfer the files across a network. Some common uses for zipped files include the following:

- **Distributing files on FTP sites and bulletin boards.** Not only are file sizes reduced by the compression, but all necessary files can be transferred in one download to reduce transfer time.

- **Sending a group of related files.** Keeping related files together makes it easier to distribute the files to a work group via e-mail or file transfer.

- **Storing files.** Compressing infrequently used files saves disk space. The files can be quickly and easily decompressed when needed.

WinZip is a Windows shareware program that both compresses files *into* zipped archives and extracts (decompresses) the files *from* zipped archives. WinZip uses the Windows point-and-click drag-and-drop interface in conjunction with a wizard interface that simplifies the process even more.

To install WinZip, use My Computer or Windows Explorer to open the Winzip folder on the CD-ROM. Then locate and double-click the winzip95.exe file and follow the on-screen instructions.

Full installation instructions and directions for using WinZip are included in Lesson 7 of this book.

USING WS_FTP LE

WS_FTP LE is a Windows shareware program used to transfer files between two computers connected by a modem and telephone line or by a network. You can connect to any remote system that has a valid Internet address and an FTP server. Once connected to the server, you can browse the directories and files and transfer files between the two systems.

To install WS_FTP LE, use My Computer or Windows Explorer to open the Wsftp folder on the CD-ROM. Then locate and double-click the ws_ftple.exe file and follow the on-screen instructions.

Full installation instructions and directions for using WS_FTP LE are included in Lesson 7 of this book.

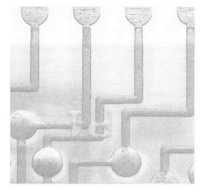

3D (three-dimensional) The visual display that exhibits the three dimensions of breadth, height, and thickness or depth. Standard 2D computer images and television displays create a flat image with only height and breadth.

A

address book An application that allows you to store full e-mail addresses as aliases that are easier to remember.

Advanced Research Projects Agency Network (ARPANET) The network funded by ARPA that served as the basis for early networking research and as a central backbone during the development of the Internet. The ARPANET consisted of individual packet switching computers interconnected by leased lines.

alias A short and easy-to-remember name that is translated from another name that is longer and more difficult to remember.

alt newsgroups An alternative list of newsgroups containing some of the more informative and provocative newsgroups on the Internet. These newsgroups are not a part of Usenet, but they operate in the same manner. It is easier to start an alt newsgroup than it is to start a Usenet newsgroup.

anonymous FTP A method for allowing FTP access to a server that bypasses the regular requirement for entering an authorized user ID and a password. Anonymous FTP is used at many university and government sites where the goal is to provide easy access to information. People accessing the site input the user ID *anonymous* and enter their e-mail address for the password.

applet A small software program written in Java that can be included in HTML documents and downloaded automatically to your computer and run.

Archie A software program that provides a method of searching archived files on Internet servers that use FTP.

archive A collection of files stored on an Internet server, most commonly called an FTP server. These archive files are often available for download by any Internet user through anonymous FTP.

attachment A file that is sent along with an e-mail message. An attachment can be any type of document—a text file, an image file, or a compressed file.

authentication The process of determining the identity and logon validity of a user attempting to access a computer network.

B

backbone The top level in a hierarchical network. Stub and transit networks that are connected to the same backbone are guaranteed to be interconnected.

bandwidth

bandwidth The difference, in Hertz (Hz), between the highest and lowest frequencies of a transmission channel. However, as typically used, a measurement of the amount of data that can be sent through a given communications circuit.

banner A narrow graphic usually found at the top of a Web page. Banners can look like a logo or a signboard and are relatively small, about 1 $\frac{1}{2}$ x 4 inches. Banners are often used for advertising and to mark a place where the reader can click to get more information.

Big Seven newsgroups The seven official newsgroup hierarchies in Usenet—comp, misc, news, rec, sci, soc, and talk. Visit the comp newsgroups for discussions of computers; the misc newsgroups for wide-ranging discussions on a variety of topics; the news newsgroups for info about Usenet; the rec newsgroups for discussions of music, sports, games, and other recreational activities; the sci newsgroups for discussions related to science; the soc newsgroups for discussions of social groups and society; and the talk newsgroups for debate forums.

binary file A file that contains information other than plain text. Binary files can contain graphics, sound, video, programs, or other information.

bit (BInary digiT) The smallest unit of information that a computer can handle. Bits are defined by either a one or a zero.

bounce The term applied to the return to the sender of an undeliverable e-mail message because of delivery problems such as a wrong e-mail address or an unavailable e-mail server.

browser A software program that allows you to view content on the World Wide Web and navigate by typing URLs in the Address bar and clicking hyperlinks.

byte Eight bits grouped together.

C

cable modem A type of modem that hooks up to a television and a computer so that you can surf the net at 100 times your current speed. Some people have their doubts about this new technology. If it takes off, the Net will never be the same!

cache A file on your computer where copies of Web pages that you've recently visited are stored. When you request a page, Internet Explorer first looks to see if the page is stored in the cache. If it is, the browser loads the page into the browser window from the cache instead of downloading the page from the Internet.

challenge phrase Data used during an authentication key exchange process.

chat A software program that enables real-time written conversation with one or more people across the Internet. Microsoft Chat allows you to animate a character to give your conversations more life.

com The last part of the host name for a domain run by a business (for example, `idgbooks.com`).

Common Gateway Interface (CGI) The standard mechanism used on Web servers to execute programs that generate dynamic documents and send them to your browser.

comp newsgroups Newsgroups devoted to computer-related information and discussion.

compression The translation of data (video, graphics, audio, or a combination) to a more compact form for storage or transmission.

conference A means of interactive electronic communication between two or more people. Conferences can be conducted through e-mail, with text- and audio-based conferencing software, or via videoconferencing applications.

congestion The term describing the situation that exists when the transmission load exceeds the capacity of a data communication path.

cookie A data file that stores information about the pages accessed at a particular Web site and the visitor's activity while at the Web site. The browser remembers information about your visit to the Web page by keeping the information in a cookie file that is stored on your computer. When you revisit a site, the server requests the cookie information, and the browser passes the information to the server by transferring the file located on your computer named cookie.txt.

cursor A small movable icon on the screen that signifies which window you are using and which part of the information in it has been selected. You can move the cursor with a variety of objects: mouse, keyboard, joystick, or trackball.

D

default The data needed to control the operation of a computer operating system or an application program. If this data is not set to acceptable values, the system or program will not run correctly, if it runs at all. Often the author of the system provides reasonable starting values that the system uses unless the user deliberately changes them.

dial up The process of connecting to a remote computer by using a telephone line.

Domain Name System (or Server) (DNS) The online distributed database of machine name addresses used to look up names of remote machines. When you enter a mnemonic domain name, the DNS translates it into an IP address.

download The process of transferring a copy of a file from a server on the Internet to another computer.

downtime The term used for the period of time that a computer is not functional. Downtime may be scheduled for maintenance or upgrades, or it may be the unexpected (and unappreciated) result of system problems.

drag and drop A mechanism for selecting one icon by clicking and holding the mouse button, dragging the icon to another icon or active area of the screen, and then releasing the mouse button to set up a link between the objects represented by the icons.

E

edu The last part of the host name for a domain run by an educational organization such as a university.

electronic mail (e-mail) A system that allows computer users to exchange messages via a communications network. Electronic mail is one of the first, and still one of the most popular, uses of the Internet.

e-mail address The domain-based address that is used to send electronic mail to a specified destination.

emoticon An arrangement of keyboard characters that are meant to be viewed sideways and reflect the emotional state of the writer of the message. Because electronic mail does not allow for body language or other emotional clues, emoticons are very useful. :-)

encryption A method of adding security to a network. Data being sent between two computers is encoded (or encrypted) so that only the intended recipient can decode (or unencrypt) the data.

F

file transfer The process of copying a file from one computer to another over a computer network.

File Transfer Protocol (FTP) The set of commands used to send files from one computer to another over a network in a more efficient way than using the `http://` protocol.

finger An Internet application that can find out if someone is currently connected to the Internet. You need to know the name and e-mail address of the person you are trying to find.

flooding The practice of intentionally filling someone else's screen with garbage. Flooding sometimes occurs during an IRC chat.

frames An organizational method used by Web page designers to divide the browser window into several windows for presenting different types of information.

freeware Software that can be downloaded from the Internet and used free of charge but that generally has little or no technical support.

Frequently Asked Questions (FAQ) A list of questions that are commonly asked by those who are new to the subject matter. Someone (such as the newsgroup moderator, a software publisher, or an expert on the subject) compiles a set of the most commonly asked questions and supplies the answers. FAQs are posted on some Web pages and maintained for most newsgroups. If you are new to a newsgroup, always consult the FAQ first. Most FAQs provide pointers to additional sources of information.

Glossary

full duplex

full duplex A data communications term indicating that both ends of a communications link can transmit data at the same time.

G

Gopher A search tool used for finding information on the Internet. World Wide Web search engines, such as those featured by HotBot and Yahoo, are now more popular.

gov The last part of the host name for a domain run by a government organization.

Graphics Interchange Format (GIF) A file format used for storing image files that is designed to compress computer-generated images.

H

half duplex A data communications term indicating that only one end of a communications link can transmit data at a given time; one end must wait for acknowledgment of its data transmission from the other end before it can start transmitting another data packet.

hit One visit by a reader to a Web site.

hotspot (also called a hyperlink) A region of text or graphics that represents a link to another document. Most hotspots are textual (in *.htm files) or are location-sensitive areas in graphics.

hyperlink A sensitive area embedded in a text document or graphic that represents a dynamic link to another document and transfers you to the document when you click the hyperlink.

hypermedia A system for storing information using embedded references to other pages, sounds, and graphics.

Hypertext Markup Language (HTML) The formatting language used to design most Web pages.

HTML editor A program that helps you create Web pages by automatically generating the HTML tags. FrontPage Express is an example of an HTML editor.

Hypertext Transfer Protocol (HTTP) The language that Web browsers use to transfer Web pages from a Web server to your computer.

History list A list of URLs that the browser automatically stores in memory for a certain amount of time. History lists are dynamic logs that document all the Web sites you visit while browsing the Web.

I

imagemap A graphic image that contains clickable images with graphical hotspots. The processing is done, at present, through the CGI mechanism.

Internet Protocol (IP) address A numerical scheme used to identify each machine on the Internet. There are more than four billion numerical combinations.

Internet site A computer connected to the Internet that contains information that can be accessed using a protocol such as http, ftp, telnet, or gopher.

Internet Relay Chat (IRC) A way for several users to log on to a communal channel and talk via their keyboards asynchronously.

J

Joint Photographic Experts Group (JPEG) A file format designed to compress digitally scanned photographs.

Jughead (Jonzy's Universal Gopher Hierarchy Excavation and Display) Software that searches for key words in Gopher menus and is often included on local Gopher servers.

jump The act of using a hyperlink to quickly move from place to place within a Web page, from page to page within a Web site, or from site to site within the World Wide Web.

K

knowbot A robot with the main purpose of gathering or filtering information.

L

linking The process of using text or graphical images to direct the reader to more information at another source.

listserv An automated mailing list distribution system.

M

mailing list A list of e-mail addresses used to forward messages to groups of people.

Subscribers use mailing lists as forums to discuss a certain set of topics.

megabyte (MB) The term for 1 million bytes (actually 1048576 bytes).

misc newsgroups A catch-all category for newsgroups that don't fit into any of the other newsgroup categories.

mirror A duplicate resource used to save transmission overheads caused by too many people trying to access one site for the same information.

moderated newsgroup A newsgroup that has a moderator who reads submissions and decides if their content and style are appropriate for posting.

Moving Pictures Experts Group (MPEG) A file format that contains moving images and can display them as a movie.

multimedia The integration of two or more types of media. Multimedia productions can include text, audio, sound, images, animation, and video.

Multipurpose Internet Mail Extensions (MIME) A transfer protocol that allows complex documents to be sent via electronic mail. A mail message can consist of several components of different MIME types and can be sent using SMTP.

Musical Instrument Digital Interface (MIDI) Computer-generated music and sound effects that can be used to compose and record musical programs.

N

Netizen An habitual visitor, resident, inhabitant, citizen, or denizen of the Internet.

Netiquette The proper and accepted way to behave on the Internet. Internet Netiquette is really just common sense; mind your manners. Use Netiquette as a keyword on almost any search engine to find plenty of advice.

news newsgroups Newsgroups devoted to issues concerning Usenet.

O

offline The state that exists when your computer is not connected to a network (such as the Internet) and you cannot transmit or receive information from other computers on the network.

online The state that exists when your computer is interactively connected to a network.

org The last part of the host name for a domain run by a nonprofit organization.

P

password A response to a query for user identification. When you log on to the Internet, for example, you are asked to enter a password. Some passwords can be recorded so that they are entered automatically by your software when required.

Platform for Internet Content Selection (PICS) A standardized format for systems rating Internet content. PICS is *not* a rating system.

post The act of putting a message into public view, usually on a Web site or a newsgroup.

Post Office Protocol (POP) A server protocol for handling e-mail delivery.

postmaster The person responsible for ensuring that a mail delivery system runs smoothly and for fixing user problems. The postmaster has an e-mail address that looks something like postmaster@site.

public domain Documents that are entirely free for public use and distribution. However, not all freely available documents fall in this category. Most Web documents and freeware are not in the public domain. Freeware usually has minimal copyright restrictions.

R

rec newsgroups Newsgroups devoted to discussions of recreational activities such as golf, motorcycling, and movies.

resource A benefit, an information source, or a necessary element. Examples of resources include available disk space, RAM, and output devices such as printers, monitors, and communication ports.

robot A computer applet that wanders the World Wide Web and automatically retrieves linked pages that contain specified keywords. The robot then builds a database of Web page URLs and indexes either all of the words or keywords within the database. The Web search engines are examples of robots.

round-trip time A measure of the current delay on a network.

S

sci newsgroups Newsgroups devoted to science news and information.

scroll The act of moving up, down, or sideways through a file or image displayed on the computer screen.

search The act of retrieving information from the Internet.

search criteria Keywords or phrases used to identify the object of a search and qualify the collected results.

search engine An application that functions much like an automated library card catalog. Search engines catalog millions of Websites. When you request information from a search engine, it lists all the catalog entries that match your search criteria.

secure server A server equipped with encryption technology to protect sensitive and confidential information. Most companies

that accept credit cards over the Internet do so through a secured server.

shareware Software that can be used free of charge for a stated period of time. If you want to continue to use the software after the trial period, you are required to pay a nominal registration fee to the developer of the program.

Simple Mail Transfer Protocol (SMTP) One of the most popular mail transfer protocols for transferring e-mail between systems.

soc newsgroups Newsgroups that discuss topics of interest for students of sociology and psychology.

spam Usually commercial messages posted across a large number of Internet newsgroups that don't contain any information of specific interest to the posted newsgroup.

spider A name for a robot that roams the Web and indexes information as it goes.

stub and transit networks Network branches that do not connect to other networks or branches (stub) or do connect to other networks or branches (transit).

surf A metaphor used to describe the action a person performs while exploring, browsing, and jumping from site to site on the Internet.

T

talk newsgroups Newsgroups devoted to Usenet's version of talk radio.

thread A list of messages that relate to each other, organized in a tree structure based on date and time of creation and the message being answered. Threads are used in Usenet newsgroups and in other structured group messaging systems.

toolbar A row of icons that is usually located at the top of an application window but can also appear as a column of icons down the side of an application window. Each icon represents a program command, so toolbars help make programs easier to use. Some toolbars can be customized; that is, they can be moved, and icons can be added, deleted, or moved.

U

Uniform Resource Locator (URL) The address that is

used to refer to a particular document on the Web.

USENET A series of computer systems (pre-Internet) on which the Usenet newsgroups were set up to exchange postings.

V

Veronica An Internet tool that allows you to search by keyword through Gopher titles and directories.

virtual reality A computer-generated environment that models some aspect of the real world. The many variations of virtual reality range from total-immersion graphics (such as headsets and force-feedback devices) to medium-performance graphics on low-cost workstations.

virtual storefront A Web-based representation of a retailer or other business that focuses on sales through the Internet.

Virtual Reality Markup Language (VRML) A method for implementing three-dimensional graphic environments and graphic objects under HTML.

W

WAV A format for storing sounds in files.

Webmaster The person who is responsible for keeping a Web site up, current, and running. The Webmaster is the first person to contact if URLs don't work or if servers are down.

Web site One or more related HTML documents available on the Internet. Typically a site presents information about a business, institution, or individual and hypertext links to other sites.

Whiteboard A communal electronic area where a group can interactively add or modify material, including graphics, online.

Wide Area Information Server (WAIS) A type of server that provides searching access to text-based databases and ranks results based on relevance to the search query.

Y

yoyo mode A state in which a computer system rapidly alternates between working correctly (being up) and crashing (being down).

A–B

C–D

(continued)

Index

E–F

Index

H–I

History list

> defined, 330
>
> returning to previous URLs, 80

hits, defined, 88, 93, 330

home page

> See also Start page; Web pages
>
> defined, 72–73

HotBot search engine, 101–103

> advanced searches, 102–103
>
> described, 98, 99
>
> search protocol, 101–102

hotspots, defined, 330

HTML (HyperText Markup Language)

> defined, 330
>
> dynamic, 13–14
>
> editors, 330
>
> formatting in Outlook Express, 201–204
>
> FrontPage Express and, 280
>
> overview, 280, 282
>
> tags, 282

http:// as superfluous, 78

> See also URLs

HTTP (HyperText Transfer Protocol), defined, 330

hyperlinks

> defined, 4, 330
>
> error messages, 75
>
> exercises, 73–76
>
> FrontPage Express, 285–286
>
> hits, 88, 93
>
> invalid, 74–75
>
> moving around with, 73–74
>
> moving backward and forward, 75–76
>
> overview, 73

hypermedia, defined, 330

I

ILS (Internet Locator Server), NetMeeting and, 265

imagemap, defined, 330

IMAP (Internet Message Access Protocol), configuring Outlook Express, 194, 196

indexing tools, searching with, 88–89

Infoseek search engine, 98

installing

> Active Desktop, 22–23
>
> components, 301–302
>
> modules from CD-ROM in back of book, 322–323
>
> self-executing files, 146–147
>
> software from CD-ROM in back of book, 320–321
>
> VRML Viewer, 132–133, 301–302
>
> WinZip, 136–138
>
> WS_FTP LE, 138–140
>
> zipped files, 142–144

installing Internet Explorer, 297–303

> Active Setup wizard, 299–300
>
> components, 301–302
>
> suite of applications, 298
>
> system requirements, 297–298
>
> troubleshooting, 303

IntelliSense features, 13

I–M

IRC (Internet Relay Chat)

> See also Microsoft Chat

> defined, 330

items, adding to Desktop, 42–43

J

Java programming, 135

JPEG format

> defined, 330

> graphics, 287

Jughead, defined, 330

jump, defined, 330

K

keys, private and public
encryption, 178

keywords, searching and, 96–97

knowbot, defined, 330

L

linking, defined, 330

links. See hyperlinks

Links toolbar

> Active Desktop, 30–31

> customizing, 159–162,
163–164

listserv, defined, 330

lurking on newsgroups, 220

Lycos search engine, 98

M

mail. See Outlook Express

mail servers, 196

mailing lists, defined, 330–331

management exercises, 111–124

> downloading Web pages, 121–122

> Favorite sites, 115–118

> Start page, 112–115

> subscribing to Web sites, 119–121

> troubleshooting, 123–124

markers, NetShow On-Demand
Player, 129–130

marquees, FrontPage Express,
290–291

MB (megabyte), defined, 331

menus

> grayed-out commands, 61

> Windows components, 60–61

Microsoft Active Desktop
Gallery. See Gallery

Microsoft Chat, 241–260

> acronyms, 249

> avatars, 244–251

> backgrounds, 246

> changing rooms, 251–252

> characters, 244–251

> Chat Room list dialog box, 252

> configuring, 243–246

> conversation options, 250–251

> conversations, 246–251

> creating new rooms, 252–254

> customizing, 244–246

> described, 16

N

Index

N

NetMeeting, 261–278

accepting calls, 271

Audio Tuning Wizard, 264–265

Chat utility, 272–273

configuring, 263–267

described, 16

file transfers, 275

ILS (Internet Locator Server), 265

IP addresses, 265

making and receiving calls, 267–271

overview, 262–263

sending and receiving files, 275

server selection, 266

setup, 263–265

sharing applications, 276

Skills Challenge, 277–278

starting conferences from directories, 268–269

starting conferences with IP addresses, 269–271

summary, 278

troubleshooting, 278

video conferencing, 262–263

Whiteboard utility, 273–274

window, 267

NetShow On-Demand Player, 127, 128–130

described, 15, 128

markers, 129–130

networks, stub and transit, 332

New Message window, Outlook Express, 200

newbie, defined, 227

news newsgroups, defined, 331

newsgroups, 219–239

+ (plus sign) and threads, 231

acronyms, 232

alt, 327

Big Seven, 328

capitalization as shouting in messages, 232

described, 16

displaying, 229

downloading messages, 234–235

Downloading Newsgroups dialog box, 223–224

etiquette, 232

finding, 225–226

Internet Connection Wizard, 221–223

lurking on, 220

marking articles as read, 231

moderated, 220

name categories, 224–225

Newsgroups window, 227

newsreaders, 220

offline reading, 235–237

Outlook Express setup, 221–225

overview, 220

posting messages, 232–234

reading postings, 230–231

Skills Challenge, 237–238

subscribing to, 226–228

summary, 239

threads, 220

troubleshooting, 238–239

types of, 220

P–Q

Index

S

security (continued)

overview, 14, 168

planning, 185–186

public and private keys, 178

restricting access to Internet, 168–169

Security Settings dialog box, 173–174

Skills Challenge, 185–186

summary, 187

troubleshooting, 186–187

zones, 172–174

Security Advisor home page, obtaining personal certificates, 176–179

self-executing files, installing, 146–147

servers

e-mail, 196

NetMeeting, 266

secure, 332

shareware

defined, 332

practice projects, 307–308

software types available on Internet, 140

Web sites containing, 145

sharing applications, NetMeeting, 276

shopping online. See online shopping

shortcuts, adding to Quick Launch toolbar, 28–29

Show Desktop button, Active Desktop, 25–26

signature files, Outlook Express, 205–206

site directories

defined, 88, 89

Yahoo!, 103–105

sizing fonts, 155–156

Skills Challenge

Active Desktop, 37–38

customizing Internet Explorer, 164–165

Desktop integration, 65–66

Favorite sites, 122–123

finding software, 147–148

FrontPage Express, 294–295

Microsoft Chat, 258–259

NetMeeting, 277–278

newsgroups, 237–238

Outlook Express, 214–216

security, 185–186

Web site searching, 105–106

World Wide Web browsing, 83–84

SMTP (Simple Mail Transfer Protocol)

defined, 332

e-mail servers, 196

soc newsgroups, defined, 332

software

bugs and, 171

downloading from FTP sites, 144–145

downloading from World Wide Web, 141–142

Skills Challenge (finding on Web), 147–148

types available on Internet, 140

viruses and, 171

software suites, 17–19

opening programs, 17–18

switching between programs, 18–19

sound. *See* audio; audio formats

spam, defined, 332

spelling errors, searching and, 100

spider, defined, 332

Standard Buttons toolbar, customizing toolbars, 159–162

Standard toolbar, FrontPage Express, 281

Start page, 94–96

See also home page; Web pages

customizing, 112–114

management exercises, 112–115

Quick for Outlook Express, 197

selecting new, 114–115

stub networks, defined, 332

subscribing to

channels, 46–49

Microsoft Network, 44–45

newsgroups, 226–228

Web sites, 119–121

suite of applications, installing Internet Explorer, 298

suites. *See* software suites

surf, defined, 332

switching between programs, software suites, 18–19

system requirements, installing Internet Explorer, 297–298

T

tags, HTML, 282

talk newsgroups, defined, 332

Task Scheduler, Active Desktop, 36–37

taskbar, Active Desktop and, 27–32

telephony, NetMeeting, 261–278

text, inserting and formatting FrontPage Express, 282–284

Text Labels command, customizing toolbars, 162

text view, Microsoft Chat, 257–258

threads

defined, 332

newsgroup, 220

3D, defined, 327

3D Web effects, VRML Viewer, 127, 132–134, 301–302

timestamp WebBots, FrontPage Express, 292–293

"Too many users, try again later" error message, 75

toolbars, 159–164

Active Desktop, 27–32

creating, 32

customizing, 159–164

default, 159

defined, 332

display and position of, 159–162

Text Labels command, 162

transit networks, defined, 332

T–V

troubleshooting

Active Desktop, 38–39

customizing Internet Explorer, 165

Desktop integration, 66–67

FrontPage Express, 295

installing Internet Explorer, 303

management exercises, 123–124

Microsoft Chat, 260

multimedia, 149

NetMeeting, 278

newsgroups, 238–239

Outlook Express, 216–217

searches, 106–107

security, 186–187

World Wide Web surfing, 84–85

"try before you buy" software, downloading process, 140–141

U

unsubscribing from newsgroups, 228–229

Update All Subscriptions command, viewing updated channel content, 49–50

upgrade enhancements, Internet Explorer, 12–14

URLs (Uniform Resource Locators), 5–6, 76–79

Autoscan, 90–91

bookmarks. *See* Favorite sites

defined, 332

domain names, 77, 78

entering, 78–79

Favorite sites, 115–118

http:// as superfluous, 78

parts of, 77

protocols, 77

USENET

See also newsgroups

defined, 332

User List dialog box, Microsoft Chat, 254–255

V

Veronica, defined, 332

video

ActiveMovie, 15

FrontPage Express, 289–290

NetShow On-Demand Player, 15, 127, 128–130

video conferencing, NetMeeting, 262–263

virtual reality, defined, 332

virtual storefront, defined, 332

viruses, downloading and, 171

VRML (Virtual Reality Markup Language), defined, 332

VRML Viewer, 132–134

exercise, 133–134

illustration, 127

installing, 132–133, 301–302

Y–Z

Y

Yahoo! site directory, 103–105
   described, 98
yoyo mode, defined, 333

Z

zipped files
   See also WinZip
   installing, 142–144
zones, security, 172–174

Now it's easy to remember what you just learned and more...

With *On-Demand*, you'll never rely on the help function again – or your money back.

roducing *On-Demand Interactive Learning*™ — the remark-
e software that actually makes corrections to your documents
you. Unlike the standard help function that merely provides
nned" responses to your requests for help or makes
write down a list of complicated instructions, *On-
mand* lets you learn while you work.

ncurrent Mode — makes the *changes for you*
t in your document.

cher Mode — *guides you* step-by-step to
ke changes safely outside your document.

mo Mode — *shows you* how the changes are
de safely outside your document.

On-Demand take care of the software commands for you.
t follow the on-screen pointer and fill in the information, and
'll learn in the fastest and easiest way possible — without
r leaving your document.

In fact, *On-Demand* makes your work so easy, it's *guaranteed* to help you finish complicated documents neatly and on time. With over eleven years in software education and a development staff that's logged more than 5,000 hours of classroom teaching time, it's no wonder that Fortune 500 corporations around the world use *On-Demand* to make learning for their employees quicker and more effective.

"On-Demand Interactive Learning for Word 97. The best training title of this group..."
—*PC World*

The Concurrent Mode Difference
Concurrent Mode guides you through learning new functions without having to stop for directions. Right before your eyes, a moving pointer clicks on the right buttons and icons for you and then lets you fill in the information.

"On-Demand lets me get my work done and learn without slowing me down." —**Rosemarie Hasson, Quad Micro**

LES AVAILABLE FOR: Windows® 3.1, 95, NT, Microsoft® Word, Microsoft Excel, Microsoft PowerPoint, Microsoft Access,
rosoft Internet Explorer, Lotus® SmartSuite, Lotus Notes, and more! Call for additional titles.

DAY GUARANTEE:
On-Demand at the introductory price of **$32**⁹⁵ (U.S. dollars) for one title or pay **$29**⁹⁵ (U.S. dollars) each for two titles. That's a
ngs of almost 10%. Use *On-Demand* for 30 days. If you don't learn more in a shorter period of time, simply return the software
TS Learning Systems with your receipt for a full refund (this guarantee is good only for purchases made directly from PTS).

Call PTS at 800-387-8878 ext. 3053 or 610-337-8878 ext. 3053 outside the U.S.

97 PTS Learning Systems   IDG103197

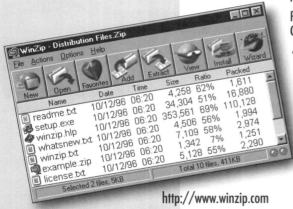

IDG BOOKS WORLDWIDE, INC.
END-USER LICENSE AGREEMENT

Read This. You should carefully read these terms and conditions before opening the software packet(s) included with this book ("Book"). This is a license agreement ("Agreement") between you and IDG Books Worldwide, Inc. ("IDGB"). By opening the accompanying software packet(s), you acknowledge that you have read and accept the following terms and conditions. If you do not agree and do not want to be bound by such terms and conditions, promptly return the Book and the unopened software packet(s) to the place you obtained them for a full refund.

1. **License Grant.** IDGB grants to you (either an individual or entity) a nonexclusive license to use one copy of the enclosed software program(s) (collectively, the "Software") solely for your own personal or business purposes on a single computer (whether a standard computer or a workstation component of a multiuser network). The Software is in use on a computer when it is loaded into temporary memory (i.e., RAM) or installed into permanent memory (e.g., hard disk, CD-ROM, or other storage device). IDGB reserves all rights not expressly granted herein.

2. **Ownership.** IDGB is the owner of all right, title, and interest, including copyright, in and to the compilation of the Software recorded on the disk(s)/CD-ROM. Copyright to the individual programs on the disk(s)/CD-ROM is owned by the author or other authorized copyright owner of each program. Ownership of the Software and all proprietary rights relating thereto remain with IDGB and its licensors.

3. **Restrictions on Use and Transfer.**

   (a) You may only (i) make one copy of the Software for backup or archival purposes, or (ii) transfer the Software to a single hard disk, provided that you keep the original for backup or archival purposes. You may not (i) rent or lease the Software, (ii) copy or reproduce the Software through a LAN or other network system or through any computer subscriber system or bulletin-board system, or (iii) modify, adapt, or create derivative works based on the Software.

   (b) You may not reverse engineer, decompile, or disassemble the Software. You may transfer the Software and user documentation on a permanent basis, provided that the transferee agrees to accept the terms and conditions of this Agreement and you retain no copies. If the Software is an update or has been updated, any transfer must include the most recent update and all prior versions.

4. **Restrictions on Use of Individual Programs.** You must follow the individual requirements and restrictions detailed for each individual program in Appendix D: What's on the CD-ROM of this Book. These limitations are contained in the individual license agreements recorded on the disk(s)/CD-ROM. These restrictions may include a requirement that after using the program for the period of time specified in its text, the user must pay a registration fee or discontinue use. By opening the Software packet(s), you will be agreeing to abide by the licenses and restrictions for these individual programs. None of the material on this disk(s) or listed in this Book may ever be distributed, in original or modified form, for commercial purposes.

8. General. This Agreement constitutes the entire understanding of the parties and revokes and supersedes all prior agreements, oral or written, between them and may not be modified or amended except in a writing signed by both parties hereto which specifically refers to this Agreement. This Agreement shall take precedence over any other documents that may be in conflict herewith. If any one or more provisions contained in this Agreement are held by any court or tribunal to be invalid, illegal, or otherwise unenforceable, each and every other provision shall remain in full force and effect.

my2cents.idgbooks.com

Register This Book — And Win!

Visit **http://my2cents.idgbooks.com** to register this book and we'll automatically enter you in our fantastic monthly prize giveaway. It's also your opportunity to give us feedback: let us know what you thought of this book and how you would like to see other topics covered.

Discover IDG Books Online!

The IDG Books Online Web site is your online resource for tackling technology — at home and at the office. Frequently updated, the IDG Books Online Web site features exclusive software, insider information, online books, and live events!

10 Productive & Career-Enhancing Things You Can Do at www.idgbooks.com

- Nab source code for your own programming projects.
- Download software.
- Read Web exclusives: special articles and book excerpts by IDG Books Worldwide authors.
- Take advantage of resources to help you advance your career as a Novell or Microsoft professional.
- Buy IDG Books Worldwide titles or find a convenient bookstore that carries them.
- Register your book and win a prize.
- Chat live online with authors.
- Sign up for regular e-mail updates about our latest books.
- Suggest a book you'd like to read or write.
- Give us your 2¢ about our books and about our Web site.

You say you're not on the Web yet? It's easy to get started with IDG Books' *Discover the Internet*, available at local retailers everywhere.

CD-ROM Installation Instructions

The CD-ROM includes the *One Step at a Time On-Demand* software. This software coaches you through the exercises in the book while you work on a computer at your own pace.

INSTALLING THE ONE STEP AT A TIME ON-DEMAND SOFTWARE

The *One Step at a Time On-Demand* software can be installed on Windows 95 and Windows NT 4.0. To install the interactive software on your computer, follow these steps:

1. Place the *Internet Explorer 4 One Step at a Time* CD-ROM in your CD-ROM drive.
2. Launch Windows (if you haven't already).
3. Click the Start menu.
4. Select Run. The Run dialog box appears.

⑤ Type **D:\Setup.exe** (where D is your CD-ROM drive) in the Run dialog box.

⑥ Click OK to run the setup procedure. The On-Demand Installation dialog box appears.

⑦ Click Continue. The On-Demand Installation Options dialog box appears.

⑧ Click the Full/Network radio button (if this option is not already selected).

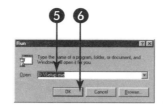

 NOTE *Full/Network installation requires 150MB of hard disk space. If you don't have enough hard disk space, click the Standard radio button to choose Standard installation. If you choose standard installation, you should always insert the CD-ROM when you start the software to hear sound.*

⑨ Click Next. The Determine Installation Drive and Directory dialog box appears.

⑩ Choose the default drive and directory that appears, or click Change to choose a different drive and directory.

⑪ Click Next. The Product Selection dialog box appears, which enables you to verify the software you want to install.

⑫ Click Finish to complete the installation. The On-Demand Installation dialog box displays the progress of the installation. After the installation, the Multiuser Pack Registration dialog box appears.

⑬ Enter information in the Multiuser Pack Registration dialog box.

⑭ Click OK. The On-Demand Installation dialog box appears.

⑮ Click OK to confirm the installation has been successfully completed.

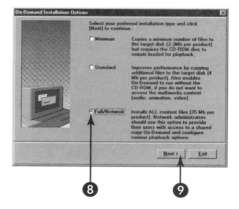

Please see Appendix D, "What's on the CD-ROM," for information about running the One Step at a Time On-Demand interactive software.